Motherhood and Social Exclusion

edited by Christie Byvelds
and Heather Jackson

DEMETER

Motherhood and Social Exclusion
Edited by Christie Byvelds and Heather Jackson

Copyright © 2019 Demeter Press

Demeter Press
140 Holland Street West
P. O. Box 13022
Bradford, ON L3Z 2Y5
Tel: (905) 775-9089
Email: info@demeterpress.org
Website: www.demeterpress.org

Demeter Press logo based on the sculpture "Demeter" by Maria-Luise Bodirsky www.keramik-atelier.bodirsky.de

Printed and Bound in Canada

Front cover image: Chloe Trayhurn
Front cover artwork: Michelle Pirovich
Typesetting: Michelle Pirovich

Library and Archives Canada Cataloguing in Publication
Title: Motherhood and social exclusion
Editors: Christie Byvelds and Heather Jackson
Names: Byvelds, Christie, 1986- editor. | Jackson, Heather, 1982- editor.
Description: Includes bibliographical references.
Identifiers: Canadiana 20190094079 | ISBN 9781772581980 (softcover)
Subjects: LCSH: Motherhood—Social aspects. | LCSH: Social isolation. LCSH: Marginality, Social. | LCSH: Loneliness.
Classification: LCC HQ759 .M68 2019 | DDC 306.874/3—dc23

To the women who have supported me in
my mothering adventure.
—C.B.

For Lyric, those who are fighting the struggle,
the single moms on welfare, prisoners,
and the writers who all inspire everything.
—H.J.

Contents

CONTENTS

Acknowledgments

As mothers who have experienced mothering and social exclusion ourselves, editing a collection on the topic has been a fascinating experience. While we were creating this collection, one of us gave birth and went from a mother of one to a mother of two little humans, whereas the other experienced a terrifying situation with her child—both episodes gave us new experiences of social exclusion.

We want to thank our contributing authors. This book would not have been possible without you. People had to experience unsafe and awful things in order for these chapters to be written, and they deserve to be heard. Your stories, research, and activism have inspired us, and we are grateful to have been able to include your work and to have played a small part in bringing them to the world. Many of you made yourself vulnerable through sharing your own experiences or the experiences of those with whom you spoke; we are confident your vulnerability will be respected and will lead to greater understanding. We extend a special thank you to artist Chloe Trayhurn—an artist and mother whose beautiful art appears both on the cover and within the collection.

This book would not be possible without the team at Demeter Press; we thank Andrea O'Reilly for giving us the opportunity to put this collection together. Lastly, given the major life events we experienced while working on this collection, we wish to thank our friends, family, and partners; without their support and encouragement, we would not have been able to work on and complete this collection.

Brook, Chloe Trayhurn

Introduction

Christie Byvelds and Heather Jackson

"Those of us who stand outside the circle of this society's definition of acceptable women; those of us who have been forged in the crucibles of difference — those of us who are poor, who are lesbians, who are black, who are older — know that survival is not an academic skill.... For the master's tools will not dismantle the master's house. They will never allow us to bring about genuine change."—Audre Lorde, 112

Although the negative effects of social exclusion are well documented, there is a paucity of research on women's experiences of social exclusion as they relate to mothering within the institution of motherhood. Social exclusion is a socially constructed concept that refers to a multidimensional form of systematic discrimination driven by unequal power in relationships. It is the denial of equal opportunities, resources, rights, goods, and services for some by others within economic, social, cultural, and political arenas. Carrying, birthing, and mothering children place women in a unique position to face social exclusion based on their role as mothers. However, perhaps at no other time in mothers' lives could we benefit more from feeling as though we are part of a community. In addition, when we, as mothers, enter into this community, we experience the patriarchal institution of motherhood. As the widely used proverb states, "it takes a village to raise a child," but it also takes a village to support mothers.

In this collection, we explore social exclusion in the context of motherhood. Our aim was to bring something new to the topic, as it seemed evident that mothers experience social exclusion. As mothers ourselves, we could certainly attest to this, and we felt it was important to dive deep into this topic.

Although women who are mothers experience social exclusion due to motherhood or motherhood-related issues—such as taking maternity leave, breastfeeding, limitations due to pregnancy etc.— they are also not immune to experiencing social exclusion more generally, however, regardless of their mothering identity, for example, due to race, sexual orientation, incarceration, or mental illness. This collection discusses all forms of social exclusion, whether directly related to motherhood or to other factors that intersect with women's identity as a mother.

While researching social exclusion in relation to motherhood, we considered the following questions. In what ways are mothers excluded? What are the experiences of socially excluded mothers? How are mothers affected by the multilevel (individual, household, group, community, country, and global) as well as the multidimensional (economic, political, social, and cultural) concept of social exclusion? What can be done to facilitate the social integration of mothers? How does the multidimensionality of disadvantage, or intersecting oppressions, contribute to social exclusion? Is motherhood itself always an experience of social exclusion? What we found was that space existed for a collection that specifically addresses the distinctive experience of mothers.

The World Health Organization describes social exclusion in several ways. It asks who is being excluded, what are they being excluded from, problems associated with their exclusion, the processes behind it, the levels at which the processes are operating, and the agents involved (Mathieson. et al.). We felt these were helpful working definitions to consider while thinking about social exclusion related to motherhood.

We received many excellent submissions, which we later divided into four sections to guide the reader through the collection. The first section explores the history of social exclusion and motherhood; the second section looks at criminalized mothers; the third delves into the complex experiences of mothers with disabilities, mothers mothering people with disabilities, and mothering and care work; and the fourth section provides insight into the experiences of mothers and social exclusion using first-hand accounts of mothers.

We believe that one of the collection's strengths is its ability to situate the topic at hand—motherhood and social exclusion—within both a historical and global context. The editors were thrilled to have authors from all over the world, including Australia, Canada, Colombia, Italy, Ireland, and the United States of America, which adds an important global dimension to the collection. As readers of the works ourselves, we enjoyed the mix of the academic and formal pieces of writing as well as those that are less so. The incorporation of research using different methodologies—whether it is quantitative methods, participatory action research, or more personal interviews— is refreshing for the reader. Personal narratives, artwork, and poetry help to change the type of reading from chapter to chapter, which creates a well-rounded collection of work.

Research on motherhood and social exclusion has so far looked at mothers within some of their intersection oppressions, such as race, age, class, chosen feeding methods, and family status,. When deciding which chapters to accept for the collection, we used the existing research as a starting point and asked ourselves what we could add to it to enrich the discussion. Geronimus (2003) argues that white individuals have adapted putting their education and employment before having children, whereas Black individuals' culture has normalized having children at a younger age. Their age and race then intersect in their oppression and exclusion as mothers. Connections have been found between socioeconomic class and age regarding when women have their first child (Hobcraft and Kiernan). In one study, those who became mothers before the age of twenty-three had higher rates of poverty later in their adult life; not surprisingly, their children were also more likely to live in poverty.

In addition to race and age, other factors influence mothers' social exclusion. Breastfeeding women experience barriers related to their independence, work, family issues, social embarrassment, and social isolation (Stewart-Knox, Gardiner, & Wright, 2003). These barriers, linked to their choice of feeding method, created the perfect environment to experience social exclusion.

In a study on mothers' experiences with their social worker, Janzen Peters finds that First Nations women experience judgment, difficulty accessing resources, and little empathy at these agencies. Health disparities among single mothers were associated with social exclusion (Johner). Rates of mental illness are higher among single mothers (Targoaz et al.), which plays into their social exclusion. Similarly, mothers of disabled children experience unique forms of social constraints (Williams and Murray).

Thus, the literature explores motherhood and social exclusion from many angles and from various intersecting oppressions. Although there is little literature on the topic, the few pieces that do exist paint a picture that is worth examining — that is, women who are mothers experience social exclusion in unique ways. We believe that building from the existing scholarship has made for a strong collection, as we continue to ask how to better understand social exclusion in the context of motherhood. We hope this collection helps in further understanding around this topic.

Even though the collection covers a wide range of topics, it is important to note its limitations. As with any collection, we could not cover all possible areas for discussion. For example, the ways in which violence against women plays into mothers' social exclusion is not explored. Similarly, there is little discussion about refugee mothers, mothers raising children born of sexual violence, and there is no discussion on the social exclusion of women who choose not to mother.. Unfortunately, due to the submissions we received, these important topics are not discussed within this collection.

The cover artwork was created by Chloe Trayhurn, a self-taught artist and mother of two living in the United Kingdom. Working in watercolour, Chloe draws inspiration from the beauty of the female form, motherhood, and physical connection. After stumbling across a piece of her beautiful work, we felt compelled to contact her to see if she would be interested in contributing something to the book, and we were thrilled when she agreed. In addition to the cover, two other pieces, called Brook and Fearless Motherhood, can be found within the collection, at the beginning of the introduction and in the "A Historical Look at Motherhood" section. We were lucky enough to receive submissions from another talented self-taught artist and mother, Flavia Testa. These four pieces are found at the beginning of each of the four sections of the collection, and each represents the theme it precedes beautifully. Testa's sketches encompass our thoughts and ideas about each theme and provide an important visual before diving into the chapters.

Part I. A Historical Look at Motherhood

This section provides a historical context to the discussion of the social exclusion of mothers. The chapters include narratives related to miscarriages in the Victorian era, behavioural issues in children and mother blaming, colonial Spain's impact on mothers who lived there, and the persecution of unwed mothers for their so-called deviant sexuality. Together, these chapters show that the social exclusion of mothers is not a new practice.

In "As If She Weren't a Mother at All: Narrating Blame and Isolation of Miscarrying Mothers in the Nineteenth Century and Today," Kathryn Huie Harrison explores Victorian perspectives on miscarriages and focuses on mother blaming. Such blaming included doctors blaming a mother's nerves and gastrointestinal problems for her miscarriage; sadly, the focus was on the mother, not other factors outside of her control. She argues that that this mother blaming persists today and that miscarriage is still a taboo topic. Clarissa Carden also explores mother blaming in her chapter "Difficult Children, Blamable Mothers? A Historical Perspective" and how behavioural issues are almost always blamed on a child's mother. She uses data from 1859 to present day from Queensland, Australia, to uncover the shift of blame onto mothers and how that has changed over time. The third chapter in this section is a piece by María Piedad Quevedo-Alvarado called "Decentring Motherhood: Social Exclusion, Ecology, and Authority in Colonial Spanish America," in which she shares a personal story of her journey through motherhood situated within historical power structures in Spain. She explores motherhood as "a state apparatus that allows certain types of social exclusion— motherhood as the reproduction of the status quo" and as "a decentring device." She uses two texts from colonial Spanish America to do this— these texts (from the sixteenth and early seventeenth centuries) portray motherhood as revealing, disrupting, and resignifying the link between motherhood and imperial power. The last chapter in this section is Karen March's "Unwed Motherhood, Social Exclusion, and Adoption Placement." The chapter highlights the way white, middle-class women's children were adopted in the early twentieth century. She discusses how previous periods of sociocultural, political, and economic change intertwined to persecute unwed mothers for their deviant sexuality and to exclude them from the social institution of motherhood. These chapters demonstrate that the social exclusion of mothers is not a new phenomenon.

Part II. Mothers and Criminalization

The chapters in the second section discuss mothers involved with the criminal justice system and richly explore their experiences. We are pleased that this section includes authors and research from Ireland and Canada, and feminist research methods.

In her chapter, "Motherhood and Social Exclusion: Narratives of Women in Prison in Ireland," Christina Quinlan explores the experiences of motherhood of incarcerated mothers in Ireland. She examines the varying degrees of social exclusion they experience based on a number of factors, including substance use, social supports, and custody of their children. The second chapter, "Addressing Social Exclusion through Collaborative Methods: Criminalized Mothers' Engagement in Research," Ashley Ward, Emily van der Meulen, and May Friedman explore social exclusion in relation to crime and use feminist participatory action research (FPAR) to gain a better understanding of their experiences. The authors felt FPAR was the best way to not only understand their experiences but also provide empowerment and inclusion. Lastly, Lucy Baldwin's chapter— "Excluded from Good Motherhood and the Impact of Prison: Reflections of Mothers after Prison"—offers insight into the emotional experiences and sense of exclusion felt by both incarcerated mothers and mothers after release. She uses primary research as well as historical research to study the experiences of social exclusion of these mothers. Her chapter discusses the value of understanding more about incarcerated mothers' lived experiences and offers recommendations in relation to such mothers. In this way, the chapter aims to minimize and compensate for the impact and effect of physical exclusion of mothers who go to prison. These chapters reveal that mothers in prison are socially excluded on many levels; they are physically and mentally excluded from the world and their children and face many barriers before, during, and after prison.

Part III. Disability, Care Work, and Motherhood

The authors in this section have an amazing array of experiences related to disability and care work. This section not only includes the experiences of mothers with disabilities and mothers of children with disabilities but also the experiences of mothers who mother their mothers with disabilities. Although this section does explore every aspect related to disability, motherhood, and social exclusion, it does demonstrate their complexities and provide many unique perspectives to the topic of disability and motherhood.

In the section's first chapter, "The Trouble with Engineering Inclusion: Disabled Mothering at the Limits of Enhancement Technology," Kelly Frisch examines the experiences of physically disabled mothers who use enhanced technologies to help them mother their children. She argues that these technologies can be helpful but do not make any large systematic or social changes. She also believes that they are not important in making disabled mothers more equal and empowered. Next, in "Exclusion, Constraint, and Motherhood: Conceptualizing the Construction of Motherhood and Mothering the Disabled Child," Karen Williams and Duncan Murray explore how mothers of children with physical and development disabilities experience social exclusion. They focus on the experiences the mothers face due to stigma, lack of support, and lack of understanding about the issues and frustrations these mothers face. Adding to the discussion of mothering children with disabilities, Yidan Zhu and Romee Lee's chapter, "Learning with Difference: The Experience and Identity of Asian Immigrant Mothers with Children with ASDs in Canada," discusses the sociocultural aspects of learning through an exploration of how Asian mothers with children on the autism spectrum experience social exclusion in learning and how these mothers produce their own knowledge in their mothering practice. In the last chapter of this section, "Daughters Who Mother Their Mothers: An Exploration of the Social Exclusion of Unpaid Intergenerational Home Care Workers," Krystal Kehoe MacLeod explores motherhood and care work. More specifically, MacLeod interviewed adult women who engage in unpaid care work by caring for their aging mothers. These adult daughters describe feeling overworked and excluded, as not many people understand what they are going through. The adult daughters also discuss feeling strain in their relationships with other family members, as they try to balance their mother's autonomy while experiencing a familial role reversal. These discussions of disability, care work, and motherhood have illuminate the intersection and complexity as well as the richness of these topics, although they only scratch the topic's surface and show the need for further research.

Part IV. Personal Narratives

These personal stories on mothering and social exclusion in this fourth and final section are both heartbreaking and heartwarming. We thank these authors, in particular, for sharing their stories. Nancy Sinclair's chapter, "The Process of (Un)Deservingness: Gestational Surrogacy and Mental Health," opens this section of the collection. She uses her story of fertility treatment and pregnancy loss to discuss surrogacy and the determination of deservingness as it relates to fertility treatment in Ontario, Canada. Next, Amber Gazso and Jason Webb use qualitative interviews with mothers to explore the role of social support in mitigating social exclusion. In their chapter, "Multiple Jeopardies and Liminality in Low-Income Mothering: Experiencing and Resisting Social Exclusion" they reveal that their social exclusion can, in fact, be created by their experiences of multiple jeopardies and liminality. They then consider whether social support networks could mitigate social exclusion. In her creative piece, "Abandon Assumptions," Rae Griffin-Carlson describes her experiences of social exclusion as they relate to her identity as a queer mom as well as partner of an Anishinaabe woman and parent of Anishinaabe children. Her short creative piece narrates her internal and external observations of the world. Continuing with creative pieces of writing, Donna J. Gelagotis Lee offers two poems. She has also included descriptions of the poems to accompany them. The first poem, "Woman from Thessaloníki", a divorced mother experiences social exclusion on an island. In her second poem, "The Step of the Door," explores the mother's role as keeper of the home, whose home life can restrict her to that space, which largely limits her social interactions to those who pass over the "doorstep" of the home. The last chapter of this section is Heather Jackson's, "Teen Pregnancy, Motherhood, and Social Exclusion," in which she discusses her experience as a teen mother and the social exclusion that she experienced as a teen and that she continues to experience into her adult life. She ends her chapter on a positive note, providing the reader with ideas and suggestions to change the ways we talk about and includes teen moms.

Conclusion

Motherhood and Social Exclusion is a collection of academic and non-academic work on the topic of social exclusion experienced by mothers. The collection hopes to bring forward new perspectives on the area and discuss topics that need to be discussed. We explore the historical complexities related to the social exclusion of motherhood, including how mothers were often blamed for miscarriages and the behaviour of their children as well as the emotional trauma related to single and pregnant women and adoption. We include chapters on women in the prison industrial complex and the difficulties of their experiences, emphasizing how being away from their children adds to the mothers' experience of trauma. This collection also touches on the experiences and complexities of mothers with disabilities and caring for children and others with disabilities. And finally, we wanted to end our collection with strong personal narratives that cover fertility, poetry, and adolescent mothering.

We hope that you find this collection informative and, perhaps, even a bit inspirational. The stories held within are beautiful, heartbreaking, and everything in between. Women who mother children need to be supported in this role and in all other areas of their life — economic, social, cultural, political, and personal. We believe it is important to use research as a catalyst for change. With this in mind, we are continuously thinking of ways to move forwards and to advance the status of women who mother. Now that this information is known, what can we all do about it? What small part can we play in including mothers within our communities and institutions? Through examining the social exclusion experienced by mothers, we can continue to work towards creating a society where women, including those who are mothers, hold equal power in their relationships and where mothering work is valued.

Works Cited

Geronimus, Arline T. "Damned If You Do: Culture, Identity, Privilege, and Teenage Childbearing in the United States." *Social Science & Medicine* vol. 57, no. 5, 2003, pp. 881-93.

Jensen-Peters, Carolyn. "Mother-Led Families with Multiple Stressors: A Qualitative Study About Mothers and Their Social Workers' Perspectives of the Social Service Experience." MSW Thesis. University of Manitoba. 2009.

Johner, Randy Lane. "The Relationship between Socio-Demographic Characteristics, Social Exclusion, and Self-Related Health in Single Mothers." PhD Thesis. University of Regina. 2009.

Lorde. Audre. "The Master's Tools Will Never Dismantle tbe Master's House." *In This Bridge Called My Back: Writings by Radical Women of Color,* edited by Chem'e Moraga and Gloria Anzaldiia, Kitchen Table, 1983, pp. 98-101.

Mathieson, Jane, et al. *Social Exclusion Meaning, Measurement and Experience and Links to Health Inequalities: A Review of Literature.* World Health Organization. 2008.

Stewart-Knox, B., et al. "What Is the Problem with Breastfeeding? A Qualitative Analysis of Infant Feeding Perceptions." *Journal of Human Nutrition and Dietetics,* vol. 16, 2003, pp. 265-73.

Targosz, S. et al. "Lone Mothers, Social Exclusion, and Depression." *Psychological Medicine,* vol. 33, no. 4, 2003, pp. 715-22.

Williams, Karen J., and Duncan W. Murray. "Negotiating the Normative: The Other Normal for Mothers of Disabled Children." *Journal of Family Studies,* vol. 21, no. 3, 2015, pp. 324-40.

PART I

A Historical Look at Motherhood

IT
TAKES
A
VILLAGE
TO SUPPORT
A MOTHER

Chapter 1

As If She Weren't a Mother at All: Narrating Blame and Isolation of Miscarrying Mothers in the Nineteenth Century and Today

Katy Huie Harrison

Two weeks after my third consecutive miscarriage, I sat in my gynecologist's office, anxious to hear my doctor's take on the test results. Their lab technician had recently taken twenty vials of blood to test for various issues that may cause recurrent miscarriage, including blood clotting disorders, thyroid problems, autoimmune diseases, and more. When my doctor walked into the room, she sat down next to me and carefully placed my chart just out of view. "I want to prepare you," she warned, as I instantly assumed the tests had revealed something terrible. I was surprised when I learned that her emotional preparation was not for the results but for the medical terminology that appeared on my chart, just barely out of view. "I want to show you your chart so we can talk through your history and test results together," she said. "But before I do, I need to explain a phrase you'll see at the top." That phrase, strategically placed so that no attending doctor could possibly miss the alert, hurt nearly as much as the multiple miscarriages themselves. I was stunned, shocked, but thankful for my doctor's forewarning when I read those ominous two words: "habitual aborter."

"Abortion," as a medical term, "derives from the Latin *aboriri*—to miscarry" (Cunningham, 215). The phrasing on my chart is a medical term that refers to "spontaneous abortion"— when a woman's body suddenly miscarries a pregnancy. A "habitual aborter" is someone who has miscarried three or more pregnancies. To most people outside of the medical community, of course, and especially to families experiencing the trauma of miscarriage, the meaning of the word "abort" is different. Although the first definition in the *Oxford English Dictionary* recognizes that "abortion" can be either "natural" or "deliberate"' in layman's terms, it generally refers to the deliberate act of removing a fetus from the mother's uterus ("Abortion"). Such a suggestion can be heartbreaking and offensive to mothers who have lost babies they desperately wanted. Regardless of political beliefs about subjects like abortion rights, in already emotionally tense moments, miscarrying mothers are subject to being labelled with terminology that is at odds with their experience, which can create feelings of confusion, anger, and isolation.

Many doctors, my own included, are aware of the vast discrepancy between the terminology used by the medical community and the emotional needs of patients. Ruth Bender Atik and Barbara Hepworth-Jones appropriately warn about the use of such language to describe recurrent pregnancy loss:

> Clinical terms can cause great distress and even anger.... It is not acceptable to use the term 'abortion' for miscarriage ... despite its historical clinical prevalence. To the lay person, 'abortion' means the elective termination of pregnancy and while they may have no theoretical objection to that procedure, they are likely to be distressed and even angered at its use in their situation. (98)

My doctor, thankfully, understood the potential emotional impact of the word, but she had no choice in the fact that it appeared prominently on my chart or each time I go the doctor; the label serves as a reminder of the discrepancy between medical rhetoric and emotionally sensitive language.

This poor choice in terminology reflects what I have discovered about the discursive practices surrounding miscarriage more generally. That is, most people in contemporary Anglo-American society lack the ability to discuss miscarriage in a way that is sensitive to the loss of a wanted pregnancy. Because approximately one in four pregnancies ends in miscarriage, many doctors treat pregnancy loss as a routine matter, failing to take into account the grief the miscarrying mother feels.[1] As Cumming et al. have explained, "The emotional burden of early pregnancy loss is commonly not recogni[z]ed by healthcare professionals, as evidenced by reports of dissatisfaction with care following miscarriage" (1138). The high prevalence of miscarriage likely explains the nonchalant attitudes of many healthcare providers—already overloaded with patients, OBs and ER doctors have little time to devote to grieving mothers when they have already witnessed multiple miscarriages that week.

Yet while medical professionals often place less weight on the emotional burden of miscarriages because of their commonality, most people outside of the medical field are unaware of their prevalence. I speak specifically within a North American context, where the subject is rarely discussed socially because of the discomfort it causes to people who have not experienced miscarriage. Our society tends to shy away from conversations that deal with grief, and there seems to be a special discomfort with grief that is directly connected to the sexualized female body, such as the loss of a pregnancy.

The result is that miscarrying mothers often struggle to find appropriate outlets for comfort—no one knows what to say, making miscarrying mothers feel silenced and isolated. As Jessica Winegar has explained, miscarrying American mothers often "feel out of place and alone, because everyone knows what to say to a woman announcing her pregnancy, but it seems that no one knows what to say to a woman sharing its loss." Because of our social lack of understanding and the resulting inability to talk about miscarriage, miscarrying mothers feel misunderstood, isolated, and (if they do not yet have living children) excluded from the practice and institution of motherhood.

The Mother's Days before and after my son was born are examples of this exclusion. On Mother's Day 2018, after four consecutive miscarriages, I finally had a living child. By the time Mother's Day came around, my son was almost a year old. I had been eight months pregnant during the previous year's Mother's Day, and even then, people were clearly uncertain how to address the day with me. My husband, knowing that I had considered myself a mother for years, planned carefully: he told me to schedule a prenatal massage, and when I came home, he had cooked me a lovely dinner. Others, though, were much more reticent to acknowledge my maternal status, even at eight months pregnant. Many people said such things as "This day will be so special next year," whereas others uncomfortably ignored the subject. In 2018, with an infant in my arms, I finally celebrated Mother's Day (in 2015 and 2016, I had secluded myself to grieve on that day), and I counted more than twenty times that someone referred to it as my first Mother's Day. Apparently, until I had had a living child, I was excluded from the motherhood club and from all celebrations included with membership. Only once I had a baby in tow—not in my womb but in my arms—could most people recognize me as a mother on this holiday.

This personal anecdote demonstrates how basic rhetorical choices tend to alienate miscarrying mothers from the social institution of motherhood. Miscarrying mothers are not usually referred to as "mothers," for instance, but as "women" — the word "mother" remaining designated for women who are fortunate enough to have birthed living children. By refusing to refer to miscarrying mothers as mothers, our society silences their experiences and erases their pregnancies from existence. Instead, our cultural rhetoric insists that only giving birth to living children warrants the status of mother.[2] As Sally Han has discussed, pregnancy, once announced, is expected to end with a live birth, not a stillbirth or miscarriage: "Pregnancy and its 'end' in the birth of a living child are treated as more or less known and given, despite the evidence that American women themselves could present from their own lives" (4). As long as a woman is pregnant, our society recognizes and assumes she will have a child, but if she loses that child, her experience as its mother is largely erased.

When I was experiencing recurrent miscarriage, I discovered how awkward it could be to tell people I had miscarried a child they hadn't known I was carrying. As a result, I started telling people earlier each time I got pregnant; I wasn't shy about my miscarriages, and I wanted the people around me to learn to deal with the sensitive nature of the subject. The most common response when I announced a pregnancy was excitement and enthusiasm; most people insisted that things would be different this time and assumed the pregnancy would work out. My experience suggests great validity to Han's assertion; even when people knew I had miscarried two, three, four pregnancies without ever carrying a successful one, and each pregnancy announcement somehow came with the assumption that I would end up with a living child. Only once in five times did that actually happen. When I announced a miscarriage, in contrast, though sympathetic, most responses erased the fact that I was ever a mother because I didn't birth a living child. People were silent, or they expressed regret and then turned away. The more miscarriages I had, the less people understood how to respond to them. "Why do you continue to put yourself through this?" I was often asked. Or there was the even more common, "Why don't you just adopt?" This shockingly flawed question somehow overlooks the fact that adoption is often a much longer, more expensive, and more rigorous process than miscarriage. Ultimately, the responses I received when I told people about more miscarriages attempted to lead to an end—adopting, considering surrogacy, or finding a different way for me to be a mother than carrying my own biological children. Few responses recognized that I had carried my own children and, thus, that I was those children's mother.

The general discomfort about recognizing miscarrying mothers as mothers appears in everyday parlance to a degree I found shocking. After four miscarriages, I had perfectly well-intentioned women, who knew about all of my losses, complain about their children. There is nothing wrong with complaining—motherhood is hard, and children are exhausting. But it wasn't that people would say, "Oh, my children are driving me nuts today" and leave it there. Instead, they'd say that and then recognize that what they said could have upset me, so they'd uncomfortably add on comments like, "Once you get pregnant and become a mother, you'll understand what I'm going through." These addendums—which were attempts to alleviate the discomfort of the speaker with my own liminal situation between mother and childless woman—essentially erased my experiences with pregnancy and motherhood. The general discomfort around me on Mother's Day when I was eight months pregnancy is especially emblematic of this erasure. Not only did people fail to recognize my previous experience as a mother and the existence of my lost children, but they also assumed that within mere months of giving birth, I still did not deserve the designation of "mother." Such a sentiment, though never ill intentioned, silenced my perspective, and it felt as though they erased my pregnancies by privileging only pregnancies resulting in live births. In Marty Heilberg's words, our society "loves pregnant women, but only if the pregnancies work" (qtd. in Layne 249).[3]

Such silencing of the miscarrying mother's maternal experience isolates mothers of loss, and it echoes the larger silence surrounding pregnancy loss, a subject Linda Layne has described as "taboo" (64). Because the subject is taboo, women experiencing miscarriage are often uncomfortable telling others about their losses, and when they do, most people are unsure how to respond, thus causing even further discomfort for the miscarrying mother. According to Laura Seftel, there is a "silence surrounding pregnancy loss" that leads miscarrying mothers to remain quiet about miscarriage until other women near them experience similar losses (15). The result of this silence, of course, is that a common experience appears uncommon; most people have no idea who in their lives has actually lived through miscarriage and, thus, they have no idea where to turn for comfort. I'm the exception—I forced the subject upon everyone around me, and the result has been that women turn to me constantly when they experience miscarriage because I'm one of the few people who they are certain understands.

This cultural silence has two particularly negative effects. First, most newly pregnant women do not know how to prepare for the possibility of pregnancy loss or what to expect when it happens. Second, once a woman experiences a miscarriage, she often has unnecessary feelings of loneliness and isolation because she is unaware that she now has a shared experience with countless women. Although there has been a cultural push to shed more light on the subject of pregnancy loss (Pregnancy and Infant Loss Awareness Day, for instance, occurs on 15 October in the United States, Canada, the United Kingdom, Norway, Italy, Kenya, and parts of Australia), the silence surrounding it is still largely the norm. As a result of this silence, miscarrying mothers are often excluded from representations of motherhood, as I have shown. The exclusion I have described thus far, though, is largely social and rhetorical.

Another problem with our silence about miscarriage—and I contend this problem has a strong historical basis—is that it is not recognized within structural institutions. Miscarriage involves a physically painful process that can be debilitating for days, even weeks, and it sometimes requires surgery. In addition to requiring physical recovery, most mothers also experience emotional trauma following a miscarriage. Yet unlike when we lose a family member, the birth of a living child, or have other types of surgery, miscarrying mothers in the United States grieve without any type of official leave from work, without a funeral (or any other type of cathartic ritual) to provide closure over the loss of a child, and usually with people telling them to "get over it" within a matter of weeks. I have known women in the United States who have been denied short-term disability to recover from miscarriages, and I have known even more who have lost jobs for missing too much work due to pregnancy loss. These issues are especially prevalent in the recurrent pregnancy loss community.

How Did We Get Here? A Historical Precedent of Silence and Blame

The Victorian period is known as an age that culturally sexualized the female body. There is a common (albeit untrue) belief that Victorians covered piano legs because they were considered too risqué. Although this trope is based on no evidence, its perpetuation demonstrates how Victorian culture has come to represent the ultimate repression of sexuality. Even pregnancy was not spoken of; women merely wore loose-fitting clothing until their pregnant bodies could no longer be hidden, at which point they began a period of confinement. I have regularly had students gasp when a birth is announced in a Victorian novel, as they had no idea the mother was even pregnant (even though I usually gave them a heads up in class). In a society where pregnancy was not a subject for open discussion, miscarrying bodies were especially silenced. I suggest that our cultural discomfort with the subject of miscarriage in present-day Anglo-American society is inherited from this Victorian-era silencing of the female body. I also believe the many ways in which Victorian women were blamed for their miscarriages continue to be echoed, though perhaps to a lesser extent, today.

Due to the large silence surrounding the subject of miscarriage, cultural and literary representations of nineteenth-century pregnancy loss are difficult to find. We see glimpses of the subject in George Eliot's *Middlemarch*, Charles Dickens's *David Copperfield*, and Thomas Hardy's *Jude the Obscure*. But even these depictions are relegated to a few lines, if even a full sentence, and that's coming from authors (especially Eliot and Hardy) who are notorious for their willingness to push the envelope of acceptability. I'll discuss these few examples later, as they demonstrate how representations of miscarriage gloss over the subject and rhetorically separate the miscarrying mother from the maternal body. These literary representations form a small part of my argument here though, because they're simply too scant. Instead, for a more in-depth look at how miscarrying Victorian mothers were silenced and blamed, we must turn, unsurprisingly, to medical writing (which is of especial interest to me once I learned that our present-day medical community today considers me a "habitual aborter").

Medical terminology, inherently, has a way of casting blame on miscarrying mothers. Although the word "miscarriage" was not a word developed in the Victorian period (the first recorded use of "miscarriage" in reference to pregnancy loss in the *Oxford English Dictionary* is from a doctor in 1615), the word itself is one that casts blame. As actress Melissa Rauch notes in a 2017 article for *Glamour*, "It immediately conjures up an implication that it was the woman's fault, like she somehow mishandled the carrying of this baby." We see this rhetorical blame clearly in the rhetoric of nineteenth-century doctors, who rarely used the word miscarriage; instead, they called the body's expulsion of a fetus, regardless of cause or circumstance, an abortion.

With this rhetorical blame already at work, Victorian doctors took things further by overtly blaming mothers for their miscarriages. Gender hierarchies were largely at play here. Most Victorian medical practitioners were men, and women needed to obey their (often absurd) instructions, lest they may otherwise fail in one of their primary duties as women—successfully carrying children. In the medical literature of the time, doctors regularly insist that women caused their own miscarriages even when medical intervention itself likely caused the loss. By blaming mothers for miscarriages, medical practitioners glossed over their own lack of understanding about the actual causes of pregnancy loss, which suggests that miscarriage was a result of inappropriate behaviour rather than of unfortunate genetic circumstances, anatomical abnormalities, or even poor medical practices. Blaming mothers for their miscarriages reinforced the notion that male doctors knew what was best for women's bodies and that when a body did not properly perform its role in pregnancy, the mother's behaviour was almost certainly to blame. By blaming mothers for their own losses, the doctors, and the literature alike, perpetuated ideas that situated women as ignorant, misbehaving "others," distancing women from their own bodies. Such language positions miscarrying mothers as culturally subversive because of their supposed refusal to follow medical advice and, as a result, their inability to carry a successful pregnancy. Certainly, Victorian medical knowledge was not what it is today, so doctors could not have known many of the common causes of miscarriage. Still, their blame is too overt to ignore.

Let's jump to present-day scientific understandings of miscarriage for a minute to be clear about what does and, especially, what does not cause miscarriage. The most common cause of miscarriage is fetal genetic abnormality, meaning that the embryo that implants in the mother's uterus has an abnormal genetic code. This is occasionally (albeit rarely) caused by a genetic translocation carried by one of the parents, which doctors discover via karyotype testing, but it is most commonly random. In most cases, such pregnancies begin healthily, but the mother's body will eventually recognize the abnormality and induce miscarriage. Factors such as sperm and egg quality come into play in this type of miscarriage; maternal age is often a factor. Other common causes of miscarriage include the following:

1. Maternal problems with the endocrine system (e.g., thyroid issues, insufficient production of the hormone progesterone, and polycystic ovary syndrome);

2. Maternal anatomical abnormalities (including problems with the shape or lining of the uterus, the ability of the cervix to seal shut, and intrauterine infection);

3. Maternal immunological factors (including, blood clotting disorders that unintentionally cut off blood flow to the fetus) (Avagliano et al. 5).

Although each of these causes begins with the word "maternal," I do not mean to indicate that the mother has any control over these circumstances; each abnormality listed above is entirely physiological. What does not cause miscarriage — stress, carrying heavy things, a cup of coffee, a glass of wine, or physical activity, unless the mother has a physiological issue that makes physical exertion a risk, such as a cervix that does not remain properly shut. This condition is known as "incompetent cervix," which is yet another example of the ways in which medical language blames mothers for physiological abnormalities.

Certainly, Victorian doctors had no understanding of genetic code, and since chromosomal abnormalities account for the cause of most miscarriages, it's no surprise that they looked to other means to understand the cause. Still, they were aware of many of the other factors, as the mid-Victorian period came with the discovery of many "intra-uterine revelations," which "promised to answer potentially all of women's diseases" including "headaches, fatigue, and transitory discomforts" (Archimedes 2).

Sondra Archimedes cites Gunning S. Bedford, a prominent mid-nineteenth century American obstetrician, in her discussion of uterine abnormalities, as he played an integral role in the discovery of uterine abnormality (which, it appears, was the cause of my own miscarriages). Yet while Bedford wrote about uterine abnormalities and their connection to many other ailments, he almost exclusively blamed miscarriage — the most logical of all ailments to arise from such anomalies — on external factors he believed to be under the mother's control. In other words, despite his interest in emerging understandings of uterine abnormalities, Bedford did not appear to have ever considered them as a possible cause of pregnancy loss. Rather, he blamed miscarrying mothers for their losses, which ideologically separated them from the women who could successfully carry and birth live infants. This blame that focused on behaviour and not anatomy suggested not a problem with the physical body but with the social one: pregnant women who neglected to follow medical advice were either unwilling or unable to carry successful pregnancies, thus threatening both social order and future generations.

In most cases, Bedford blamed miscarriage on either the mother's nerves (which his language suggests he thought were under her control) or on some sort of forbidden behaviour, such as dancing, horseback riding, or carrying heavy items. Physical exertion was considered to be such a risk factor that some doctors suggested that walking and visiting friends were too strenuous activities for pregnant women to safely undertake. Even when Bedford did attribute a miscarriage to a medical cause, his rhetoric still implicitly criticized the mother. He warned, for instance, that diarrhea—a gastrointestinal problem over which the mother has no control—could lead to miscarriage. Although this idea would appear to suggest that the mother is not responsible for her loss, Bedford's rhetorical choices cast blame; he says that diarrhea "may, by debilitating the system, give rise to unpleasant results; but *what is most to be apprehended is its tendency in women of great nervous susceptibility to produce miscarriage*" (Bedford 147).

The use of italics for emphasis is especially crucial to the rhetorical importance of Bedford's message. He does not even mention the medical ailment he is concerned with in the clause he chooses to stylistically highlight, but instead he focuses on the mental instability of women who are likely to have miscarriages as the result of a weakened system from diarrhea. These women, who are not mothers until they have birthed living children, are susceptible to miscarriage because of psychological causes, which Victorians believed to be largely controllable. Such emphasis, even when supposedly attributing a medical cause to the loss of a pregnancy, implicitly blames pregnant mothers for their own susceptibility to miscarriage. The implication is clear: if only a woman could control her anxious mind, then she could also carry her baby. This emphasis on nervous tendencies establishes miscarrying mothers as distinctly "other" from healthy pregnant and maternal bodies, whose diarrhea, and whose minds, is less likely to lead to miscarriage. (I should note that diarrhea is, at times, a symptom of miscarriage, but it is certainly not a cause.)

For Bedford, because miscarriage was so often caused by "general nervousness" (241), the best methods to prevent miscarriage when it was threatened was to give an actively miscarrying mother a cordial, put her feet up, and offer "cheerful and encouraging assurances that things are going on well" (246). This medical advice emphasizes not that an anatomical or genetic issue causes the loss of pregnancy but that a mother's mental state determines her ability to carry a child successfully. In subsequent pregnancies following miscarriage, Bedford said, the pregnant mother should be prescribed laudanum to ensure she remained calm and did not cause another spontaneous loss (246). These suggestions clearly blame the mother's mental state for her losses, never physical, biological, or care-based causes. Prescribing laudanum, we now know, could very well cause a miscarriage, but Bedford's insistence that miscarriages were the result of nervousness erased any possibility that his own treatment regimen could have been responsible for pregnancy loss. Rather, in case studies, Bedford blames the mother and her nerves time and again. It's also worth noting that this cause has maintained a stronghold over present-day understandings of miscarriage. Survey anyone who has experienced fertility trouble, and she will not be able to count on both hands the number of times she's been told to "Just relax," as if her nerves are her problem.

The blame Bedford places on his patients highlights another problem with nineteenth-century medical rhetoric about miscarriage: although women supposedly had enough control over their bodies to be responsible for their miscarriages, Bedford did not grant them enough agency to believe they actually understood what their bodies were experiencing. "When summoned to a female who supposes herself to be menaced with a miscarriage," Bedford writes, "the first and obvious duty of the practitioner is to ascertain whether she is in fact menaced, or whether her fears are without foundation" (244). This language silences the agency and the understanding of the pregnant mother. She is incapable of determining with certainty whether she is miscarrying (a difficulty even for doctors today if not for the availability of blood tests and ultrasound technology). If she is not miscarrying, her fears are said to be without foundation, as if the extensive cramping and bleeding that likely led her to call for the doctor in the first place are not valid reasons for concern. Furthermore, Bedford says the doctor must first ascertain whether the mother "*really* is threatened" (244, my emphasis). The word "really" highlights not only that the mother is incapable of making such a determination herself but also that the doctor's assumption is actually that she is mistaken in her concern. Additionally, the words Bedford uses to describe the miscarriage minimize both the physical and emotional impact of pregnancy loss on the mother, as the words "menace" and "troubles" suggest a mere disturbance, not the physical and psychological pain that accompany labouring and birthing a sleeping child.

Some nineteenth-century doctors had more nuanced under-standings of the causes of miscarriage than Bedford, but their rhetoric was still largely accusatory and isolating. Edward Tilt, an English obstetrician and eventual president of the Obstetrical Society of London, researched and discussed "uterine deviation" in great detail, and he recognized some physiological medical causes of miscarriage, such as "ulceration of the cervix" (9). Still, Tilt's rhetoric demonstrates a continued separation between the emotional and physical experience of miscarriage and medical discursive practices, and his rhetorical choices (certainly not his treatments) are similar to those used in contemporary medical practice. He uses the words "miscarriage" and "abortion" practically interchangeably in his writings, and he suggests the monthly application of leeches to the cervix of patients for whom "abortion has become habitual," which are nearly the exact words that appeared on my medical chart a century and a half later (Tilt 124).

Tilt also blamed miscarrying mothers for their losses. After a woman to whose cervix he had applied leeches miscarried the day following his treatment, Tilt claimed that the leeches could not have caused the loss. Instead, he insisted, "It is probable that the miscarriage was caused by the patient having danced a great deal on the previous evening, although she had been told to keep quiet" (124). Through such language, Tilt perpetuates the accusatory rhetoric that blames miscarriage on over-excitement or nerves. Despite a likely physical cause, which would have been the doctor's fault, Tilt not only blamed the mother's behaviour but also highlighted the subversive nature of that behavior because it ignored male medical instruction. Tilt also suggested that young brides should celebrate their marriages less in order to avoid miscarriage. As Tilt writes, "The succession of visits and gaieties in honor of the bride, the sight-seeing and other fatigues of continental trailing, are well calculated to bring early miscarriages," which blames women for their losses because of their insistence on indulging in excess (292).

These two doctors form prime examples of the ways in which medical rhetoric of the time ignored even the science that was understood about miscarriage. Instead, they insisted on casting blame on miscarrying mothers. It was as if the language doctors used formed a mechanism of control over their patients: do as I say, or else the consequences are on you. Other examples are abundant, but I chose these two because of their specific notoriety: Bedford was an instrumental player in the discovery of uterine anomalies, and Tilt was leader of London's major obstetrical society. The rhetoric of blame that these, and most other medical practitioners, perpetuated is echoed in the few literary representations of miscarriage available.

The blame doctors attributed to miscarrying mothers made its way into the few fictional representations of the subject. One of the more detailed depictions of nineteenth-century miscarriage appears in George Eliot's *Middlemarch*, in which Rosamond miscarries after horseback riding. Even this seemingly thorough consideration is granted a mere two paragraphs of discussion—to use Doreen Thierauf's words, it is a "non-depiction" due to its largely taboo subject (480). In the short paragraphs that do discuss Rosamond's miscarriage, the narrator directly blames Rosamond for her loss. In response to a commonly held belief that horseback riding regularly caused miscarriage, Rosamond's husband, a doctor, warns her not to ride during her pregnancy (Greaves 13-14). When Rosamond defies his wishes and goes riding with his cousin, she miscarries their child. Not only does such a depiction paint Rosamond as an uncontrollable, misbehaving woman, but it also blames her loss specifically on that misbehaviour, implying that a more appropriately submissive woman would have carried the pregnancy to term.[4] The culpability of mothers for their own miscarriages in fiction suggests that medical rhetoric permeated outside the medical realm; the subject of miscarriage was barely discussed, but when it was, social practice, much like the medical one, was to blame the mother for her loss.

In addition to blaming mothers, the non-depictions of miscarriage in Victorian fiction highlight the silence surrounding the subject, a silence that, to a large extent, continues today. In most novels, miscarriage is a minor footnote in a much larger plot, as the mother's experience is largely ignored in the minimal space granted to the subject. In Dickens's *David Copperfield*, for instance, Dora's pregnancy and miscarriage are described in a mere three sentences that are easy for most readers to overlook. David explains, "Dora was not strong. I had hoped that lighter hands than mine would help to mould her character, and that a baby-smile upon her breast might change my child-wife to a woman. It was not to be. The spirit fluttered for a moment on the threshold of its little prison and, unconscious of captivity, took wing" (Dickens 495). Such a brief and vague discussion of the subject demonstrates the unspeakability of miscarriage; the words "pregnancy" and "miscarriage" never actually appear, nor is Dora ever imagined as a mother. Rather, the focus is on the life lost, with no regard to the effect of that loss on the mother. She has no voice in her story.

The explanation of Sue Bridehead's miscarriage in Thomas Hardy's *Jude the Obscure* perhaps best demonstrates the silence surrounding the subject of pregnancy loss. The loss of Sue's pregnancy receives surprisingly minimal attention in this late-century novel that otherwise breaks numerous social taboos, including descriptions of cohabitation and pregnancy out of wedlock, as well as a murder-suicide scene. Sue's emotional state endangers her pregnancy after the murder-suicide of all of her living children by the eldest child, who kills himself and his siblings to save his poverty-stricken parents from bearing their expense any further. Although the act of the murder-suicide is not depicted in the novel, the narrator describes the scene in detail vivid enough that many scholars consider it the most shocking moment in Victorian fiction. Yet although Hardy provides details about the murder-suicide of children by a child, Sue's subsequent miscarriage is told briefly and from a distance. When Sue miscarries (we could perhaps classify her loss as a stillbirth; the details are too scant to be sure), the reader sees neither Sue nor her lost child. Instead, the experience is described as a secondary account, in passive voice, when Jude receives "intelligence" that "a child had been prematurely born, and that it, like the others, was a corpse" (Hardy 406).

This example from Hardy's novel most aptly demonstrates the unspeakable nature of miscarriage because it immediately follows the breaking of other social taboos. A gruesome murder-suicide scene can be discussed in greater detail than the account of pregnancy loss, which must be conveyed passively. By refusing to examine the female experience of miscarriage (every fictional account here comes from a male character and the medical discussions necessarily came from male doctors), women's experiences as miscarrying mothers are explicitly silenced. This silence has in many ways and for centuries perpetuated and propagated mother-blame even when it's incorrect and inappropriate, causing miscarrying mothers to feel isolated from their surroundings, their doctors, and their bodies.

Guilt and Isolation: The Experiences of Miscarrying Mothers Today

Although contemporary mothers are not blamed for their miscarriages with the overtness that Victorian mothers were, the rhetoric of blame is still pervasive. I was lucky in that my own doctors repeatedly emphasized that there was nothing I could have done to have caused or prevented my miscarriages. But through discussions with hundreds of other women who have experienced multiple miscarriages, I hear very few such stories. Their doctors do not overtly blame them, but few take the time to emphasize that the mother is not to blame. It's for this reason that almost every miscarrying mother I have ever encountered has described guilt as one of her primary emotions.

Medical language can be isolating, and social discourse still maintains elements of accusatory rhetoric that either blame the miscarrying mother or minimize the loss she experiences. Due in part to the "emphasis on self-determination" that has worked to secure women rights to contraception and abortion, there is now an "unintended and unexamined consequence" in that "women may be assumed to be responsible for their pregnancy loss" (Layne 241).

I've already discussed how frequently women experiencing miscarriage (or other infertility issues) are told to "just relax," which insinuates the same notion Bedford espoused in the Victorian period— that pregnant mothers' nerves are to blame for their losses. Another accusatory statement I have heard derives in part from my physical location—I live in the Bible Belt of the Southern United States— as I have been told by multiple people that I "just need to pray harder next time. Such comments simultaneously blame me for my losses and minimize my experience. Although women who suffer from recurrent miscarriages, at least those with the financial and geographical means to seek medical counsel, often go through expensive and invasive testing to determine and rectify a genetic or physiological cause, any suggestion that a miscarrying mother should do something differently in the future implies that her previous losses occurred because she did not do that thing well enough during previous pregnancies.

Furthermore, the use of the word "just" (which somehow always seems to accompany such suggestions) minimizes the experience of a major loss by indicating that the solution to avoid it in the future is small and simple. Other well-meaning people compare our losses to even greater tragedies in attempt to make us feel better. As Linda Layne has explained, "Others minimized my loss by comparing it to what were, at least to their minds, worse hardships, such as being unable to conceive" (3). Such attempts to help miscarrying mothers see the bright side ultimately diminish their experiences; certainly, it would be worse for most people to lose a living child than to miscarry during the first trimester of pregnancy, but pointing out that "at least" a more terrible thing didn't happen only has two possible outcomes. Either it causes miscarrying mothers to feel guilty for their own pain, or it reiterates their feelings of isolation because the people around them clearly cannot connect with their experience.

The ultimate result of such responses tends to be that miscarrying mothers become silent; they feel so stunned by much of what people say regarding their losses that rather than explain the ways in which comments are hurtful or offensive, they quietly either leave the conversation or change the subject. In most instances, the offending commenter never understands the impact of their words, whereas the grieving mother, reminded of the social difficulty of discussing miscarriage, isolates herself and silences her experience in order to avoid the painful reactions from others. The result, of course, is that no useful conversation ensues, no one learns, and no progress is made—a cycle we appear to have been stuck in for centuries.

From a coping perspective, self-blame is a common concern for mothers following miscarriage, and social ideas that perpetuate that blame further isolate miscarrying mothers from the people around them. As a study by Carolyn Huffman and coauthors have demonstrated, mothers who feel guilty about their miscarriages are more likely to experience isolation and blame (32). Either because they cannot reconcile their loss with all they did to try to prevent it (eating right, avoiding certain medications, exercising without over-exercising, etc.) or because others place blame on the mother. Miscarrying mothers who have feelings of guilt also tend to experience feelings of isolation.

In order to help miscarrying mothers feel less isolated, we must understand and discuss miscarriage in a way that recognizes the mother's experience without minimizing it. Because the experience of carrying a pregnancy that doesn't produce a live birth is so poorly understood, miscarrying mothers are often excluded from social understandings of motherhood, usually without most people recognizing the impact of how they define motherhood. By removing the taboo from discussions of miscarriage, we can redefine—or as I would prefer, "undefine"—motherhood to recognize the experiences of women whose pregnancies do not result in happy endings, an inclusion that would make great strides in helping miscarrying mothers through their times of grief. Miscarrying mothers are often told, "You'll get to be a mother someday," but few people recognize that miscarrying mothers *already are* mothers, albeit not fortunate enough mothers to have living children. Mother's Day and Father's Day, as already discussed, are mere examples of institutionally recognized as well as socially constructed celebrations of only the best outcomes of pregnancy.

I highlight the problems with the many people's lack of understanding about the experiences of miscarrying mothers not to blame anyone but to demonstrate a larger point. As a society, we simply aren't educated enough about the subject of miscarriage to recognize how the ways we discuss and embody motherhood unintentionally exclude miscarrying mothers, especially those who do not yet have living children. Changing these norms, however, is complicated and requires cooperation from multiple fronts.

When talking about motherhood, we all need to be aware of the potential impact of our words on families who have experienced miscarriage. Miscarrying mothers themselves, when comfortable, need to speak out about their experiences. The medical community needs to consider ways that they can discuss miscarriage that will be both medically beneficial and emotionally sensitive for patients. As with the Victorian example, because most discussions about miscarriage occur in medical communities, the rhetoric inherently influences social perceptions of the subject. Additionally, Linda Layne has suggested creating "culturally sanctioned rituals by which to mark a pregnancy loss in our societies"—a step that would inherently help miscarrying mothers feel connected to those around them because rituals work specifically to "reaffirm" a "connection to others," thus reaffirming the miscarrying mother's "sense of belonging and identity" (247). Only by improving communication about miscarriage from so many angles can society create a place for it in social discourse and normalize a common experience to help miscarrying mothers feel included rather than excluded.

Such social steps are also necessary to make institutional progress, such as providing miscarrying mothers with benefits like health or bereavement leave. Many miscarriages end in surgery, whereas non-surgical miscarriages after eleven to twelve weeks of gestation regularly result in the mother experiencing contractions and actually giving birth. Only women with access to paid sick or personal leave can miss work without penalty while their minds and bodies recover, yet the need to use a strictly allotted number of sick days for such a physically and emotionally traumatic experience is unacceptable. This is also the reason that many women I know who suffer from recurrent miscarriage have lost jobs because of it—there simply are not enough sick days to cover the doctor's appointments and diagnostic tests in addition to the physical experience of miscarriage, whether vaginal or by dilation and curettage.

Some women, if they have access to such coverage, can use short-term disability to cover leave for miscarriage, whereas others (like myself) are lucky enough to go through such experiences while working for understanding employers. For many women, though, these benefits do not exist—I know many women who have worked through miscarriages, despite the immense physical and psychological toll the experience takes on a woman's body. I've known others who lost their jobs for missing work, a particularly common problem for women who suffer from recurrent miscarriage. Other women feel so unprotected institutionally that they are not even comfortable being honest about the reason for a usually necessary absence; a 2010 article in the *National Post*, for instance, tells the story of a woman who "simply told her boss that she was not feeling well—to have been completely honest would have tipped him to a possible maternity leave in her future" (Vallis A8). Such benefits as the ability to maintain a job and take sick leave should not be contingent upon having understanding employers; miscarrying mothers need to be guaranteed the right to care for their bodies and their minds. These institutional structures need to change, but until strides are made in understanding the commonality of miscarriage and its impact on societies and families, little progress will be made.

What Inclusion Can Look Like

I'll close with a brief anecdote about a time when I was *included* in social perceptions of motherhood and the impact that it had to demonstrate the importance of making such strides. My friend and colleague Rebekah, with whom I shared an office at the time of all four of my miscarriages, found out that she was expecting her first child at the same time that I learned I was pregnant with my third. Because we shared such close physical proximity, we confided in each other, but within a few weeks, she was celebrating seeing a heartbeat on an ultrasound while I was recovering from a methotrexate injection to dissolve an ectopic pregnancy.

One day, Rebekah walked into our office and requested my permission to ask a "sort of weird question." She described a sensation she was feeling in her abdomen, and said, "You know what the first trimester is like a lot better than I do. This feeling is normal, right?" When I tell this story, most people look at me with horror, unable to imagine that this apparently audacious friend was willing to remind me of my own lost pregnancies by comparing it to her healthy one. What those people don't understand is that my pregnancies are erased far more often than they are recognized—people pretend my pregnancies never occurred because recalling them makes them uncomfortable. Until I gave birth to my son, my fifth pregnancy, I was mostly treated as if I had never been through an experience that I actually knew better than most.

In asking this question, Rebekah was the first person ever to include me as a mother; she validated my pregnancies and acknowledged my vast experience *being* pregnant. I was amazed to feel so recognized, so validated, and so included. It wasn't until I was *included* in a discussion about the changing maternal body that I became fully aware of the plethora of ways in which miscarrying mothers are traditionally *excluded* from the social and institutional understandings of motherhood. Having spent the past year-and-a half of my life perpetually stuck in the first trimester, I had not even as much as a baby bump to show for it. Rebekah was the first person to openly recognize that I had experienced pregnancy, multiple times, that I'm attune to every feeling, every emotion, and every twinge— that I'm more aware of the what it's like to live in the first trimester than most mothers who have successfully carried pregnancies to term.

In the time since my recurrent losses (as I finalize edits for this chapter, my son is over a year old), Rebekah remains one of the people I'm most comfortable discussing miscarriage with because she's one of the only people who has never experienced miscarriage who still consistently validates my experiences as a mother. I see other children who were born at the time when my miscarried babies would've been due, and I feel a slight sting. But when I look at her son, I just see my younger little boy's friend, not a reminder of a life that didn't get to be.

This is the result of inclusion and validation.

It is relatively easy for miscarrying mothers with Internet access to find support systems through women experiencing the same loss, but finding support systems in people who have not shared this experience is much more difficult and may be nearly impossible for women without easy access to online resources. Those systems are essential, but they are not likely to become more frequent until we, as a society, become more aware of and comfortable understanding the experience of miscarriage. By creating more dialogue about miscarriage, we can achieve multiple goals that will allow miscarrying mothers to find much more such support. We can prepare women who will someday attempt to become pregnant for the possible experience of miscarriage and develop the necessary terminology and social structures to move miscarriage from "a private space of shame" to a "public space of solidarity" (Layne 239). Finally, such a shift would move us in the direction of creating effective institutional systems — such as appropriate leave structures to accompany revised definitions of motherhood — which would help miscarrying mothers to finally be included in social understandings and representations of motherhood.

Endnotes

1. According to the American Pregnancy Association, an estimated 10 to 25 percent of all recognized pregnancies end in miscarriage ("Miscarriage"). This number is potentially much higher when including pregnancies that never make it to the point of a viable ultrasound; Carolyn Huffman claims that between 20 and 25 percent of all pregnancies end in miscarriage — the same statistic my reproductive endocrinologist told me.

2. For women who experience late-term stillbirth, or whose children die in infancy, social designation of the role of "mother" tends to be more nuanced. Many people acknowledge that such women deserve to be called mothers, whereas others choose to ignore that fact, largely likely due to their personal discomfort of reminding the mother of her loss. In the case of the woman who has lost her only living child, the more time that passes following the loss, the less likely it is that people will remember to recognize the grieved mother.

3. The original quote comes from Heilberg's "Out of Place," published in *UNITE Notes* in 2001. I have not been able to access the original source.

4. Thierauf has persuasively argued that Rosamond's miscarriage was actually an intentional abortion; see "The Hidden Abortion Plot in George Eliot's *Middlemarch*" in *Victorian Studies*.

Works Cited

"Abortion." *Oxford English Dictionary Online*. Oxford University Press, 2016. Accessed 6 July 2015.

Archimedes, Sondra M. *Gendered Pathologies: The Female Body and Biomedical Discourse in the Nineteenth-Century English Novel*. Routledge, 2005.

Atik, Ruth Bender, and Barbara E. Hepworth-Jones. "Talking to Patients about Lifestyle, Behavior, and Miscarriage Risk." *Recurrent Pregnancy Loss*, edited by Ole B. Christiansen, Wiley Blackwell, 2014, pp. 86-102.

Avagliano, Laura, et al. "Miscarriage: Definition, Prevalence, Causes, and Symptoms." *Miscarriages: Causes, Definitions, and Symptoms*, edited by Andrea Luigi Tranquilli, Nova Biomedical, 2012, pp. 1-10.

Bedford, Gunning, S. *Clinical Lectures on the Diseases of Women and Children*. 8th ed. William Wood & Co., 1866.

Cumming, G.P., et al. "The Emotional Burden of Miscarriage for Women and their Partners: Trajectories of Anxiety and Depression over 13 Months." *BJOG: An International Journal of Obstetrics and Gynaecology*, vol. 114, no. 9, 2007, pp. 1138-45.

Cunningham, F. Gary, et al. *Williams Obstetrics*. 23rd ed. McGraw Hill, 2010.

Dickens, Charles. *The Personal History of David Copperfield*. Bradbury and Evans, 1850.

Greaves, George. "Observations on Some of the Causes of Infanticide." *Transactions of the Manchester Statistical Society*, 1862, pp. 2-24. *Hathi Trust*. babel.hathitrust.org/cgi/pt?id=ncsl.ark:/13960/t0bv7gr0t; view=1up;seq=7. Accessed 3 Nov. 2016.

"Habit, n." Def. 9. a. *Oxford English Dictionary Online*. Oxford University Press, 2016. 17 Nov. 2016. Accessed 6 July 2015.

Hardy, Thomas. *Jude the Obscure*. Harper & Brothers, 1896.

Heilberg, Marty. "Out of Place." *UNITE Notes*, vol. 20, no. 3, 2001, p.4.

Huffman, Carolyn S., et al. "Measuring the Meaning of Miscarriage: Revision of the Impact of Miscarriage Scale." *Journal of Nursing Measurement*, vol. 22, no. 1, 2014, pp. 29-45.

Layne, Linda L. *Motherhood Lost: A Feminist Account of Pregnancy Loss in America*. New York: Routledge, 2003.

"Miscarriage." *American Pregnancy Association*. American Pregnancy Association, 2016, americanpregnancy.org/pregnancy-comp lications/miscarriage/. Accessed 6 July 2015.

"Miscarriage, n." Def. 4. a. *Oxford English Dictionary Online*. Oxford University Press, 2016. Accessed 6 July 2015.

Nelson, Claudia. *Family Ties in Victorian England*. Praeger, 2007.

Rauch, Melissa. "Actress Melissa Rauch Announces Her Pregnancy and Reflects on the Heartache of Miscarriage." *Glamour*, 11 July 2017, www.glamour.com/story/actress-melissa-rauch-announces-pregnancy-and-reflects-on-miscarriage. Accessed 3 September 2018.

Seftel, Laura. *Grief Unseen: Healing Pregnancy Loss through the Arts*. Jessica Kingsley, 2006.

Thierauf, Doreen. "The Hidden Abortion Plot in George Eliot's *Middlemarch*." *Victorian Studies*, vol. 56, no. 3, 2014, pp. 479-89.

Tilt, Edward John. *A Handbook of Uterine Therapeutics and of Diseases of Women*. William Wood & Co., 1881.

Vallis, Mary. "The Lonely Pain of Lost Pregnancy; Tests Raise Hopes that Can Be Crushed by an Early Miscarriage." *National Post*, 6 Mar. 2010, p. A8.

Winegar, Jessica. "The Miscarriage Penalty: Why We Need to Talk More Openly about Pregnancy Loss in Academe." *Chronicle of Higher Education*, 29 Nov. 2016, www.chronicle.com/article/The-Miscarriage-Penalty/238526. Accessed 3 September 2018.

Chapter 2

Difficult Children, Blamable Mothers? A Historical Perspective

Clarissa Carden

Introduction

W hen a child is unable or unwilling to live up to society's standards of good behaviour, they open themselves and their families up to blame. That blame, all too often, falls disproportionately on the mother. This chapter explores the practice of mother-blame in an historical context. Drawing from the historical record in Queensland, Australia, it argues that historical discourses holding mothers to be blamable for the behaviours and failings of their children are replicated in contemporary discourse focusing on parents.

Previous researchers have pointed out that mothers generally bear the burden of blame and work associated with children's troubles in education, including disciplinary ones (e.g., Dudley-Marling). The burden on mothers concerning childrearing and associated tasks is one that affects middle-class mothers, as this group devotes a significant amount of time to developing the talents of their children (Francis 927). As a result, mother-blame exists across all social classes: all mothers, in varying ways, stand in relation to their children in a position that is both privileged and difficult. If their children behave admirably, they are open to praise, but if their children are unable or unwilling to conform to expected standards, they become blamable.

Much of this blame is implicit. Public commentators rarely choose words that explicitly point the finger at mothers for the behaviour of children. Instead, the language used implies the culpability of the mother while couched in more general terms. Often *parents* are blamed for problems, but the discourse of failed *mothers* is implied. In this chapter, I trace the history of this discursive construction of failed mothers and present fragments from the history of mother-school relations in Queensland, Australia. In doing so, I demonstrate the existence of a high level of historical continuity in the gendered nature of parent-blame.

Stigma, Blame, and the Contemporary Mother

Erving Goffman, in *Stigma*, states that individuals who are "related through the social structure to a stigmatized individual" may find themselves sharing in the discredit of the stigmatized person to whom they are attached (Goffman 29). Stigma can be overt and in the public sphere, or it can primarily exist in the subjective experience of the stigmatized person (Francis 928). Mothers to children whose behaviour is deemed problematic can experience a stigma that is as severe, and often more so, than that experienced by their child. This stigma is the result of the close social proximity between mothers and children and may thus be conceptualized as a courtesy stigma rather than a stigma associated with the specific actions of the mother (Francis 928). The notion of courtesy stigma has been previously applied to research on the mothers of mass murderers (Melendez et al.). It has also been applied to mothers of children with mental health disorders, such as attention deficit hyperactivity disorder (ADHD) (e.g., Koro-Ljungberg and Bussing). The notion of courtesy stigma, however, is somewhat lacking in relation to the experiences of mothers whose children do not conform to socially prescribed behaviours. Courtesy stigma is different to blame: it occurs due to the proximity of a person to a stigmatized other, whereas blame involves stigma as the result of a person's perceived traits (Francis 929). Courtesy stigma is, thus, different to the stigma associated with perceived bad parenting (Francis 939). The two can, however, go hand in hand, as is demonstrated in this chapter. Blame is intensified in the context of a culture of experts. Psychological expertise, for example, in the form of discourses surrounding children's behaviour in schools, such as school bullying, has been shown to lead to parents being blamed for child behaviour (Herne 263).

The contemporary experience of mothering children with behavioural difficulties is characterized by expert interference, stigma, and blame, which can be attributed in part to the culmination of specific historical circumstances that made prominent and acceptable a discourse of child discipline which positions mothers as uniquely responsible for child behaviour. This discursive construction is neither natural nor inevitable. An analysis of public discourses reveals both an enduring culture of mother-blame and a number of alternative pathways. It also reveals the way in which discursive constructs that do not explicitly position mothers as blamable can, nonetheless, imply that the failure of mothers is responsible for poor child behaviour.

Opinion pieces blaming mothers for failing their children position their arguments in relation to the rights of the child. One such article—published in Queensland's only major printed newspaper, *The Courier Mail*, in 2001 and which questions the validity of attempts to encourage mothers to enter the workplace—states that "we as a community should not be arguing about whether mothers have a right to stay at home. We should be giving all mothers our utmost support to ensure that the central focus—the children—are cared for in the best possible way" (Whaley). The author suggests that this will assist in the prevention of poor behaviour. In 2000, an article was published in the same newspaper lamenting what was perceived as the over-prescription of medication for ADHD. This article spoke about doctors and parents, but it bore the title "Mother's Little Helper" and quoted a mother whose child was prescribed the medication (Retschlag). In both of these examples, the discursive construction of "good mothering" held against "bad mothering"—good mothers put their children's good ahead of their careers, in the first instance, and refuse unnecessary medication, in the second. The latter article demonstrates a puzzling contradiction. Mothers must operate within the context of a culture of experts—the very culture that renders opinion articles on the craft of mothering profitable—but must also be willing to defy expert advice in cases such as the medical prescription of medication for ADHD, where the problem being treated by expert advice is viewed as inherently one associated with the skills of the mother.

Child Behaviour and Mother-Blame—Historical Change and Continuity

The historical record in Queensland demonstrates that the precise nature of concerns over child behaviour has shifted considerably over the past century and in line with dramatically altered social conditions. Despite such changes, the association of blame with parents—particularly mothers—has remained largely the same. During the early stages of the British occupation of Australia, white Australian children were viewed as a source of danger, whose socialization must be achieved perfectly to allow British society to prosper in the antipodes. Although the British colonists were certain of their own civilized state, they were uncertain as to whether civilization could thrive on the Australian frontier (Russell 44). With limited educational provision required until into the early twentieth century, the manners and behaviour of children in colonial and early federation society were, therefore, the responsibility of their parents, particularly their mothers. There was a strong geographical aspect to the discursive constructions of child behaviour. Those children who grew up in isolated regions in the bush, who mixed little with the more respectable portions of colonial society, and who had few opportunities to engage in formal schooling were open to censure. So, too, were city children a source of concern. The former lived a life that was depending on the discursive formation in use at any particular time, simple, natural, wild, untamed, and neglected. The latter was either exposed to the benefits of urban society or lived a life marked by moral hazard and affectation (Russell 197). In Queensland, such concerns were amplified by fears about the impact of tropical and subtropical climates on the health and morality of white children (Carden, "Reformatory Schools"). There was little agreement as to how or where children ought to be brought up in order to obtain results that could be viewed as civilized. There was, nonetheless, a general belief that many of the problems facing adults could be avoided if children were raised to be well-mannered and gentle (Russell 214).

It was from this context—a context of colonial violence and fear, and in which children were positioned both as the positive future of the state and as the sign of a deteriorating race—that the focus on the mother as responsible for child behaviour was developed. It must be explicitly noted here that the mother analyzed and commented upon was undoubtedly white until the middle of the twentieth century. It was the white racial future that discursive constructions of child behaviour and motherhood were concerned.

The discourse of parental responsibility for school behaviour was prevalent from the introduction of state education in Queensland. The type of discursive construction surrounding parents and their children is evidenced by an 1888 article published in the *Brisbane Courier* (later the *Courier-Mail*), which states that "the lawless youth – (and no one can deny that lawlessness is strikingly conspicuous among us)— follows the impulses of a high-spirited young animal." It goes on to argue that this lawlessness is almost invariably due to the failure of parents. Here, however, fathers are described as the force through which (male) children should be controlled. The article, which begins by describing the indiscipline discussed therein as "one of the most marked features of the present age," asks the reader to consider the following: "Who can expect a lad who does not acknowledge the claims of his family upon his obedience, upon his regard for its interests, to admit the claims of what to him must be at least more or less of an abstraction, namely, his country." Having explicitly brought forward the problem of future citizenship, the article then describes the young person who due to a failure of parental discipline behaves in such a manner as to ensure that little hope may be held out for their future reformation:

> It is not enough that a man should send his children to school. The discipline of school life fails almost wholly unless it is supported by the weight and authority of parental discipline, for it is to the parent's view of things that the child peers instinctively, and the burden and responsibility of turning out a boy who will become a good citizen lies pre-eminently with the father, and can be shifted by him to no one else's shoulders.

The positioning of male children as the responsibility of paternal, rather than maternal, authority represents a conception of men as the educators and defenders of manhood. Mothers were considered to be responsible primarily for the behaviour of daughters. Their willingness and ability to carry out this responsibility was a source of public debate, but they were far from universally maligned. A1893 a letter to the editor of the Brisbane Courier defends the girls of Queensland and calls a previous letter writer to task for slandering "the mothers of our Australia, who, we are glibly told, are so engrossed in the pursuit of pleasure as to have little time to devote to their daughters' welfare" (Graham 2). This demonstrates an important aspect of dominant discursive constructions: they do not necessarily go unchallenged. That letter, written in defence of Queensland's mothers, does not question the position of the mother as moral authority over the child. Instead, it questions the notion that they failed in their role. Suspicion over the abilities of mothers was amplified during and after the First World War. Without fathers present as disciplinarians and sources of authority, mothers were brought into the spotlight. Lady Gibbs, writing for the newspaper *Week* in 1926, describes youth as "contemptuous of discipline," with "even schoolchildren likely to strike" (32). Mothers during the war, Gibbs states, were left without fathers to discipline and to support them. Their children had become uncontrollable, with discipline remaining at a low ebb even after the war. This construction of mothers as incapable of controlling their children continued through the twentieth century. A columnist for a local newspaper in the regional city of Rockhampton, going by the penname "Jill's Mother," argued in 1938 that schools are "usually right" and that mothers should recognize that "counsel ... given to their children on the subjects of hygiene and behaviour" are not a rebuke to their parenting but instead helpful advice, impersonally given (Jill's Mother 10). Mothers who disagree with the advice of their child's school were, therefore, positioned as being overly sensitive. The Second World War brought another rash of concern about the ability of mothers to discipline children without the aid of a male authority figure. A 1943 article published in the *Daily Mercury*, in rural Mackay, states that children were skipping school at higher levels than prior to the Second World War and that working mothers and "the relaxed discipline" in "broken-up families" were to blame ("Boys Wag School While Mothers Work" 4).

By the mid-twentieth century, blaming mothers for disciplinary problems within the school became more explicit. "Medical Mother," a person presenting as a doctor and mother writing a columnist for Brisbane's *Courier-Mail*, wrote in 1954 that she occasionally wished she was not a working mother. In the column, she states that the school teachers of Queensland had noticed that those naughty children who could not be controlled were often those whose mothers worked outside the home (Medical Mother 9): "The tragedy of it is that so often all her hard work and sacrifice in carrying on two hard jobs is in vain for, if her child has, in the meantime become a delinquent, or even 'out of hand,' he is now incapable of profiting by the opportunities she has worked so hard to provide" (Medical Mother 9).

The 1959 Dewar report into the problems of youth states that "deep and widespread ignorance" existed among parents in relation to childcare and that "it solves nothing to blame parents who seek to do the right thing by their children, but fail through lack of knowledge or training" (Dewar et al. 2). The report argues that education ought to focus on preparation for future domestic tasks, including parenthood. Discipline within the home was perceived as often at fault, being either too lenient or too harsh for the benefit of the child. No outside influence, including the school, could make up for a lack of appropriate discipline in cultivating a future citizen (Dewar et al. 2).

This government report demonstrates that people in positions of power viewed parents as incapable, often through no fault of their own, of teaching their children the right way to live. The committee indicates that training for citizenship should begin in the earliest years of schooling, potentially at the age of four (Dewar et al. 2). The school is, thus, a means through which the defects of the educational provision by families and society may be corrected. Citizenship education is a form of disciplinary action: a form of moulding what Foucault describes as "docile bodies" (135). Through providing explicit instruction in the way children ought to behave as members of a society, and through doing so at an early and impressionable age, the committee aims to alter the way children think about themselves as individuals within the community. That this role is conceived as one appropriate for the state represents a serious alteration in the way that self-discipline in young people is understood. No longer is it an inherent trait or something to be gained through interactions with parents and peers. It becomes teachable, and the lack of self-discipline becomes correctable when intervention is sufficiently early. The space in which it cannot be successfully taught is the home. This foreshadowed the concern with the ability of the family to protect and manage children in later years, which was to become a key factor in the perceived disintegration of school discipline.

Bassett et al., in a 1963 text on techniques for headmasters, go further than suggesting that parents and teachers need to work together to address disciplinary problems. They explicitly state that many problems in school are the result of a failure in home environments: "It can readily be admitted that the disciplinary problems of a school are in part derived from outside the school. A child is learning (or not learning) self-control in the home and in the street, as well as in the school, and the disciplinary problems that a school may experience may well be not of its own making, or within its control" (9).

Parents, then, were viewed as responsible for a lack of self-discipline among the young as well as a lack of application to schoolwork and a lack of self-control in the classroom. This stance held that the school was not to be blamed for the disciplinary problems occurring under its purview. Instead, parents failed to exercise adult authority to that extent that would encourage pupils to behave in sanctioned ways.

Towards the end of the century, the sense that a failure of adult—particularly maternal—authority within the home was affecting the school took on greater urgency. The 1990s marked the emergence in Queensland of a prevalent discourse of school discipline as in crisis. Concerning parents, this discourse argued that parents refused or were unable to teach children how to behave in public spaces. One 1998 article from *The Courier Mail* says that contemporary parents were unwilling to employ "any consequence that serves to prove, once and for all, that parents mean business—permanently" (Rosemond). Although the article describes parents, the author provides the example of a parent who resisted suggestions that their child had ADD and instead used harsh punishment to correct their child's behaviour—the parent was the mother. The clear implication here is that if children cannot be controlled in the home or in the school, the fault is with the mother who is too weak to control the behaviour.

The source of authority drawn upon by those aiming to evaluate and control the behaviours of children continued to shift. Child behaviours were co-opted by medical authorities, as in a 1999 report on alcohol, cigarette, and illicit drug use among students in Queensland secondary schools, which was produced by the Centre for Health Promotion and Cancer Prevention Research (Stanton et al.). These behaviours remained an education issue, as evidenced by the co-operation of the Department of Education in the production of the report and the report's mention of education programs undertaken on the use of such substances (Stanton et al. 5). They were also taken, however, into the realm of healthcare. The continuing factor was that aspect of children's upbringing which had, historically, been understood as the domain and responsibility of their parents, became understood as the responsibility of the state.

These fragments, extracted from the history of the twentieth century, demonstrate a lengthy preoccupation with the role of the mother as moral educator. The moral role of mothers in raising children has long been a focus of historians, potentially at the expense of fathers (Olsen 766). Moments such as those above, therefore, serve to demonstrate what is widely understood: mothers occupy a unique discursive position in relation to the behaviour and morality of the child. It is that discursive position that renders possible the present conceptions of mothers as blamable for child behaviour.

Contemporary Others

Into the twenty-first century, similar discursive constructs of failed parenting have continued. The term "parents" continues to be employed rather than "mothers." The historical account above demonstrates the way in which the "parents" has been used as a descriptor that is explicitly more inclusive than "mothers" but which, nonetheless, exists within a history of mother-blame and implies that mothers are primarily responsible for parental failure. This discourse of "parent-blame" was employed by members of the Queensland Parliament in 2013 in the process of passing a piece of legislation granting school principals additional powers to suspend and expel pupils. Independent MP Liz Cunningham of Gladstone spoke in favour of the Bill and said the following:

> I have heard so many people of my generation and even the generation below mine talk about difficulties with the "younger generation". If students do not learn discipline at home—and that can be for a variety of reasons—school is the place where they begin to learn the frameworks and the parameters within which they function. (Queensland Parliamentary Debates 31 October 2013, 3806)

More recent events in Queensland highlight the extent to which the stigma emerging from mother-blame can be associated with, and compound, existing forms of social exclusion. In 2016, the only primary school in the remote Indigenous community of Aurukun, in Far North Queensland, was closed twice. On both occasions, violence behaviour from young people in the community led to school staff being evacuated. Rather than tackle the pressing issue of Indigenous disadvantage, many Queensland newspapers explicitly or implicitly blamed the parents of Aurukun for the closure of the school (Carden, "As Parents Congregated at Parties"). The well-worn narrative of mother-blame, here repositioned as parent-blame, bolsters narratives of Indigenous deficit or failure, obscuring other, more complicated, explanatory narratives.

In 2016, an article in *The Courier Mail* suggested that well-publicized problems with violence and ill-discipline in Aurukun could be the result of fetal alcohol syndrome —in effect suggesting that Indigenous mothers had set their children up for failure in utero (Perkins 20). Both the historical discourse of "failed mothers," which referred primarily to white mothers, as well as a separate history of the marginalization of Indigenous people and families are relevant. This article, written by a psychologist and researcher, draws on the authority of the expert to excuse young people for their behaviour while simultaneously pinning the blame on their mothers. Other parents used the same incidents to position themselves as good mothers who discipline their children while calling for other parents to do the same (e.g., Geiger). The mayor of Aurukun joined in on this parent-blaming. He was reported in the *Cairns Post* as having blamed the community for the problem, including for "a lack of respect and discipline in the households," which, he stated, contributed to the issue (Radke 8).

A similar sense of loss in relation to community control of children and support for parents has been evident for some time. A 2002 government report states the following:

The increasing number of working mothers, single parents, and single mothers in particular, cannot be held solely accountable for an apparent inability to control boys or for a decline in parenting skills generally. Their counterparts in earlier generations are likely to have enjoyed more support and assistance from friends, family and neighbours. While the hard evidence is not available to support the assertion, few people would dispute that a generation ago it was much more common for neighbours to assist each other in the supervision and routine discipline of each other's children. It is also true that a generation ago more parents had the support of an extended family network. (House of Representatives 55)

The attitude espoused in this statement is symptomatic of a nostalgic turn. There is a sense that children were better behaved in the past, families were stronger, and mothers had a greater degree of control over their children. The same report, which invokes nostalgia to eschew placing the blame for children's behavioural issues solely on parents, also indicates that "certain parenting styles" may be related to learning and behavioural problems (House of Representatives 55).

Conclusion

Much of the contemporary discourse of blamable mothers is nostalgic: it invokes a sense that, in some distant past, parents, but particularly mothers, were good and disciplinary. This paper demonstrates that this is not so: there has never been a historical moment, at least in the history of Queensland, at which public discourse held mothers up as exemplary disciplinarians. Indeed, the opposite is true: mother-blame has a lengthy history that appears to be associated less with the conduct of an individual mother and child than with a general perception that where children misbehave, mothers are to blame. It is against this historical background that contemporary discussions of failed parents must be read.

The history of Queensland not only demonstrates that mother-blame is continuous but also that its specific form and content differ according to historical context and existing attitudes towards the specific mothers who are to be blamed. As the case of Aurukun demonstrates, mother-blame can contribute to and amplify existing negative perceptions and forms of social marginalization. Although the use of the term "parents" appears to de-gender accusations of parental failure, the similarity of the parent-blame discourse to historical and contemporary accusations of maternal failure cannot be ignored.

Works Cited

Bassett, GW, et al. *Headmasters for Better Schools.* University of Queensland Press, 1963. "Boys Wag School While Mothers Work." *Daily Mercury,* 15 Mar. 1943, p. 4.

Carden, Clarissa. "'As Parents Congregated at Parties': Responsibility and Blame in Media Representations of Violence and School Closure in an Indigenous Community." *Journal of Sociology,* vol. 53, no. 3, Sept. 2017, pp. 592-606.

Carden, Clarissa. "Reformatory Schools and Whiteness in Danger: An Australian Case." *Childhood,* 2018, pp. 1-11.

Dewar, A.T., et al. *Report of the Committee on Youth Problems.* Committee Report, Queensland Government, May 1959.

Dudley-Marling, Curt. "School Trouble: A Mother's Burden." *Gender and Education,* vol. 13, no. 2, June 2001, pp. 183-97. *Queensland Parliamentary Debates,* Queensland Government, 2013, pp. 3798-818.

Francis, Ara. "Stigma in an Era of Medicalisation and Anxious Parenting: How Proximity and Culpability Shape Middle-Class Parents' Experiences of Disgrace." *Sociology of Health & Illness,* vol. 34, no. 6, July 2012, pp. 927-42.

Foucault, Michel. *Discipline and Punish: The Birth of the Prison.* Translated by Alan Sheridan. 2nd ed. New York: Vintage Books, 1995.

Geiger, Dominic. "Mother's Call for Discipline." *Cairns Post,* 27 May 2016, p. 7.

Goffman, Erving. *Stigma: Notes on the Management of Spoiled Identity.* Simon and Schuster, Inc, 1986.

Graham, W. Edward. "Letter to the Editor: Our Girls and Boys." *The Brisbane Courier,* 27 Jan. 1893, p. 2.

Herne, Karen E. "'It's the Parents': Re-Presenting Parents in School Bullying Research." *Critical Studies in Education,* vol. 57, no. 2, 2016, pp. 254-70.

House of Representatives Standing Committee on Education and Training. *Boys: Getting It Right.* The Parliament of the Commonwealth of Australia, Oct. 2002.

Jill's Mother. "Teacher Is Usually Right: A Plea to Mothers to Co-Operate with School." *Evening News,* 22 Oct. 1938, p. 10.

Koro-Ljungberg, M., and R. Bussing. "The Management of Courtesy Stigma in the Lives of Families With Teenagers With ADHD." *Journal of Family Issues*, vol. 30, no. 9, Sept. 2009,

Lady Gibbs. "Special Article: Problems of Parenthood No. 7: Should Discipline Be Maintained?" *Week*, 6 Aug. 1926, p. 32.

Medical Mother. "Working Mothers and the Juvenile Delinquent." *The Courier Mail*, 1 Oct. 1954, p. 9.

Melendez, Michael S., et al. "Mothers of Mass Murderers: Exploring Public Blame for the Mothers of School Shooters through an Application of Courtesy Stigma to the Columbine and Newtown Tragedies." *Deviant Behavior*, vol. 37, no. 5, May 2016, pp. 525-36.

Olsen, Stephanie. "The Authority of Motherhood in Question: Fatherhood and the Moral Education of Children in England, 1870–1900." *Women's History Review*, vol. 18, no. 5, Nov. 2009, pp. 765-80.

Perkins, Meg. "Punishment Not the Answer." *The Courier Mail*, 30 May 2016, p. 20.

Radke, Brendan. "Mayor Doesn't Pull His Punches." *Cairns Post*, 14 May 2016, p. 8.

Retschlag, Christine. "Mother's Little Helper." *The Courier Mail*, 14 Jan. 2000, p. 17.

Rosemond, John. "When the Going Gets Tough." *The Courier Mail*, 21 Apr. 1998. Factiva.

Russell, Penny. *Savage or Civilised? Manners in Colonial Australia.* University of New South Wales Press Ltd, 2010.

Stanton, Warren R., et al. *Alcohol, Cigarette and Illicit Drug Use among Year 7 to 12 Students in Queensland, 1999.* Centre for Health Promotion and Cancer Prevention Research, University of Queensland Medical School, 2000.

The Brisbane Courier. "Tuesday, June 19, 1888." *The Brisbane Courier*, 19 June 1888, p. 4.

Whaley, Maria. "Who's Caring for the Children?" *The Courier Mail*, 15 June 2001, p. 21.

Chapter 3

Decentring Motherhood: Social Exclusion, Ecology, and Authority in Colonial Spanish America

María Piedad Quevedo-Alvarado

A few years ago, I picked up the results of my pregnancy test at the health institution where I was affiliated. I was asked for my identity document in order for the results to be handed to me. Next, the nurse looked into a drawer for the test results and once she found them, she looked inside, took my identity card, and left to another room without saying a word, only indicating with gestures for me to follow her.

In that other room, she sat in front of a computer and entered my personal information into some kind of register. She was still not talking to me. Then she prepared some medical forms, including a prenatal control card, which she marked with my name and age. She put together a couple of fliers on pregnancy, handed me this newly prepared package, and said, "Here's this stuff, mom." I thought: "Mom? Am I *your* mom? Can you call me that?" Could this very same situation happen to other women picking up their pregnancy test results? Such a lack of communication and consideration? Such violence? Such sudden blurring of one's own identity? "Mom." I suddenly was not María Piedad, with all the varied, contradictory, multifaceted feelings, ideas, experiences, and expectations converged in that name; rather, I was "mom" to someone I had never seen before in my entire life and to someone who was in no way related to me. What was the basis of such an invasion? Why did this nurse think she had the right to take my identity away and call me mom and input my personal information into a computer without first letting me know the test results and without asking me if I would choose to continue with the pregnancy and have the baby? Why was she depriving me of my own body, my choices, my name, and my rights as a woman? The pregnancy test results were known first by a database of the state. Only after this were the results given to me, the one whose body and life this affected first and foremost. How could such a thing possibly happen? This situation made me question the value of my own individuality within the state. It showed a health system regulated by a state imposing its authoritarianism over me—a state more concerned with the costs of the health system rather than the guarantee of coverage for its people—as well as a health system characterized by wide misinformation, precarious health coverage, corruption, and lack of recognition of sexual and reproductive rights, especially women's.[1]

There, in that room, I was standing in front of the state, its authoritarianism, its power, and its politics. My female body was standing in front of the patriarchal body of the state and had no possibility of speaking. I felt and thought that it was violent and that motherhood, in terms of the state, was also violent—a device of control and discipline, and a device for state reproduction in the most literal sense.

This was the very first moment I experienced motherhood as a type of political exclusion and as the cancellation of my own individuality and rights. It carried the imposition of a social role defined by the state and controlled by society. Although we do not often associate motherhood with the lack of rights or with the impediment of full social participation, it can entail a kind of social exclusion due to the number of normative discourses linked to its dimension as an institution—marriage, family, heterosexuality, maternal instinct, unconditional love, sacrifice, etc.—and can restrict women in many different areas, including legal, medical, social, economic, and labour[2] ones as well as others.[3]

Determined to overcome the social prescriptions of motherhood I decided to have my baby and become a critical mother, undisciplined and disobedient. I was not willing to lose myself into motherhood or to accept its social impositions to satisfy others or fulfill their expectations. Choosing motherhood did not mean renouncing my identity and desires or adhering to conservative perspectives, but it did mean hard work, resistance, courage, sensibility, creativity, and love. As a female scholar interested in literature and history, one of my most difficult struggles has been the building of motherhood as a place of thinking in order to enhance, enlarge, and enrich my space of living and writing.

My aim in this work, then, is to explore motherhood as a state apparatus that allows certain types of social exclusion—dominance, subalternization, depriving of rights, even racism, (i.e., motherhood as the reproduction of the status quo)—in contrast with its dimension of political resistance and displacement of the authority on which that state is founded (i.e., motherhood as a decentring device). Thus, I would like to refer to a couple of texts of colonial Spanish America where I find a characterization of motherhood that confronts and disrupts the link between motherhood and official, imperial power from the experience and aspirations of two colonial individuals from the final decades of the sixteenth century and the first decades of the seventeenth century: Don Diego de Torres, cacique of Turmequé, in the New Kingdom of Granada; and Garcilaso Inca de la Vega, born in Cuzco, in the Viceroyalty of Peru. These two individuals present motherhood as a destabilizing device of the imperial and colonial structure.[4]

The *Relación* of Don Diego de Torres: Breastfeeding as a Political Ecology of the Empire[5]

Don Diego de Torres (1549–90), the cacique of Turmequé, was a *mestizo* (born of Spanish and Indian parents) born in the New Kingdom of Granada. He was son of the conquistador and *encomendero* (a trustee of Indian tribute) Juan de Torres, and Catalina de Moyachoque, sister of the cacique of Turmequé. Don Diego inherited the *cacicazgo* (chiefdom) from his uncle but was deprived of it by the Royal Audiencia, who gave it to his half-brother who was Spanish born, not mestizo. Don Diego travelled to Spain and obtained a meeting with King Philip II, who restituted his cacicazgo. However, when he returned to the New Kingdom, the colonial authorities did not recognize the royal decree, and Don Diego was accused of instigating a rebellion. He, then, had to run away, and after some difficulties, he fled to Spain again to continue his claims, which produced a document known as *Relación de Don Diego de Torres*, in which he denounces and explains to King Philip II the sufferings of the Indians of the New Kingdom of Granada under Spanish rule, especially the cruelties committed under the encomienda system.

Most of the studies concerning the figure and words of Don Diego de Torres focus on his mestizo condition, his exciting escapes, and his confronting of colonial law the performing of his subjectivity in front of the law (Rappaport; Restrepo). I am going to try here a more modest approach. My interest is in the way Don Diego uses motherhood to delegitimize the colonial government in his *Relación*, and as a term to be associated with the economies of the Spanish Empire. Although the colonial system celebrated masculinity, and its capacity for imposing order through violence, Don Diego developed an image of colonial power as unproductive for the economic interests of the Spanish Crown; he used motherhood as an argument against the devastation and infertility of the Indies caused by Spanish colonization.[6] In other words, Don Diego uses motherhood as tool to both critique the Spanish occupation of the Indies and to reestablish the productive dimension of the Spanish occupation of the Indies that favoured both colonizers and colonized.

Against a tapestry of devastation of nature, human injustice, and colonial oppression of the Spanish rule, Don Diego projects motherhood and breastfeeding of the Indians as devices of production and fertility. This political ecology is presented by Don Diego as an unbalance, which can be restored by the Crown through the protection and the recognition of the services of the Indians.

His document refers to the use of female Indians who have just given birth as breastfeeders for Spanish women. Three or four female Indians were used as breastfeeders for Spanish babies, and they performed other occupations in the Spanish homes. According to Don Diego, the male Indians kept their babies in their towns but could not take good care of them because they could not nurture them. Therefore, the babies often died because of the absence of their mothers and, even worse, died without being baptized. Within his account, Don Diego speaks with the language of empire, and in that sense, the lack of a Christian ritual, baptism, would be seen as a disservice to the king as well as would be the taking of Indian mothers for the breastfeeding of Spanish babies. This use of the female Indians as wet nurses is presented in the *Relación* as a way of taxation, as an economy of the empire—an economy resulting in devastation, death, and the looting of royal incomes.

When Indian mothers were taken to support Spanish mothers, Don Diego reports, the male Indians went to their caciques and governors seeking help. However, they did not find any comfort or solution, which showed that they lacked power within the colonial rule. Indian authorities were supposed to be heard by colonial governors; the competence of the caciques and other chiefs acknowledged by the law that was being overruled. Where, then, could the Indians find the king's authority and protection?

The image that Don Diego represents is interesting: male Indians with their crying babies in their arms, going from their towns to the houses where the Indian mothers were taken and from these houses to the Indian authorities, not knowing what to do. In the absence of the mother's body, there was no other body to take its place. The body of the father was not useful, as Indian men could not work or collect tribute while they cared for their babies; as a result, babies were dying. In my view, the absence of the mother's body and the insufficiency of the father's body replicate the absence of the king's body and the insufficiency of his law in replacing it. Indian women nurturing Spanish babies reproduced the social exclusion of Indian groups within the colonial system—the dispossession of their own bodies to make them work for others. Against that, Don Diego uses motherhood to affirm the Indians' contribution to the Spanish Empire as well as a device to obtain the restitution of his cacicazgo. By so doing, Don Diego reintegrates motherhood's meaning of fertility, abundance, and richness as something associated with the colonized people, undermining the colonial official's authority and overcoming social exclusion by projecting the Indians as legitimate interlocutors for the king.

Not only the death of the Indians was cruel—since they were subjects of the king, as much as the Spaniards, and their deaths could have been avoided—but it was also inefficient for the political and monetary economy of the empire. But beyond the purely economic argument for improving the treatment of Indians, Don Diego interrogates the Crown and asks King Philipp II what he is doing in favour of his subjects, in favour of the Indians.

In his argument, Don Diego proposes a balance, a sort of political ecology between the exploitation of nature, Indian labour, and colonial power. Motherhood becomes part of the balance he is requesting in terms of preservation and reproduction. The argument defends not only Indians but also the Spanish Empire itself, as it is being plundered by its own agents.

If we return to Las Casas's *Brevissima* in which the Dominican friar shows the Spaniards to be wolves (cannibals) devouring the helpless sheep (Indians), could not the death of the Indian babies be viewed as a form of cannibalism? A sort of devouring by Spanish greed? Are not the Spanish mothers devouring the native babies? In this revision of cannibalism—a kind of inhumanity usually attributed to Indians—Don Diego presents Spanish motherhood, or colonial motherhood, as a kind of monstrosity. By so doing, he reorders the terms of the dominance, showing it not only as illegitimate but as inhumane.

Mastering the Mother Tongue: Authority and Self-Invention in the Works of Garcilaso Inca de la Vega

Born in Cuzco and the son of a Spanish captain of Pizarro's army and of an Inca princess, Gómez Suárez de Figueroa (1539–1616) was a colonial subject proud of his double origin. He enjoyed some privileges as a descendant of a Spanish conquistador and *corregidor* (mayor); he received a careful education and was trained in legal matters by a notary friend of his father. However, Gómez Suárez also experienced the social exclusion of being an illegitimate son (noble Spaniards were banned from marrying Indians, as was the case of captain Garcilaso, his father), a mestizo, and a member of the colonized groups (he grew up among the defeated royal Inca family). After the death of his father, Gómez Suárez travelled to Spain with the money of his inheritance and established there, starting a new life.

Having arrived in Spain at age twenty and been denied the economic compensation for his father's services to the Crown—who was accused of betrayal for sympathizing with the then rebel Pizarro—he first decided to enroll in military service to King Philip II, but he did not receive any recognition from the Crown either. Then, Gómez Suárez de Figueroa began his career in the letters; he changed his name to Garcilaso Inca de la Vega, adopting the name of the Spanish love poet of the time—Garcilaso de la Vega—who was born in Toledo and was related to him by his father's aristocratic ascendancy. In doing that, he was not only appropriating the literary authority of the Toledan poet as much as his military figure,[7] as Roland Green has affirmed, but also endowing his lettered project with a poetic dimension, specifically amorous.

The first work of Garcilaso Inca (1590) was a translation of a Neoplatonic love treatise written in Italian by Jehudah Abrabanel, who had been expelled from Spain for his Jewish ascendancy.[8] In this work, he proudly claims his Peruvian origin and years later, in the prologue to the second part (1617) of his major work, *Comentarios reales* (*Royal Commentaries*), he will refer the scene of a conversation with a Spanish scholar who had diminished his work as a translator –almost twenty years after its publication and canonization– to underline not only the importance of his cultural achievement but, from there, the unjustifiable disdain with which his Andean origin (and with it his entire culture), was dismissed. From the very title of this first piece "La Tradvzion del Indio..." ("The Translation of the Indian...") to the final reference in his last work, Garcilaso establishes a double dimension of the word, alluding to his Indian origin as his main recognition as author/translator, and unfolding it to involve his interest in language (from Italian into Spanish, one foreign language to another), and more specifically in the language of the Indian (Inca) empire, Quechua, his mother tongue. As Susana Jákfalvi-Leiva has stated about this translation as a rewriting, it "condenses the transitivity from the maternal space to the inclusiveness into the European Renaissance context" (5).

Garcilaso is also interested in establishing a link between language and territory in which the mother tongue is central to affirm a place – geographical, cultural– of belonging. It also alters the center point from which the colonizers have defined the new world languages (and its inhbitants) as barbarians. From this place enabled by the mother tongue, Garcilaso can refer the Spaniards as corrupts and barbarians, as he says in the prologue to the first part of the *Royal Commentaries* (1609): they "como extranjeros en aquella lengua, interpretaron fuera de la propiedad de ella" ("as foreigners in that language, interpreted it improperly"). This identification of the colonizers as foreigners, even if obvious, repositions their assumed authority as inappropriate and reminds that the Andean land is actually not their territory. As the proper interpreter Garcilaso claims to be, he elevates Quechua as an authoritative source about history, power, cultural sensibility, and legitimacy.[9]

Therefore, the focus of my inquiry here is how Garcilaso Inca constructs a discursive and historical space of existence for someone like him—a socially excluded subject as well as a mestizo of double nobility who had no space of belonging within the imperial structure—through the proud affirmation of his mother tongue, as a source of knowledge, understanding, and authority. He refers to it as "*la lengua que mamé en la leche*" ("the tongue I was breastfeed with"), which involves a profound sensibility of Inca history and culture, unknown and inaccessible for Spaniards. He fashions himself as an expert interpreter and linguist, whose authority and knowledge come from his Inca origin because, as he says, "*soy indio*" ("I am an Indian") and in this history, the *Royal commentaries*, he will write as an Indian to allow his reader to know the Quechua in "its property and purity".[10]

I want to focus on the trope of lactation, which brings him close to Don Diego's arguments discussed above, but here Garcilaso Inca develops it as a device to delegitimize European authority. It also disrupts the linguistic and political episteme of the colonizers. We need to have in mind that at the beginning of the seventeenth century lactation was understood not only as nutritional but also as a source of well-being or to the detriment of social order. The use of wet nurses was considered by some men as undesirable for Spanish babies because they could influence negatively the behavior and customs of the children (Meléndez 2009, 368). Garcilaso Inca, on the contrary, revalidates lactation as a source of authority and uses it to write, think, and intervene in the text of history. He declares not to be interested in contradicting the Spanish historians who have written about the conquest of Peru but "to serve as a comment and gloss, and interpreter in many Indian words." As José Rabasa has stated, by doing so he was also transforming the categories in which that history was being narrated and made official (206).

This link between lactation and language accentuates the Indian origin of the Inca and reevaluates its minor position within the colonial system—not for the purpose of taking the place of the dominant, but to enhance the transatlantic communication with his fellow Peruvians for whom he "points with his finger the principles of their language" to avoid its corruption and loss. Here, the mother tongue shortens the geographic distance between Garcilaso and his land and people, and strengthens the quality of Quechua to fight against cultural extinction.

Margarita Zamora has shown that the blood purity statute of the Spanish empire did not apply to the naturals of the New World but to Muslims and Jews. But the question of purity of blood had to do not only with faith and fidelity to the Christian god, but with matters of ethnic and national identity. We can see the cultural and political unity implied in the Castilian language disrupted by the linguistic corpus of Quechua. It also questions the constructed legitimacy of Spanish occupation through the exercise of Castilian as a language of history and power. If Garcilaso carries the burden of illegitimacy in his recognition as a mestizo, identified as an "infamous and vile being, prone to the vices acquired in the breasts of the Indian mother" (Zamora 373), he turns this illegitimacy into a condition of cultural authority and resistance.

If, as Zamora states, we cannot think of Garcilaso as lacking purity of blood, we certainly can think of him as overflowing impurity of (breast)milk. The mixing of cultures and tongues his very name testifies and the grounds Quechua provides for the rewriting of history intensify the recognition of the textual corpus of the mother as actively critical, politically conscious, and culturally committed.

Final Considerations

Social exclusion is important when thinking motherhood. It is hard not to notice the many and sophisticated ways motherhood serves to discipline and marginalize women and other subaltern subjects in order to reproduce the status quo. But it is also an experience that can be informed by love, courage, desire, and critical thinking. Nowadays, there are new articulations of motherhood—dietetic, neoconservative, disembodied, passive, or unproductive—that work to exclude mothers and motherhood from the action of history. But as this piece shows, not only can motherhood be a device of questioning, disrupting, and undermining the dominant order, it can also be used to create new territories of reality. It can be a way to transform the order of the world.

From the *Relación* of Don Diego as much as from the works of

Garcilaso Inca de la Vega, it is possible to note the way in which, by motherhood, a metaphorical as well as a real subaltern feminine body, transcends the masculine, patriarchal body of the law of Spanish Empire to reorganize relations of power. Moreover, motherhood in the works of Don Diego and Garcilaso Inca perturbs and undermines the masculine order of power that excludes them from social rights and privileges. It also perturbs the Reason of power.

Don Diego's complaints show that colonial Spanish law is not a reasoned discourse, whereas Garcilaso Inca demonstrates that the epistemological authority of the Empire can be altered, questioned, and modified by the affirmation of the culture and knowledge of the (m)other. In both cases, social exclusion is questioned and intervened by a de-centered discourse on motherhood.

We cannot ignore the strong relation between motherhood and Indians in the texts examined above. Even if we can recognize today that women and Indigenous peoples have been historically oppressed, my interest, however, is not to reproduce this association. Rather, I would like to push forwards this link in terms of seeing motherhood as an important part of the political imagination of early Modern Spain but in a sense that writes back to the history of power.

I would like to return to that scene in the room of the health institution where I was given my pregnancy test results. I would like to return to the silence of the nurse, and I would like to try to end it or, at least, to disturb it in the way that Don Diego and Garcilaso Inca did. These two subjects overcame—even if only temporarily—the social exclusion of the colonial system by critiquing with their words and writing the bureaucratic apparatus that deprived them. They altered the language of power by using it with another agenda. They reshaped it as the language of the (m)other. By so doing, motherhood became a device of restitution of the deprived body: whereas Garcilaso Inca's tongue projects epistemological and political authority, Don Diego's eyes, voice, and hand report to the King the cruelties committed by his officials, and my body gives birth and my hand writes against the state dimension of motherhood.

That female nurse who acted as a state official, with her databases, registers, forms and fliers, and who deprived me of my own body and voice is an example of how the state is performed and also of how it is constituted by a bureaucracy. The nurse's silence towards me speaks of the vertical dimension of state bureaucracy, which does not allow communicating with concrete individuals. Even if I had said something to the nurse, my response would not have been heard nor would it have changed the bureaucracy, since language was among the things I was being deprived of in that room. I was neither allowed to speak or be heard. My words were powerless; they were not part of the language of the state.

Even though I did not say to the nurse how violated I felt because of her actions, I have been able to process it through the years and to reshape this experience into a locus of thinking and writing. In doing that and in studying Don Diego and Garcilaso Inca from this perspective, I have been able to redefine the state, since I do not define it as rigid or monolithic; rather, I think it is possible to undermine, disrupt, and weaken it through experience, language, desire, and creativity. Indeed our critiques, claims, and writings can refashion the state[11]; thus, motherhood as a form of thinking and acting can become a potent force of history.

Endnotes

1. In 2006, ironically under the right-wing government of president Álvaro Uribe Vélez, the Constitutional Court of Colombia, through sentence C-355, found in favour of women's sexual and reproductive rights and decriminalized abortion in three specific cases: sexual abuse, fetus malformation, or danger to the life or health of the mother. However, this decision has not been applied in most cases that women have asked for an abortion—many of them have been underage—because the doctors have objected to providing one on conscientious grounds–even judges have alleged it, which is actually against the law. Many of these women have returned to using clandestine abortions, with great risk for their health and life, and others have been simply obliged to continue with their pregnancy while still fighting for their right to an abortion. Tribunal strikes and administrative barriers within the health system also infringe upon their right to an abortion.

   Medical discourse, with its epistemological privilege, has also contributed to spread of the dominant idea of motherhood as natural, which has naturalized certain expected behaviors associated to motherhood and, therefore, has stigmatized women who become mothers as much as women who do not. Recently, a female magistrate of the Constitutional Court revised sentence C-355 with the purpose of reducing the number of weeks a pregnant woman could access an abortion. After deliberation, the Constitutional Court maintained the original terms of the sentence.

2. For example, through the law 1822, passed 4 January 2017, the President of Colombia Juan Manuel Santos Calderón extended maternal leave in Colombia from fourteen to eighteen weeks. Business associations declared their opposition to the law and warned, as a result, many companies would not hire women.

3. In the context of gender, class, race, sexual, or religious inequalities, motherhood can reinforce the conditions of vulnerability or make them more difficult to overcome. It can face other kinds of social exclusion in situations of war, migration, sickness or disability.

4. Social exclusion was a constitutive part of the Spanish colonial structure in the Indies. Cultural differences such as religious beliefs or the lack of alphabetical writing were used by conquistadors and colonizers as arguments for military occupation, evangelization, and the establishing of a new political order ruled by the Spaniards.

   The colonial context, despite the recognition of limited authority to indigenous chiefs and noble indigenous families over its people, favoured Spanish descendants as officials of the Crown and also as owners of the land. Indians, mestizos, and blacks, therefore, were excluded from political participation as much as from economic and social advantages.

5. The reading I propose here is framed in a research project on Don Diego de Torres with prof. Emiro Martínez-Osorio, from York University, Toronto, Canada.

6. In my view, Don Diego's thinking about colonialism follows that of the Dominican friar Bartolomé de Las Casas. Don Diego uses arguments favouring the peaceful governing of the Indians already used by Las Casas in his *Brevissima relacion de la destruycion de las Indias* (1552, *A Brief Account of the Destruction of the Indies*). That is not to say that Don Diego was in total favour of the Spanish rule, but he was a mestizo who needed to negotiate with the imperial power to protect him and his people. In this sense, he was complaining and

legitimizing his claims within the languages of the empire. He was a colonial subject, and he used this language to denounce injustice and to claim protection from King Phillip II because the Indians were his subjects and the king was not protecting them. Also, for clarification, I use "Indians" to refer the original inhabitants of the territory later called New Kingdom of Granada.

7. Garcilaso de la Vega, the Toledan poet, was also a soldier of the King, and died at age thirty-three in a battle at Nice.

8. Garcilaso Inca published this work under the title "*La tradvzion del indio de los Dialogos de amor de Leon Hebreo*" (*The Translation of the Indian of the Dialogues of Love by Leon Hebreo*).

9. In his other works, *La Florida del Inca* (1605) and *Royal Commentaries* (1609 and 1617), translation is a key point of epistemological authorization as well as of political legitimation. Garcilaso is interested in showing a coherence between the exercising of power and the uses of the tongue, in which the Inca empire is his best example.

10. As he says in the Prologue to the first part of the *Royal Commentaries* (1609). We can understand this statement as a form of destabilization and disavowal of the official historiography of the Inca Empire and its conquest by the Spaniards. Garcilaso Inca presents himself as a linguist who is correcting the terms of history.

11. I am aware that the state within which my experience is shaped is not the same state of Don Diego and Garcilaso Inca. However, this modern state has retained and strengthened a lot of legislation, practices of power, and forms of establishing relations with the people that come from the colonial period.

Works Cited

Archivo General de Indias. Patronato 231. *Relación de Don Diego de Torres*. N. 6, R 5. 1584.

Garcilaso de la Vega, Inca. *Obras completas*. Biblioteca de Autores Españoles, 1965. 4 vols.

Greene, Roland. *Unrequited Conquests. Love and Empire in the Colonial Americas*. The University of Chicago Press, 1999.

Gupta, Akhil. *Red Tape. Bureaucracy, Structural Violence, and Poverty in India*. Duke University Press, 2012.

Jákfalvi-Leiva, Susana. *Traducción, escritura y violencia colonizadora: un estudio de la obra del Inca Garcilaso*. Syracuse University, 1984.

Mazzotti, José Antonio. *Encontrando un Inca. Ensayos escogidos sobre el Inca Garcilaso de la Vega*. Axiara Editions/Academia Norteamericana de la Lengua Española, 2016.

Meléndez, Mariselle. "Educando a la mujer criolla en la prensa hispanoamericana de la Ilustración." *Poéticas de lo criollo. La transformación del concepto "criollo" en las letras hispanoamericanas (siglo XVI al XIX)*, edited by Juan M. Vitulli and David M Solodkow Corregidor, 2009, pp. 353-77.

Rabasa, José. ""Porque soy indio": Subjectivity in Garcilaso's *La Florida del Inca*". *Writing Violence in the Northern Frontier. The historiography of Sixteenth-Century New Mexico and Florida and the Legacy of the Conquest*. Duke University Press, 2000, pp. 199-225.

Rappaport, Joane. "Buena sangre y hábitos españoles: repensando a Alonso de Silva y Diego de Torres." *Anuario colombiano de historia social y de la cultura*, vol. 39, no. 1, 2012, pp. 19-48.

Restrepo, Luis Fernando. "El Cacique de Turmequé o los agravios de la memoria". *Cuadernos de Literatura*, vol. 14, no. 28, 2010, pp. 14-33.

Restrepo, Luis Fernando. "Narrating Colonial Interventions. Don Diego de Torres, Cacique of Turmequé in the New Kingdom of Granada." *Colonialism Past and Present. Reading and Writing about Colonial Latin America Today*, edited by Alvaro Félix Bolaños and Gustavo Verdesio, State University of New York Press, 2002, pp. 97-117.

Zamora, Margarita. "Sobre la cuestión de la raza en los *Comentarios reales*." *Renacimiento mestizo. 400 años de los Comentarios reales*, edited by José Antonio Mazzotti, Iberoamericana/Vervuert, 2010, 361-79.

Fearless, Chloe Trayhurn

Chapter 4

Unwed Motherhood, Social Exclusion, and Adoption Placement

Karen March

G offman defines social stigma as an attribute that discredits a person because it draws the negative attention of others to that attribute. He perceives these attributes (i.e., stigma traits) emerging through an interaction process by which others categorize and label certain individuals as being unworthy of social acceptance. The majority of studies using Goffman's model tend to examine social stigma "as something *in the person* rather than a designation or a tag that others affix to the person" (Link and Phelan 366). This tendency to isolate stigma traits, personalize stigma impact, and identify stigma management strategies at the individual rather than the structural level limits our conceptualization of stigma outcome to an understanding of idiosyncratic tactics and management schemes rather than as a behavioural choice constrained by sociocultural context (Link and Phelan).

In this chapter, I examine how different sociocultural, economic, and political environments have shaped the social processes of labelling, stereotyping, separation, and status loss experienced by North American white, middle-class unwed mothers[1] during the twentieth century. Such an examination focuses on the association between social structure, sociocultural context, and adoption. Recognition of the historical change in social attitudes towards unwed mothers underscores how women can be excluded from the social institution of motherhood and denied the status of mother accorded to them through pregnancy and birth. More importantly, the identification of the fundamental social mechanisms underlying the social stigma of unwed motherhood provides a stronger understanding of adoption placement as a social response as well as a personal act.

North American adoption practices have always been influenced by wider cultural beliefs concerning sexual purity, the essentialism of motherhood, and perceptions of biological inheritance. For example, at the beginning of the twentieth century, white, middle-class unwed mothers were stigmatized socially and were ostracized by their family and community when a pregnancy revealed they had broken purity norms by having sexual intercourse before marriage.

Adoption was not viewed as a viable option because the mother-child bond was considered sacrosanct. It was also assumed that keeping her child would give the unwed mother a constant reminder of her transgression thereby making her less likely to sin again. Additionally, the science of eugenics was prominent at the time, and many community members feared respectable families would be tainted if they adopted children who had inherited defective germ plasm from their degenerate unmarried parents (Berebitsky 21). Unwed mothers with a child could not find gainful employment, however, and public assistance programs banned them from benefits in fear that such actions would support illicit sex, undermine the institution of marriage, and produce a financial drain on the state. Most had to place their children in orphanages and take menial jobs; they hoped of a future marriage to a husband who would accept and raise the child as his own. This event rarely happened due to the stigma trait they carried as sexually loose women unfit for respectable marriage.

Recognizing the unsavory conditions of orphanages, some unwed mothers made informal adoption arrangements and/or contacted community service agencies for placement assistance (Kunzel). In its own recognition of the negative environments of many orphanages, the social work profession also began a program of changing public attitudes towards adoption through focused investigations of biological family backgrounds, the development of infant testing, and in-depth home studies of potential adoptive parents. These processes eased some of the stigma that illegitimate children acquired from their mothers' unsanctioned sexual behaviour. As the twentieth century progressed, adoption laws were instituted, placement rates increased, and adoption came to be viewed as a more credible means of family formation.

A major change in adoption acceptance occurred in the early 1950s after the termination of the Second World War. Returning military men sought the stability of home and family, and the women who had waited for them desired fulfillment of postponed motherhood. Assisted by a surge in economic prosperity, a pronatalist climate emerged in support of early marriage, large birth rates, and child-oriented households (Adams). A noticeable number of infertile couples turned to adoption. Politically astute, this parent group endorsed adoption legislation, promoted positive images of adoptive families, and pressured adoption agencies for babies. Their desire for adoptable babies was easily fulfilled because women were still stigmatized for the immoral act of having sex before marriage and lacked social and financial support for keeping and raising any children born out of wedlock.

During the same time period, a social worker named Leontine Young published *Out of Wedlock*, a book based on her eighteen years of work in maternity homes across the United States. Young lessened some of the sense of immorality attached to unwed motherhood in her presentation of this pregnancy as a symptom of a neurotic personality. Specifically, the unwed mother was a girl who had made a mistake rather than a sexual deviant. As such, she possessed little interest in either her baby or the biological father except as a means of expressing her pathology (6). Recovery could occur only by disconnecting her from the "product of her neurotic behavior" and helping her "concentrate on achieving good mental health" (7). Separation would not be a problem because her neurosis had blocked the natural process of mother-child bonding. In fact, adoption was a better option for these children because it removed them entirely from the negative effects of neurotic mothering and placed them under the care of mature, married couples capable of rearing them into successful adulthood.

Social workers trained in Freudian psychology welcomed Young's model. The idea of clients who could be treated through counselling responded more appropriately to their educational training and professional skills than did the previous provision of religious assistance to fallen women (Kunzel 146). The apparent lack of trauma over losing her child to adoption also made the neurotic unwed mother a much more appealing placement candidate than the grieving sinful one. Interestingly, family practitioners tended not to notice "the absence or miraculous disappearance of neurosis exhibited by the much larger population of unwed mothers who got married during pregnancy" (Rains 5). Neither did they recognize how conveniently the children they chose for adoption matched the socioeconomic and racial characteristics of the largest group of adopters seeking their services (Berebitsky). Instead, adoption was portrayed as beneficial for all parties. Through adoption, the unwed mother could be restored to good mental health, her child could be given the opportunity to reach its full potential, and the family needs of prospective adoptive parents could be met. In this way, the essentialism of motherhood that had tainted previous adoptions became superimposed by an ideological image of family. Notably, that image tended to match the adoption worker's own life experience—that is, the experience of being raised by a white, middle-class heterosexual married couple who possessed the ability to rear a child with similar values to their own (Spensky 108).

The community-at-large also embraced the neurotic unwed mother model. The Cold War was threatening the economic prosperity of the 1950s and the political system upon which such fortune relied. In contrast, the family served as a symbolic institution of the moral strength and social stability inherent in the democratic way of life (Adams). Unfortunately, a noticeable rise in teenage pregnancy rates violated the normative standards of premarital purity and marital fidelity upon which the North American family was based (Rains). Young's analysis of teenage pregnancy as the by-product of an individual girl's neurosis eased public anxiety over the moral breakdown of North American culture at the same time as it endorsed family norms through adoption.

The presentation of teenage sexuality as neurotic behaviour also alleviated the distress of individual family members. Specifically, parents who feared they would be judged socially for not imparting the appropriate gender role expectations of unmarried virginity and married motherhood to their children were calmed by the knowledge that deviation from such behaviour was due to individual pathology. And if a pregnancy occurred, adoption offered a "moral reprieve" (Rains 6). Sons could abdicate responsibility because they were victims of an oversexualized girl's psychological illness. More importantly, evidence of a daughter's mistake could be expunged, and any stigma she might carry for breaking the norms of virginity before marriage would be removed. She could go away in secret, have the baby, place it for adoption, return to her community, get married, have more children, and assume a socially acceptable family life as if the pregnancy had not happened. Coincidentally, this secrecy process had been reinforced by the simultaneous enactment of nondisclosure laws that sealed adoption records and kept the identity of all adoption triad members—that is, adoptive parents, adopted persons, and biological parents confidential. Given these social contexts, it is not surprising that the smallest percentage of adoption placements occurred before 1950 and the largest in the mid-1960s (Evans B. Donaldson Institute).

To summarize, the forgoing description highlights the primacy of sexual purity for women before marriage during the first half of the twentieth century in North America and how white, middle-class women were stigmatized due to an unwed pregnancy. Although these unwed mothers experienced social disgrace for breaking this normative standard and carried a spoiled social identity, each generation of women encountered a different process of social labelling, stereotyping, status loss, and community and family response based upon the sociocultural, economic, and political environments in which they carried out their everyday lives. Larger structural components influenced the stigma theories applied to their behaviour (e.g., sinful or neurotic), which, in turn, affected their motherhood choices (e.g., orphanage or adoption) as well as the tactics they used to manage their stigma trait (e.g., responses to public shaming or secrecy). Specifically, it was through wider, socially constructed discriminatory practices that their options for successful motherhood were shaped, their ultimate exclusion from the social institution of motherhood occurred, and adoption as a formal, legal system of family formation emerged.

Today, the social norm of sexual purity and the practices of stigmatizing women for unwed motherhood are disintegrating due to a new era of change in the sociocultural, political, and economic environments. In the 1970s, continued economic growth from the postwar era had created a significant expansion of women into the paid labour force. The civil rights and feminist movements of the 1960s had advanced a more liberal agenda and the promotion of human rights. The legalization of contraceptive devices and easier access to abortion had fostered a sexual revolution whereby more tolerant attitudes towards women's sexuality emerged, and losing one's virginity before marriage became more socially acceptable. A noticeable increase in divorce and remarriage rates had initiated stronger social acceptance of alternate family forms. Significantly for adoption, family practitioners had begun to reject psychoanalytic theories of neurosis in favour of more complex socioeconomic theories and started to acknowledge the significance of bonding between the unwed mother and her child.

The intersection of these changes altered the unwed mother's position as a social outcast. It began through a process whereby noticeable numbers of mature, employed unwed mothers decided to keep their babies (Ludtke). These women were absorbed easily into a larger group of divorced mothers, widows, and deserted wives who were also working and raising children alone. The successful childrearing practices of this group of mothers encouraged ideas that all unwed mothers might be able to raise their children if given financial and social support. Laws were enacted making it illegal for schools to expel pregnant teens; job development programs were created for mothers on welfare, and governments established subsidized daycare for poor women seeking employment. The label of single mother replaced the socially stigmatized label of unwed mother, and the inferior legal status of illegitimate was eliminated.

The label of single mother is applied differently, however, depending upon how a single mother is categorized. Adult, employed middle-class single mothers tend to be praised for their ability to keep and raise their children alone, whereas teen single mothers are depicted as a high-risk population requiring substantial amounts of state resources, parenting intervention, and community support (Strong-Boag). This social distinction appears mainly as an issue of maturity and masks how factors such as family background, education, employment, geographical district, race/ethnicity, or access to independent income affect motherhood (Jackson and Mannix). Thus, although neither category of single mother is denounced for breaking a moral code of sexual purity and unmarried virginity, teen mothers are stigmatized socially for having made a bad choice by becoming pregnant before they are capable of raising a child effectively. Given the current face of adoption in North America, their motherhood is also contrasted negatively against the better opportunities offered by adoption applicants (Shaw) in ways that portray them as selfish and placing their own needs above those of their children's future wellbeing. In consequence, there is still a group of women who suffer social stigma for their motherhood and who, as a result of that stigmatization process, must develop tactics to manage this spoiled identity and to protect their children from the effects of having a mother who is considered to be socially unacceptable.

David Frost defines discrimination as "instances when people or groups are denied equality and treated differently because of their stigmatized status" (825). He views such incidents being "supported by stereotypes or commonly held generalizations about qualities of people based on their membership in stigmatized groups or possession of a stigmatized attribute" (825). Frost also notes that discrimination occurs at both the institutional and the interpersonal level in ways that affect the decisions individuals make in conducting their everyday life. As can be seen in the historical analysis presented above, past women were subjected to distinctive types of social discrimination that were informed by specific stereotypes of unwed motherhood. This process denied such women equality as mothers, obstructed their ability to raise their children effectively, and pushed them towards orphanages and/or adoption placement. In comparison, the single mother of today may not be not judged and stigmatized for her sexuality, but her position in the institution of motherhood is affected significantly by her access to such resources as a good education, stable employment and family or peer group support (Kilty and Dej).

Further knowledge of the relationship between social discrimination and motherhood exclusion requires a stronger focus on how the application of stereotypical labels affects the identity of women who have children outside the boundaries of marriage. Only then, can we truly recognize how particular types or groups of women become constrained in performing motherhood. When our understanding of those labels is intertwined with an understanding of the sociocultural, economic, and political practices in which women conduct their everyday lives, the decisions they make as mothers become clearer and, in some cases, more appropriately supported. Of particular interest for the study of adoption, current research indicates that the social programs and minimal financial funding provided to contemporary single mothers has created a detectable attitude in North American society, whereby adoption placement is viewed as the selfish and heartless act of a depraved woman (March and Miall). From this perspective, the choices single mothers make may still be constrained by the interconnections of social standards, public perceptions, structural policy, and organizational procedure. It may merely take another era of economic, social, and political change to introduce new discriminatory practices that may, once again, exclude them from the social institution of motherhood altogether—or, hopefully, aid them in gaining a position that enables them to become the mothers they envision and all mothers wish to be.

Endnote

1. The term "unwed mother" is used here to describe white, middle-class, unmarried mothers. This population represents the largest group of women to place children for adoption in Canada, Australia, Britain, New Zealand, and the United States during the twentieth century (Evans B. Donaldson Institute). Adoption is mainly a white institution designed to assist white, heterosexual, middle-class married couples. This fact is supported by researchers (Berebitsky, Kunzel, Rains, Solinger, and Strong-Boag) who analyze the processes by which Black, Indigenous, ethic, and working-class mothers were eliminated as viable adoption placement candidates. Space limitation precludes my ability to discuss these other works and/or compare these other populations of mothers.

Works Cited

Adams, Mary Louise. *The Trouble with Normal: Postwar Youth and the Making of Heterosexuality*. University of Toronto Press, 1997.

Berebitsky, Julie. "Family Ideals and the Social Construction of Modern Adoption: A Historical Perspective." *Adoptive Families in a Diverse Society*, edited by Katarina Wegar, Rutgers University Press, 2006, pp. 29-42.

Evans B. Donaldson Institute. *Safeguarding the Rights and Well-being of Birthparents in the Adoption Process*. New York Press, 2007.

Frost, David. "Social Stigma and its Consequences for the Socially Stigmatized." *Social and Personality Psychology Compass*, vol. 5, no. 11, 2011, pp. 824-39.

Goffman, Irving. *Stigma: Notes on the Management of Spoiled Identity*. Prentice-Hall, 1963.

Jackson, Debra, and Judy Mannix. "Giving Voice to the Burden of Blame. A Feminist Study of Mother's Experiences of Mother Blaming." *International Journal of Nursing Practice*, vol. 10, 2014, pp. 150-58.

Kilty, Jennifer, and Erin Dej. "Anchoring amongst the Waves: Discursive Constructions of Motherhood and Addiction." *Qualitative Sociology Review*, vol. 8, no.3, 2012, pp. 6-23.

Kunzel, Regina. *Fallen Women, Problem Girls: Unmarried Mothers and the Politics of Reproductive Control*. Beacon Books, 1993.

Link, Bruce G., and Jo C. Phelan. "Conceptualizing Stigma." *Annual Review of Sociology*, vol. 27, no.1, 2001, pp. 363-85.

Ludke, Melissa. *On Our Own: Unmarried Motherhood in America*. Random House, 1997.

March, Karen, and Charlene E. Miall. "Reinforcing the Motherhood Ideal: Perceptions of Biological Mothers who make an Adoption Plan." *Canadian Review of Sociology and Anthropology*, vol. 43, no. 4, 2006, pp. 367-86.

Rains, Prudence. *Becoming an Unwed Mother: A Sociological Account*. Chicago: Aldine-Atherton, 1971. Print.

Shaw, Anita. "Media Representations of Adolescent Pregnancy: The Problem with Choice." *Atlantis*, vol. 34, no. 2, 2010, pp. 55-65.

Solinger, Ricki. *Beggars and Choosers: How the Politics of Choice Shapes Adoption, Abortion and Welfare in the United States*. Hill and Wang, 2001.

Solinger, Ricki. *Pregnancy and Power: A Short History of Reproductive Politics in America*. New York University Press, 2007.

Solinger, Ricki. *Wake up Little Susie: Single Pregnancy and Race before Roe v. Wade*. Routledge, 1992.

Spensky, Martine. "Producers of Legitimacy: Homes for Unmarried Mothers in the 1950's." *Regulating Womanhood: Historical Essays on Marriage and Motherhood and Sexuality*, edited by Carol Smart, Routledge, 1992, pp. 100-119.

Strong-Boag, Victoria. *Finding Families, Finding Ourselves: English Canada Encounters Adoption from the Nineteenth Century to the 1990s.* Oxford University Press, 2006.

Young, Leontine. *Out of Wedlock.* McGraw-Hill, 1954.

PART II
Mothers and Criminalization

Perfect Mothers Are a Myth

OTHER MOMS ARE PERFECT...

Chapter 5

Motherhood and Social Exclusion: Narratives of Women in Prison in Ireland

Christina Quinlan

This chapter considers one aspect of contemporary experiences of socially excluded mothers—that is, experiences of motherhood of women in prison in Ireland. The experiences detailed in the chapter are presented within a brief historical and theoretical framework that highlights some salient aspects of experiences of Irish motherhood, within the country's conceptions and apparatuses of social justice. The chapter provides insight into mothering and social exclusion in Ireland and the uneven power relations that have shaped women's experiences of mothering. A number of personal narratives from women in prison are presented, each of which was selected based on the capacity of the narrative to illustrate an experience of motherhood. The chapter provides insight into the mothering experiences of some of the most socially excluded women in Ireland: women in prison.

A Brief Review of the Literature

With its Catholic ethos and habitus, Ireland has had particularly idealized notions of motherhood and particularly narrow notions of appropriate femininity. This has had serious implications and consequences for women and mothers, but especially mothers who find themselves involved with the criminal justice system. These notions have also affected women who have not contravened the law but whose attitudes and/or behaviours are deemed to be in need of adjustment and correction. Much of women's engagement with the forces of correction in Ireland, including the criminal justice system, has been related to or has been as a consequence of women's experiences in terms of sexuality, reproduction, and abortion (Quinlan, "Policing Women's Bodies"). Indeed, recently for many women in Ireland, their experiences of corrections were related, more than anything else, to their experiences of mothering (Quinlan; O'Sullivan and O'Donnell; Garrett).

For centuries in Ireland, and continuing to this day, unmarried mothers have been harshly treated. The shocking experiences inflicted on these women are well documented (Quinlan, "Policing Women's Bodies"). Currently, for example, excavations are being carried out in the burial places of babies and children who died in the Tuam Mother and Baby Home. Tuam is a town in County Galway County, in the west of Ireland. The Home is a former institution for unmarried mothers run by the Sisters of the Bon Secours. On 13 March 2017, *The Irish Times* (the newspaper of record in Ireland) published a list of the names of the 796 babies and children who died in the Home between 1925 and 1960. As evidenced by the list, the death rate among the children was particularly high. For example, in the month of April 1926, twenty-two children died in the Home. In the month of December 1936, twenty children died. In the month of June 1947, twelve children died. The youngest children to die were two babies, named Baby Walsh and Baby Haugh, both lived just ten minutes. The oldest child to die was Kathleen Cloran, who died in 1932, when she was nine and a half years old.

The death records show that the children died of illnesses, such as tuberculosis, convulsions, measles, whooping cough, influenza, bronchitis, and meningitis. The list of names of the children who died in the Home was compiled by Catherine Corliss, a local historian in Tuam. Her research led to the establishment of a Commission of Investigation into Mother and Baby Homes. The investigation into the Tuam Mother and Baby Home established that "significant quantities of human remains had been discovered in structures designed to contain sewage." The remains of children who died in the home were disposed of in the sewage system. The large number of children who died, coupled with their place of burial, is the latest trauma in a long catalogue of traumas that the Irish people have had to come to terms with in relation to the treatment of some mothers and their children in the country.

Historically, motherhood outside of marriage was a scandal in Ireland (Quinlan, "Policing Women's Bodies"), and the Irish state provided no support for single (unmarried) mothers (Luddy, 2011). This changed in 1973, when the first social welfare payment was made to an unmarried mother. Known as "the unmarried mother's allowance," it was a weekly payment of £8.50 (see One Family: Our 45 Year History). Prior to this date, there was no support whatever for mothers who were unmarried (Luddy). If these women did not have the support of their families, and many did not, it just was not possible for them to keep and care for their babies. Often, the women "were thrown out of their homes, lost their jobs, and were rejected by their communities" (One Family). Until the last decades of the twentieth century, women were dependent on their relatives, their husbands if they were married, for financial support. Indeed, in the 1970s in Ireland, only 7 percent of married women were in paid employment (O'Connor 7). Pamela O'Connor (2006) attributed this feature of Irish society to a marriage bar—an instrument of the state designed to exclude women from certain occupations. When a woman married, she was obliged by law to resign from her job. Introduced in the Civil Service Amendment Act of 1925 and developed in later legislations (Crowley and Kitchin), the marriage bar was finally removed in 1973 (Rodger).

Through legislation and through society and culture, Ireland produced a harsh environment for women who offended sexual mores. For every individual woman who was said to have, in the phrase used at the time, "gotten into trouble," the "trouble" she was in was that she was pregnant and unmarried. Both her pregnancy and her baby were evidence of sexual immorality. From the moment she became aware that she had conceived, she had to learn to live with the stigma that came with being a single and an unmarried mother. Along with that stigma came the stigma of illegitimacy. The child born outside of marriage was legally, social, and culturally deemed to be illegitimate. It was not until 1987 that the status of illegitimacy was abolished in Ireland (Ferriter 524). Internationally in the twentieth century, experiences such as these were common for women and were driven by, arguably, "a post first-wave feminism deepening conservatism" (Connolly 68).

The treatment of some single mothers in recent Irish history is as painful as the treatment of some mothers in the distant past (Quinlan, "Policing Women's Bodies"). One example of this is the reduction of lone parents' social welfare allowance in the post-Celtic Tiger economic collapse. The Celtic Tiger economy should be understood as an economic boom that developed within a broader bubble economy (O'Flynn et al.). This boom ended in a spectacular financial crash in 2008, and the Irish government provided six banks with approximately €400 billion in leveraged loans, which generated enormous financial losses. Eurostat figures show that at a time when the banking crisis was costing an average of €192 per capita in Europe, the cost of the banking crisis in Ireland was "a staggering €8,981" per capita (O'Flynn et al. 11).

All of Ireland's citizens were forced to carry the financial burden of bailing out the banks. This was brought about in part through a particular political process that operates in Ireland (O'Flynn et al. 5). This process consistently and persistently protects powerful interests and the status quo. One of the most common weapons of the process is scapegoating, which was used in the post-Celtic Tiger era. This scapegoating was evident throughout the banking crisis, in hegemonic political discourse, and in mainstream media. Political discourse and the media were, throughout, generally supportive of the socialisation of private banking debt and the subsequent policies of austerity. These policies were rooted in class interests and neoliberal ideology (O'Flynn et al.).

Throughout the economic crash, a public discourse developed in Ireland that blamed everyone for the economic crisis. The discourse highlighted 'inefficient' public services as well as the serious problem we in Ireland were said to have with social welfare fraud. The concerns articulated in relation to claims of welfare fraud developed around a discourse about migrants flying into the country to claim benefits and then flying out again—a phenomenon known as "welfare tourism." And long after its worst effects of the crisis had abated, this discourse was still persistently and consistently articulated by those in power.

One consequence of this was that, again, in the twenty-first century, single mothers, and particularly single mothers who had children with different men, became for some public commentators a focus for public moral outrage. This kind of commentary created a public discourse that labelled these women as "immoral," and this was used to rationalize cuts to social welfare (O'Flynn et al. 18), which included cuts to payments for one-parent families. The Central Statistics Office in Ireland published figures for 2011 that show that, in that year, there were 89,612 lone parents (of children under 15) in Ireland, and 83,476 of them (93 percent) were single mothers. It is quite extraordinary what can be hidden in an aggregate statistic. The cuts to this allowance cruelly cut the income of 83,476 single women caring for their children.

Discourses that scapegoat lone parents, mostly women, caring alone for their children threaten their livelihoods and wellbeing, and, consequently, the welfare of the children. The readiness of hegemonic political discourse and media discourses to engage in this kind of scapegoating in response to the failures of private capitalism evidences the broad power imbalances of the system, its essential meanness, and its fundamental lack of fairness. Whereas the profits of banks and big businesses are private, wholescale losses in the sectors can be socialized, even when the costs of that socialization serve to further impoverish those among the most vulnerable in society—in this case, single mothers eligible for social welfare support.

Research Methodology

This chapter explores experiences of mothering and motherhood of a group of women who are among the most socially excluded women in Irish society—women in prison. In Ireland, women account for about 3.5 percent of the prison population. On any day, there are about 150 women in prison. Most women in prison are serving short-term prison sentences for nonviolent relatively minor offences (Quinlan, "Women in Prison"). The statistics on the numbers of women in prison in Ireland mirror the gender breakdown in prison populations internationally. Prison populations are predominantly male, and, generally, prisons are designed and built to accommodate men. It is widely acknowledged that men and women experience prison differently and that women in prison have very specific needs. These needs relate in part to the fact that many women in prison are mothers of young children, and some of them struggle with their parenting responsibilities because of their personal circumstances and their own unmet needs (Quinlan,

"Women in Prison). The UN Bangkok Rules, adopted in 2010 and voted unanimously for by the 193 countries that are members of the United Nations, acknowledge that women in criminal justice systems do have gender-specific characteristics and needs ((Penal Reform International). Through their circumstances and vulnerabilities, women can become trapped in criminal justice systems, and alternative ways, including noncustodial measures, need to be developed to deal with women's offending behaviours.

The chapter details experiences of motherhood as narrated by women in prison in Ireland. It considers the role of mothering in the lives of these women, the support they rely on in mothering, and the difficulties and obstacles they encounter in their lives that obstruct them in both their wish and their need to mother. The methodology used in this study is narrative analysis. The narratives drawn on are those of women in prison in Ireland; they form part of a broader ethnographic study that has been published (Quinlan, *Inside*). Although they inform the previous study, these narratives have not been published before now. They stand alone as a dataset and are useful in terms of the insight they provide on the experiences of motherhood of some of the most socially excluded women in Ireland. Throughout the chapter, pseudonyms are used to protect the identities of the participants in the study.

In all, there were thirty-three narratives from mothers in prison. Among them, there were three narratives from expectant mothers and two from mothers who were also grandmothers; they each had one grandchild. Of the thirty-three mothers, five were married, two were widowed, and five were divorced or separated; the rest were single parents. Thus, two thirds of the mothers were lone parents. In terms of mothering support, six of the mothers said that they were supported by the fathers of their children. Seventeen of the mothers said that family members, in almost all cases the women's own mothers, had assumed responsibility for childcare while they were in prison. Most of the women said that they would return to their mothering roles when they left prison.

Narratives of Motherhood and Social Exclusion

The stories the women told were essentially stories of motherhood and social class. Most of the women in prison, and consequently most of the mothers, were poor women from socially marginalized backgrounds. There were some middle-class women and middle-class mothers, but not very many of them. Addiction, violence, and abuse were key features of some of the stories. These factors of abuse, addiction, violence, crime, and prison can be seen as the factors shaping the life experiences of several of the women who participated in the study—particularly, the lives of the most socially excluded women. The factors can be conceived of as a cycle, and they are represented below in Figure 1.

Figure 1: The Vulnerable Woman and Prison Cycle

For this project, the key themes to emerge from the analysis of the narratives were the women's good and bad experiences of mothering, the support they had with mothering, and their experiences of mothering being interrupted. These key themes are outlined in the paragraphs below.

Experiences of Mothering: Good and Bad

The women talked about their own experiences of mothering, including the advances made in Irish society in terms of the support available to poor mothers, the changes in Irish society regarding the acceptance of unmarried mothers, and the struggles of mothers who are overburdened and have few resources.

The women talked about their own experiences of being mothered, and most of the women described good experiences of being mothered. They talked of their own mothers lovingly. They explained how close they felt to their own mothers and recounted narratives that showed the support they received from them. Lucy, a single mother, outlined her experience as follows: "I never actually left home. I live in a three-bedroom house, and I share a room with my three sisters. My child is four years old. My mother rears her. She stays with my mother. Her father is in Australia, he writes letters and he sends money every second week." Lucy's narrative reveals the acceptance that there is now in Ireland for young women who become pregnant outside of marriage. Indeed, even though she become pregnant and gave birth to a baby, Lucy never actually left home. She lived at home, when not in prison, with her parents, her sisters, and her young child.

Another of the women, Catherine, shared a similar experience. She said that she lived at home with her mother, her siblings, her baby, and her sister's baby: "There are six of us in the family, and I never left home. I'm still with my mother. We have a three-bedroom house. My sister is there, with her baby too. We're all there together. It's good fun." Catherine's narrative highlights her happiness, sense of security, and the wellbeing she feels in relation to her home and her baby's home.

Although some of the women felt supported by their families in mothering and their experiences of motherhood, others talked about the lack of support that their mothers had had with mothering and some of the consequences of that. They described how their mothers had their patience tested and were pushed to their limits as they tried to care for their children without adequate support.

Diana talked about growing up as one of six children. Her dad died when she was nine, but she did not know why he had died. She said that her mother used to hit them because, she said, they would "drive her to it." She felt sorry for her mother, because she was alone with six kids.

Alcoholism and drug addiction featured in the narratives of some of these women. It was these women who described the most difficult experiences with their mothers and families. Geraldine talked about her mother's addiction to alcohol and the impact it had had on the family. She explained that she had been brought up by her grandparents: "When I was seven, I found out that my grandmother, who I thought was my mother, wasn't. That's when I started to get angry with my mother. They took thirteen of us off my mother, seven girls and five boys." Such anger, rooted in past traumatic experiences, was described by a number of the women, and for some of the women, it led to experiences of self-harm.

Addiction issues were the cause of the problems for some of the women. One of these women, Ellen, explained that she was an alcoholic, and she talked about her behaviour being so problematic that when she was drinking her mother would change the locks to keep her out of the house. She said that when she was arrested and charged, her mother offered to pay bail, but she did not offer her accommodation; fortunately, her social worker offered to help her with this. Ellen described herself as a binge drinker—someone who wouldn't drink every day but could go for months without a drink and then go on a binge. Ellen's sister and her sister's husband were now caring for her children as their legal guardians.

Although some of the women reported troubled relationships with their mothers, a small number of the women had had truly dreadful experiences. One of the women, Jane, was twenty-two years old, and she had spent much of her childhood in foster care, moving from home to home. She had suffered violent abuse. She recounted the following narrative:

My dad has been a prisoner all his life. I've been in and out of foster care all my life. I went into care at two years of age; I think I was with me ma until I was two. Then from two to twelve, I was with one foster family. They used to beat me up, and I don't like to think about them. From twelve to thirteen, I was with another family, just a standby place. Then after thirteen, I was with me ma again.

Tara, who was a Traveller woman, described her family, the violence she experienced in her family, and her memory of being mothered:

My da tied my ma to the wheel of a cart, cut her hair off, broke her teeth, and scarred her face so that no man would look at her. He wasn't the man who put bread on the table. He was the man who put pints [of beer] on the counter. Me da was a bastard, and when he dies, I'm not going to the funeral. Me ma gave birth to me in the back of a tent. She fed me and dressed me and begged for me.

Hilary, who was twenty-six years of age, said, "my mum used to get people to abuse me. She hurt me more than anyone. I don't feel safe with her. I left home at fifteen." A number of the women had left home at very young ages. Some of them spoke of being in a juvenile home; others spoke of being in foster homes. Some of the women spoke of being on the streets from a young age.

These narratives also showed how violence and addiction harmed them, their children, their families, as well as their relationships. But they also showed the support that mothers and families in Ireland provide for their daughters when they are pregnant and when they are mothers in need of support, as lone parents and/or as mothers in prison. These support are fundamental in enabling these women to mother through the security and the relatively well-resourced environment of the family home. The children of these imprisoned mothers are given the critically important life opportunity of growing up in a loving household where resources and responsibilities are shared. This is a fundamental change in Irish society. The experiences of these children and their mothers are in stark contrast to the experiences of the children and the mothers of the children of the Tuam Mother and Baby Home, as detailed earlier in this chapter.

Mothering Support

The women talked about the support they had with mothering. Some of the women talked about the support they received from the fathers of the children; others recounted narratives detailing the support they received from the state, as their children were in foster care or in the care of the state. Other women talked about the support they received from their families, particularly their mothers, who were caring for their children while they were in prison. For most of these women, being a mother and receiving support with mothering were fundamental to their lives and to their identities.

One woman, Joy, had been married for three years and separated for four; she described the support she received from her mother as follows: "I have a little girl, she's eleven. My child is with my mum. She knows I'm her mum. I went home to her every weekend. I was moving back in with them, just before I came here [into prison]." Joy explained that she was not concerned about her daughter because while she was in prison, her daughter continued to live with her mother, who cared for her. Although she appreciated the support of her mother, clarity around her role as her daughter's mother was important to her. While her mother assumed a surrogate mothering role with her daughter while Joy was in prison, she did not usurp Joy's rightful position as the child's mother.

Another woman, Jackie, worried about losing her mothering role through being in prison: "I have one child, a boy; he's six. He's at home with my mam. He knows I'm his mam, but he calls his nanny [grandmother] mam sometimes." Kath explained that she lived at home with her mother and father and that they had legal custody of her son: "I have one child, a boy; he's seven. My mam and dad have had full custody of him since he was two, but I'm back home with him. I live with my mam and dad. I'm home now, and he knows I'm his mammy." Fundamental to Kath's experience of motherhood was the fact that her child lived in the safety and the security of her family home and that her parents had legal guardianship of her son. Central to Kath's sense of wellbeing was her awareness that she could mother her son when she was able to do so, and when she was not in prison. She knew that when she left prison she would return to live with her son and her parents in her family home.

Helen, who had grown up in foster care, talked about the support she received from her foster mother, and she explained that she shared the role of mother to her daughter with her foster mother. She was happy to do this, and she viewed the role of her foster mother in mothering her daughter as supportive; she did not feel challenged or threatened in terms of her mothering role, her mothering rights, or her mothering experience: "I have one child, a girl. She's six, and I'm expecting a baby. My child is with my foster mother. She thinks of us both as mam." Helen, who was expecting a baby, had a scan of her baby on her bedside table (see Photograph 1). The photograph was displayed on a bedside locker in a room in the Dóchas Centre, the women's prison at Mountjoy Prison in Dublin, Ireland. The photograph provides a perspective on the vulnerabilities of mothers caught up in criminal justice system and in prison. The photograph gives a sense of Helen's youthful vulnerability. In the photograph, the scan is propped up against a soft drink carton from a fast food restaurant, and there's a crumpled packet of candy and an ashtray filled with cigarette ends in front of the scan.

Photograph 1: Fetal scan from a room in the Dóchas Centre (the women's prison in the Mountjoy Prison Complex in Dublin) (Source: Christina Quinlan)

Another woman in the group, Jill, was pregnant, and she talked about her husband and the support he gave her: "I'm married and I have one child, a girl, she's one year old and I'm pregnant. My daughter is at home with my husband. He's a carpenter, and he's very good to us. I'd be lost without him. He's the best thing that ever happened to me." Another woman, Anna, also talked about the support she received from her children's dad: "I have four children, two of each, two boys and two girls. Three of the children are with their dad. One son is with me; he's with his dad now I'm in here [in prison]." Gina talked about the support she received with mothering from her son's paternal grandmother. She explained that her son was three years old, and living with her ex-boyfriend's mum. She said, "I'll get him back when I leave [prison]."

Alice recounted a sad narrative about her son's father. She said that he had "gotten a couple of chances to come up and see his son, but he never came." She explained that he had come from "a broken home," and, as a result, she felt that he was deeply troubled. "I don't know," she said, "people who come from broken homes, I think they're just doomed."

Marie, a Traveller woman, recounted the following narrative illustrating her experience of being a lone parent as well as a separated mother with five children to support and only with the social welfare allowance:

I lived with a bloke for ten years, and I had five kids. I buried two, cot deaths. When I used to cry, he used to say that I was embarrassing his family. So I left with the kids and got a flat in Dolphins Barn [a suburb in Dublin]. I was living on the top floor, and the little one asked for a horse, and another one wanted a pony. I asked them, "how could I do that on the children's allowance." He works, and he said to them, "I'll buy you the horses if you tell the social worker that you want to live with your da and not your ma."

The struggles of mothers lone-parenting their children in difficult financial circumstances were evident in some of the women's narratives, as was the terrible impact of addiction. These women talked about their addictions and how they had undermined the support they received from their families and from their mothers. Their narratives illustrate the impact of addiction on the women's lives, on their mothering experiences, and on the support they received with mothering from their mothers and their families.

Tracey, who was twenty-five years old, said that although her mother was caring for her child, she herself wanted to be "a proper mother" to her child. She said that when she was out of prison, she helped her mother to look after her child sometimes, but she said that since she had gotten involved in drugs, her mother "had kind of washed her hands of her." Jenny talked about the enormous amount of support she got from her mother, and she talked about the lengths to which her mother would go to try to help her. She also talked about the impact of drug addiction on her, on her family, and on the support she received with mothering:

> My son will be two years old in August. He's with me ma. I reared him until I came in here. I always got a lot of help from me ma. Me ma doesn't like me fella. That can be a problem. If we're drug-free, me ma has no problem with us. When he got out [of prison] the last time, me ma was great to him. But then we slipped [back into drug use]. Me ma just doesn't want to know us when we're on drugs, and I don't blame her.

Julie's children had been taken from her and were being cared for by the state. She spoke of having HIV and said that the father of her oldest child also had the virus. Her partner, the man she was with currently, not the father or her children, was also an addict. He was in Coolmine, an addiction rehabilitation centre in Ireland. Julie said that she didn't get any support from her family. She said that they didn't come to see her in prison, she didn't have a good relationship with her ma and da. She said that "they were fighting, mostly about me drinking, being on drugs, and being in prison." Julie had started getting into trouble in her twenties, getting involved in drugs, drinking, and fighting. She engaged in sex work for drug money.

The supports these women received were central to their mothering and motherhood experiences. These women were able to mother their children and to develop good motherhood experiences with and for their children because they had these supports. Through living with their mothers and, in some cases, their fathers and siblings, these women were helped in coping with their limited financial means, generally their only income was a social welfare allowance. Sadly, the narratives of some of the women provided clear evidence of the profoundly destructive effect of drug and alcohol addictions on these women's mothering as well as their familial relationships.

Mothering Interrupted

The following paragraphs detail the women's sense of their mothering experience being interrupted, either by prison (for all of them) or by addiction (for some of them). Lucy Baldwin writes about mothering, the maternal experience for mothers in prison being disrupted and even destroyed by an experience of imprisonment. Imprisoned women often feel separated and isolated from their children and helpless in terms of their need to care for their children. Women worry about being in prison and not being able to care for their children.

One of the women, Vera, explained her experience of her mothering being interrupted by her term of imprisonment as follows: "I have one son; he's six. He's with my mother. I'm his ma, and when I leave here, I'll be his ma again." Vera spoke of the father of her son. She said that the boy's father was in London and that he didn't support the child. He had ended their relationship and she acknowledged that she missed him.

Grace, who was twenty-four years old, provided the following narrative: "I was never married. I have three children, two boys and a girl, aged five to one year old. They're with my mother. I am their mother and I will be their mother when I leave [prison]. Their father is near the kids, but he's not with the kids. He doesn't support us." Lisa, who struggled with psychiatric problems, narrated this story:

> I saw a psychiatrist three times. She put me in strips [in a strip cell, a cell with no furnishings]. It made me more depressed, but I didn't tell her that. I cut myself once in here [in the Dóchas Centre, the new prison at Mountjoy Prison in Dublin] and once in the old prison. It was just anger. I was just so angry. The cutting made me less angry. All I think about is me baby out playing and wondering did me ma bring him off somewhere for the day, if it's a nice day.

Lisa's narrative shows the pain and suffering of mental illness, as well as the harsh treatment sometimes provided in prison to women with mental illness difficulties. Her narrative also details the support she receives from her mother in terms of caring for her child. Although she is mentally ill and in prison, she can imagine her son at home with her mother, safe and happy and cared for; she knows that when she leaves prison, she will re-join her family and recommence caring for her child.

Sarah talked about her experience of motherhood being interrupted by her term of imprisonment. She talked about being away from her little girl, and about returning to her mothering role when she left prison: "There's just me mam and me brother and me baby. Me baby is two years old. She's with me mam. I'll be her mam again when I get out. I was never away from her side since she was born. I think her dad is out [of prison] in Limerick." When Sarah talked about her own father in prison, she said that she hated him and that she didn't want to know anything about him. She talked about having been sexually abused by him. Many women in prison have been victims of violent abusive offending behaviour (Quinlan, *Inside* 96-97). Violence and abuse are key features in vulnerabilities and the prison cycle, as outlined in the model in Figure 1 presented earlier in this chapter.

Drug and alcohol addictions featured again in the narratives of motherhood being interrupted. One of the women, Clare, had very serious addiction issues and had, as a consequence of them, lost custody of her daughter and lost her mothering role. She recounted the following narrative: "I have a child, a little girl. She's four and a half. She's in foster care, long term. She has been taken off me until she's eighteen. Even if I don't get her back, I'd like to see her." Kay, who also had drug addiction problems, lost custody of her children, who were under the care of their grandparents. She recounted the following narrative:

I'm single, and I have three children, two boys and one girl, aged fourteen to seven. My oldest boy lives with my mother: he's good for her. The other two are with their (other) granny, they're across the road from each other. I did try to rear those two myself ... if I had never gone near drugs. Now those two, I'd say, will stay with their granny. But I hope they'll come back.

Another woman, Rose, suffered from addiction and talked about her husband, who had died at thirty-four from cirrhosis of the liver.

She said that she had two boys, aged seventeen and nineteen. She said that they lived on their own in their own flat looking after themselves and that they looked older than they were. She said that Concerned Parents against Drugs—an organization that was setup up by local inner-city communities in Dublin in the early 1980s to combat drugs—wouldn't let her go near her children because of her addiction.

Throughout these narratives, there is evidence of each of the women's need to mother their children. The narratives show that most of the women did feel that they had a mothering role with their children, and this was so even when many of them shared this role with their own mothers. In fact, it was because the women could share their mothering role and responsibilities with their mothers and their families that they were able to experience mothering and enjoy their experiences of mothering and motherhood. The support that their families provided for them made these mothering and motherhood experiences possible. The love and acceptance that most of the women enjoyed within their families and their family homes was evident throughout the narratives.

What was also evident in some of the narratives was that it was violence, abuse, and addiction that disrupted family life and destroyed familial relations. Furthermore, the narratives showed that, sadly, it was the women with serious drug and/or alcohol addictions who lost their mothering roles and their experiences of motherhood. For the most vulnerable and the most socially excluded women, it was the destructive factors of abuse, addiction, violence, crime, and prison shaped, created, and developed for them their difficult life experiences.

The narratives of the women were full of the love they had for their children, and they were full, for most of the women, of the love and respect that they had for their own mothers, their fathers, their siblings, and their family homes. Their narratives were also full of the hopes and dreams they had for motherhood and their mothering roles. These narratives are so far apart from the ugly narratives of the public discourses that scapegoated single mothers during the economic crash that ended the Celtic Tiger economy. Public discourses promulgated by powerful public commentators provided a rational for cutting social welfare allowances, including cuts to the allowance paid to eligible lone parents—95 percent of whom were single mothers.

Discourses are ways of seeing the world; they are ideological flows of information through which the social is constructed and communicated (Quinlan, *Inside*). How the powerful construct and communicate public discourses that shape the lives and the life experiences of the most vulnerable needs constant public critique. A public discourse that scapegoats poor women, vulnerable women, and women eligible for social welfare payments is reprehensible. So too is a public discourse that scapegoats sexually active women and women who are lone parenting their children. Such discourses are particularly reprehensible in Ireland, where, historically, the harshest treatments in terms of public scorn, opprobrium, and social exclusion were reserved for sexually active women and single mothers and their children.

Conclusion

This chapter details the motherhood narratives of imprisoned women in Ireland. The chapter outlines their experiences of mothering, the support they receive, and their experiences of mothering being interrupted. The narratives highlight the importance of motherhood for these women and the challenges they face in mothering. The main support for these women in their mothering roles was their own family; for most of the women, their own mothers were the most important support in their lives. Many of the women lived with their mothers prior to their incarceration, and some lived in multigenerational households with their mothers, fathers, grandparents, brothers and sisters, nephews and nieces, as well as their own children. Most of the women were secure in the knowledge that they would return to their families and to their mothering roles when they left prison.

The most socially excluded women among the mothers in the study were the women with serious addiction problems. It was these women who lost custody of their children and who lost the support of their families. The majority of the mothers in the study were lone parents; they did not have life partners, they were not married to the fathers of their children. In financial terms, they were poor women, and they were among the lone parents whose social welfare allowances were reduced by the Irish state in order to bail out the banks after the economic crash of 2008. These poor women were among the women scapegoated and demeaned in public discourses which were developed and promoted in Irish society and used to justify those social welfare cuts.

Works Cited

Baldwin, Lucy. "Motherhood Disrupted: Reflections of Post-Prison Mothers." *Emotion, Space and Society*, 2017, pp. 1-8, wephren.tghn. org/site_media/media/articles/ESS_final_article__11orl7Z.pdf. Accessed 10 May 2019

Connolly, Eileen. "Durability and Change in State Gender Systems." *European Journal of Women's Studies*, vol. 10, no. 1, 2003, pp. 65-86.

Crowley, Una, and Rob Kitchin. "Producing 'Decent Girls': Governmentality and the Moral Geographies of Sexual Conduct in Ireland (1922-1937)." *Gender, Place and Culture. A Journal of Feminist Geography*, vol. 15, no. 4, 2008, pp. 355-72.

CSO (Central Statistics Office). "Census 2011 – This is Ireland" CSO, 2011, www.cso.ie/en/media/csoie/census/documents/census 2011pdr/Pdf_6_Tables.pdf Accessed 11 May 2019.

Ferriter, Diarmaid. *Occasions of Sin: Sex and Society in Modern Ireland*. Profile Books, 2009.

Garrett, Paul Michael. "'Unmarried Mothers' in the Republic of Ireland." *Journal of Social Work*, vol. 16, no. 6, 2016, pp. 708-25.

Government of Ireland. *Mother and Baby Homes Commission of Investigation*, 2018, www.mbhcoi.ie/MBH.nsf/page/index-en. Accessed 10 May 2019.

Luddy, Maria. "Unmarried Mothers in Ireland: 1880-1973." *Women's History Review*, vol. 20, no. 1, 2011, pp. 109-26.

O'Connor, Pamela. "Private Troubles, Public Issues: The Irish Sociological Imagination." *Irish Journal of Sociology*, vol. 5, no. 2, 2006: pp. 5-22.

O'Flynn, Micheal, et al. "Scapegoating During a Time of Crisis: A Critique of Post-Celtic Tiger Ireland." *Sociology*, vol. 48, no. 5, 2014, pp. 921-37.

One Family. "Our 45 Year History," *One Family*, onefamily.ie/about-us/our-history/. Accessed 10 May 2019.

O'Sullivan, Eoin, and Ian O'Donnell. "Coercive Control in the Republic of Ireland: The Waning of a Culture of Control." *Punishment and Society*, vol. 9, no. 1, 2007, pp. 27-48.

Penal Reform International. "UN Bangkok Rules," *Penal Reform*, www.penalreform.org/priorities/women-in-the-criminal-justice-system/bangkok-rules-2/. Accessed 10 May 2019.

McAuliffe, Nora-Ide. "Tuam Mother and Baby Home: Names of the 796 Children Who Died," *The Irish Times*, 13 Mar. 2017, https://www.irishtimes.com/news/social-affairs/tuam-mother-and-baby-home-names-of-the-796-children-who-died-1.3008263. Accessed 10 May 2019.

Quinlan, Christina. *Inside: Ireland's Women's Prisons, Past and Present.* Irish Academic Press, 2011.

Quinlan, Christina. "Policing Women's Bodies in an Illiberal Society: The Case of Ireland." *Women and Criminal Justice*, vol. 27, no 1, 2017, pp. 51-72.

Quinlan, Christina. "Women, Imprisonment and Social Control." *The Routledge Handbook of Irish Criminology*, edited by Deirdre Healy et al., Routledge, 2016, pp 500-521.

Quinlan, Christina. "Women in Prison: The Need for Radical Reform," *The Irish Independent*, 14 May 2017. www.independent.ie/life/women-in-prison-the-need-for-radical-reform-35706365.html. Accessed 10 May 2019.

Rodger, John. "Family Policy or Moral Regulation," *Critical Social Policy*, vol. 15, no. 43, 1995, pp. 5-25.

Chapter 6

Addressing Social Exclusion through Collaborative Methods: Criminalized Mothers' Engagement in Research

Ashley Ward, Emily van der Meulen, and May Friedman

For nearly two decades, feminist motherhood scholars have noted the increasing social and cultural emphasis on intensive mothering (Hays) and the centrality of mother blame (Caplan). Dominant discourses of motherhood portray good mothers as submissive and selfless, erasing maternal subjectivity and instead presenting mothers only as accessories to their children. Increasingly, the "good enough" mothering proposed by Donald Winnicott has become lost in the impossible expectations and child-centred discourses that focus on maternal perfection. Shari Thurer, Sharon Hays, and Andrea O'Reilly suggest that the demands on mothers to behave as selflessly as possible are growing at the same time that mothers are expected to be increasingly economically productive, resulting in what Hays terms the "cultural contradictions" of motherhood. Even these contradictions, however, can at times be emblematic of privileged and normative experiences of motherhood. For mothers who are marginalized through conditions of poverty and other structural oppressions, and/or who engage in stigmatized activities such as substance use or sex work, the unreasonable standards of modern motherhood may come at an unsustainable cost.

As a trio of researchers interested in developing an interdisciplinary view of criminalization, motherhood, and participant involvement in research processes, we begin by considering the ways in which criminalization produces conditions of social exclusion for some mothers. By situating mothers' experiences through the theoretical lens of criminalization, we can operationalize mother blame as a system that uniquely and disproportionately disparages and oppresses particular women within a legal or criminal justice context, thus leading to their lived (and often multiple) realities of social exclusion. We then advocate in favour of collaborative research methods as a way to begin addressing and mitigating criminalized mothers' experiences of exclusion, focusing especially on feminist participatory action research (FPAR). We suggest that FPAR is an ideal approach to challenge exclusion, as it aims to produce socially meaningful knowledge with participants in the research process and can enable a plurality of contributions to the body of scholarly research, theory, and praxis about criminalized motherhood. In this discussion, we consider both the benefits of collaborative approaches and some of the potential challenges that may arise during such processes.

Social Exclusion through Criminalization

Although romanticized and intensive views of motherhood are not new (Douglas and Michaels; Hays; Maushart), the increasing shift of these standards into child protection and criminal contexts is cause for alarm. Indeed, suspicions of criminality expose women who have broken no laws but contravene norms of motherhood—especially those who are racialized and/or low-income—to heightened mother blame, state surveillance, regulation, and potential incarceration. These mothers are held to ever higher standards of maintaining the health and safety of their children, with the result of outcomes that lead to prosecution. There is a large and growing number of these instances reported in newsmedia. Eileen DiNino, a 55-year-old White mother of seven from Reading, died serving a 48-hour jail sentence because she could not afford to pay $2000.00 in legal fees from her two teenage sons' truancy cases (Kilgore). DiNino experienced a number of health problems, and once incarcerated did not have access to her medications for high blood pressure, anxiety, and bipolar disorder.

Debra Harrell, a 46-year-old Black woman from South Carolina, was incarcerated for allowing her 9-year-old daughter to play at a nearby park while she worked her shift at McDonald's (Friedersdorf). More recently, a study by Smirnova and Gatewood Owens reported on the criminalization of mothers taking nonmedical prescription medications from their doctors for postpartum depression, mental and/or physical health problems related to experiences of abuse and victimization, and recovery from caesarean section childbirth deliveries. These women, initially motivated by the desire to be "good" mothers and comply with prescriptions from their doctors, realized the pills also eased their multiple stresses and demands related to caretaking of their children and families – particularly in contexts of experiencing intimate partner violence and entrenchment in poverty. Their extended use of these medications outside of prescription led to their criminalization and incarceration, and separation from their children and families.

The term "criminalization" often refers to one's engagement in explicitly or potentially illegal activities that can result in criminal charges and that may include consequences such as probation, restitution, and penal incarceration. Criminalization can also be understood more broadly as the ways in which legislative and policy mechanisms, as well as other forms of social control, are enacted against certain people in unequal ways, exacerbating their social and structural oppressions. Drawing from Pat Carlen's theory of criminalization as a set of attitudes, expectations, and performances that position certain bodies as more criminal than others, we recognize that the term can additionally be used to represent the social and legal treatment of certain communities and individuals even prior to arrest and/or incarceration. Similar to Danielle Laberge, we identify criminality and criminalization not as an individual activity or characteristic but as a complex discursive process that requires a consideration of women as criminalized rather than as criminal. The ways in which criminalization affects the lives of women spans from the level of individualized blame, stigma, and shame experienced by mothers, to the isolating effects of alienation from social and community connections, and to the institutional barriers to securing employment, education, food security, and housing. Considered as a set of discursively produced effects for mothers who are criminalized, social exclusion becomes not an individually located deficit, pathology, or deviance to be remedied, but a set of socially, historically, and institutionally produced effects that render mothers as morally abject and ultimately criminal.

Dominant discourses of maternity position mothers' antisocial behaviour as selfish and delinquent—thus lacking the essential qualities to adequately perform as a good mother. This has implications for women who are then punished, corrected, and surveilled for their actions. The need for women to atone and transform their so-called deviant behaviour is seen as necessary to reduce children's negative outcomes as a result of inherently poor caregiving. Women are frequently subjected to increasingly unreasonable burdens and losses of equitable rights as they become networked into child protection, mental health, social service, and criminal justice systems. The effects of these institutions and systems in women's lives can lead to grave personal and social consequences: increased state and/or police surveillance, mental health and substance use labels and forced treatment, criminal justice sanctions, unwanted child welfare interventions, and loss of housing. The inordinate amount of effort required for women to demonstrate their legitimacy in their roles as mothers, friends, partners, employees, and others becomes an oppressive task downloaded individually onto these women, and they can become systemically excluded from full and active social participation.

Processes of criminalization are particularly evident in the lives of certain mothers—namely those who are engaged in stigmatized activities and/or who are poor or racialized—as criminalization is deeply intertwined with racialization and colonialism (Brown and Strega). For example, behaviours that are considered antisocial but are not explicitly illegal, or are at the limits of legality, may nonetheless result in state action against women and their children under the guise of child protection. Mothers who are involved in such activities—including sex work and drug and/or alcohol use—may hide or modify behaviours out of concern for how these activities could be perceived by child protection workers. In Canada, Indigenous and racialized mothers experience greater surveillance and scrutiny from such authorities. Comprising disproportionate numbers of women in contact with the criminal justice system, the discriminating consequences for these women are devastating: high levels of unemployment, frequent charges for intoxication and substance use, more frequent mental health systems contact (community and carceral), and systemic and interpersonal violence. Thus, from a feminist research perspective, capturing the nuanced intersections of these women's experiences is crucial for theory and praxis, and particularly for equitable and inclusive policy, practice, and social supports for criminalized mothers.

Beyond these diverse social contexts, the academic literature exposes the ways in which criminalized mothers face systematic exclusion. There has been a consistent advancement and growth in studies on criminality and gender, especially in the scholarly fields of social work, sociology, child development, child welfare, criminology, legal studies, psychology, and women's studies (Balfour and Comack; Belknap; Bortich; Campbell; Horn; Razack; Sudbury). The field of motherhood studies has been similarly burgeoning (diQuinzio; Friedman; Hays; Kinser; Thurer), and there is a robust body of feminist criminological literature devoted to the topic of motherhood while in or exiting prison (Balfour and Comack; Bosworth; Carlton and Segrave; Eljdupovic and Bromwich). Across disciplinary social science boundaries, however, motherhood and criminality are often framed within moralizing discourses that view criminal behaviour as especially reprehensible when committed by mothers. A common message within the literature is that being a good mother is incompatible with the commission of behaviours deemed antisocial or criminal. Good mothering is thus positioned as salvational for criminalized women—an identity that can reconcile previous misconduct behaviours and can provide a source of hope for women negotiating a criminalized existence.

Although research on mothers in prison has been important for uncovering significant issues related to their past histories of abuse and social disadvantage (Allen et al.; Berry and Eigenberg; Brown and Bloom; Ferraro and Moe; Opsal), further research would be beneficial for adding nuance to the extant social and structural locations and realities of the women. The scope of analyses on incarceration and motherhood is quite broad in breadth and depth, yet it remains disproportionately quantitative and top-down in research design and methods. Broader understandings and considerations of mothers who are criminalized through their engagement in certain activities such as drug/alcohol use or sex work tend to be undertheorized in their intersections with maternity. As Mary Daly and Chiara Saraceno argue, a social exclusion lens "is dynamic and process-oriented; it has the capacity to turn the spotlight on the ex/includes and the ex/included, and it facilitates the type of multilayered analysis that is necessary for a fuller understanding of gender and other complex social relations" (85). In spite of the plurality of scholarly disciplines and approaches to the subject matter of criminalized mothers, research that includes mothers themselves as empowered participants or collaborators is rare.

Collaborative and Participatory Research

One potentially successful way to address and challenge criminalized mothers' social exclusion is to engage in research undertakings with them. Conducting research and working alongside criminalized mothers can allow for more diverse and comprehensive representations and understandings of their lives and experiences. Collaborative approaches have been found to increase the reliability of collected data, increase effectiveness of research findings, and better advance social justice aims for marginalized populations (Bradbury-Huang; Brydon-Miller et al., "Why Action"), making this approach ideal for research as praxis with this population of women.

We argue that there is a need for studies to begin with the lived experiences of mothers as they encounter mechanisms of social control and to draw on the significant insights of feminist motherhood scholars on the need for empowered motherhood, which emphasizes "maternity agency, authority, autonomy and authenticity" (O'Reilly 15). As of yet, however, such an analysis is rarely applied to marginalized mothers whose lives are governed by processes of criminalization. Feminist and antioppressive theories inform research practices that do not assume expertise about mothers' lives; instead, they encourage full collaborative involvement in research to minimize problematic power differentials (Brown and Strega). Indeed, collaborative approaches have the potential to disrupt dominant discourses beginning with their very application—a bottom-up research agenda involving the participation of affected women, from planning research questions and research design to data collection, data analysis, and dissemination of findings (Brown and Strega;

Brydon-Miller et al., "Why Action"). Conducting research *with* criminalized mothers on topics they deem important, applying broad definitions of "motherhood" and "criminalization," and ensuring that collaborative, participation-based methodologies are utilized can facilitate the emergence of more nuanced understandings of mothers' experiences. Also important is to capture the ways in which women have enabled experiences of empowerment, success, and agency through adaptation, resilience, and resistance. Although collaborative and participatory approaches have been effective in research with women experiencing assault and domestic violence (Langan and Morton; Maguire; Parnis et al.), as well as with sex workers (O'Neill; Shannon et al.; van der Meulen), women in prison (Fine and Torre; Martin et al.), women exiting prison (Baldry et al.), and women with mental illness (Rebeiro et al.), they are still relatively rare in research generally (Dupont) and certainly remain to be fully explored with mothers who experience other contexts of criminalization.

Feminist scholars have long encouraged the use of collaborative methodologies that emphasize political action to challenge inequality and benefit women (Cancian, "Conflicts"; Cook and Fonow; Sprague; Elwood Martin et al.). FPAR, for instance, combines collaborative research and critical feminist theory by incorporating women's involvement in each part of the research process, including developing the research questions to be examined, completing the research activities, and interpreting and disseminating the findings (Reid et al.). Feminist research specifically brings forward an analysis of gender in participation, issues, structures, and language; collaborative methodologies target involvement by community and a high degree of social and political change (Cancian, "Participatory Research"). Inclusiveness is emphasized in FPAR such that multiple perspectives of women are understood and valued from a critical, intersectional orientation, while at the same time researchers confront and challenge assumptions they bring to the process (Brydon-Miller et al., *Travelling Companions*; Ristock and Pennell). Further, in feminist participatory studies, community members and researchers can benefit from sharing and learning from each other's knowledges, dismantling traditional hierarchies in the research setting, enhancing the relevance of research processes and outcomes, and effecting social and political change with the research results.

In applying collaborative approaches to the study of criminalized mothers, these methodologies would allow for women to partake in the research at all levels of the process, bring community organizations together, and create the conditions for beneficial policy and practice change. FPAR has the potential to interrupt themes of good and bad mothering, and add counter-narratives to dominant discourse. The rhetoric around mothers who use drugs, for example, would seem to engender at times hostility or helplessness by suggesting that these mothers somehow do not or cannot care enough about their children, suggesting that substance-using mothers cannot help but be bad. In contrast, an analysis must be taken up, as Susan Boyd and Lenora Marcellus suggest, through the lens of gender, class, and race, and must consider the broader discursive shifts that see "drug user" and "mother" as unyielding and contradictory identity markers.

Additionally, by situating the research process in the varied experiences of mothers themselves, FPAR has the capacity to offer more nuanced representations of mothers' diverse parenting roles, relationships, and responsibilities. Many studies on motherhood do not explicitly define or describe the term, implying that the care of biological offspring occurs exclusively by cisgender women. Conversely, Sandra Enos asserts the need for mothers and mothering to expand beyond children and their mothers. What about incidences of daycare and babysitting, she asks? How do women conceptualize motherhood, and how would this differ from researchers' ideas about motherhood? How do ideas about mothering intersect with race, given that racial differences exist in mothering practices? Moreover, some criminalized mothers do not fit the binary gender structures dictated by dominant discourses of femininity and heterosexuality. In research studies that uphold traditional concepts of the nuclear family, parenting, femininity, and mothering, individuals falling in the margins of these social constructions continue to be excluded from research, and the ways in which they are discounted by social institutions go unchallenged. A participatory and collaborative research framework can allow for the inclusion of diverse ways of mothering by the myriad ways of being a woman; this approach can expand our understanding of how people are affected by a range of systems of social control.

These kinds of more nuanced approaches can encourage deeper, intersectional analyses of criminalization and mothers' race, class, ability, gender and sexual identity, and additional social locations, offering valuable information that challenges and provides possible solutions to current policy and practice in transcarceral systems. We suggest, therefore, that future research and knowledge creation would benefit from engagement with participatory approaches—specifically if it were to be undertaken with mothers who have experiences with criminalized activities and interactions with criminal justice systems, rather than on them (van der Meulen).

Studies employing participatory approaches often find the data to be of enhanced validity, as women may fear repercussions of particular disclosures when asked by researchers with whom they are unfamiliar and, thus, may answer questions in such a way that adheres to socially expected values and behaviours. When immersed in a climate of risk management and surveillance, the consequences for women who disclose behaviours viewed as morally reprehensible are very real. In studies where the individuals who collect the data have connections with the community, or are themselves members of the study population (often called peer researchers or community-based researchers), the responses to research questions can be more honest and authentic (Alexander and Richman). Peer researchers, in this case criminalized mothers themselves, may be viewed as more trustworthy than unknown individuals or those associated with academic institutions. Better data mean better information for theorization and for program and policy development. Including criminalized mothers in the study, as researchers or in other capacities, is an important avenue for the collection of quality information.

One example of the highly successful use of a participatory action methodology for marginalized mothers is a study by Kathleen Kenny and Amy Druker that explore women's experiences of grief following the apprehension of their children to child protection services. This context of maternal grief has received little attention in research. It occupies relatively invisible space in society as a result of the judgment of mothers who transgress not only their socially sanctioned gender and maternity roles of caretaking and selflessness, but potentially legal regulations; the status of loss as undefined in terms of being temporary or permanent; and the systemic demands of child protection services on mothers after apprehension has occurred. Kenny and Druker's study involved the participation of nine women from Toronto, Canada, inviting them to share their experiences of losing a child. Simultaneously, individual (e.g., mental health struggles due to isolation, hopelessness, trauma, etc.) and structural (e.g., loss of rights and loss of trust in others, lack of supports and instability, targeted programs, etc.) dimensions of grief were conceptualized by the researchers and the participants; the mothers identified the barriers and facilitators for coping with the loss of their children. Based on the information provided by the women, a program titled The Grief and Loss Education and Action Project was initiated by two collaborating community agencies that provided a series of weekly sessions for women to tell their stories, raise awareness and consciousness around their experiences, and to process their loss using art and coping strategies with a facilitator or counsellor. Additionally, a meeting was arranged with the program participants and a child protection service worker in order to educate the worker about the impact of the child welfare system on the mothers, their negative experiences with it, and their suggestions for change, including a "best practices" document. The women related this experience as resoundingly positive and empowering.

Collaborative research approaches, of course, are also not without their challenges, and there are numerous logistic and structural issues that can arise while engaging in such methodologies. Generally speaking, collaborative models, with their emancipatory and political aims that challenge taken-for-granted priorities and conventions, include a range of complications regarding the theoretical and social questions being answered, recognition of the ethics and values behind the research, the kinds of publications that are prioritized, who obtains credit on published products, and the closeness of participants to researchers (Cancian, "Feminist Science," "Participatory Research"). Furthermore, in studies that include peers in data collection roles, it is important to actively consider issues related to confidentiality and privacy. Although some research participants may be more comfortable engaging with peer researchers, others may not wish to disclose or be in contact with particular familiar individuals, especially if peers are to also incorporate practice interventions or are otherwise connected to community organizations where participants seek services (Guta et al.; Flicker et al.; Roche et al.). There are also possible ethical issues in terms of what information is disclosed and what must be done with particular kinds of information, especially if peers are affiliated with social agencies or institutions. Additionally, although funding bodies are increasing their expectations of and support for community-academic partnerships, collaborative studies often comprise very lengthy processes and can require substantial amounts of funds, which despite the rhetorical support, still tend not to fit within granting body expectations and requirements.

In addition to logistic and structural complications, a key challenge for FPAR with criminalized mothers is the political climate of the carceral state, which heavily controls the kinds of research projects allowed to be carried out. The challenges of such work in the carceral state (Goodman; Larsen and Walby; Watson and van der Meulen; Watson; Yeager, "The Freedom," "Getting the Unusual") and specifically with women in prisons (Hannah-Moffatt; Martel) have been discussed elsewhere, but for our purposes, we acknowledge how this can affect studies with criminalized mothers more generally. Although particular research questions may be answered through access to information requests (Brownlee and Walby), the data received may be less relevant for research that takes an explicitly feminist approach and that aims to explore women's complex lived experiences. Indeed, collaborative feminist researchers bring with them a critical lens while pushing possibilities for resistance and inclusion from the margins to the fore. As noted by Michael Mopas and Sarah Turnbull, collaborative methods demand that researchers be flexible, reflexive, and creative.

Conclusion

The social context for criminalized mothers is one in which the regulation and surveillance of their bodies, reproductive choices, and mental health is particularly prominent (Campbell; Chan and Rigakos), and their social exclusion is a resulting factor. Although feminist analyses may situate these choices in a broader context of structural and systemic oppressions, too often women have been deprived of agency in the name of either judging or patronizingly excusing criminalized behaviour, both of which position mothers negatively. This chapter suggests that a broader definition of criminalization can allow diverse groups of mothers to respond to the limitations in existing knowledge about their experiences. Although some feminist literature on criminalized mothering has suggested a more participant-driven, strengths-based focus, there seems to be limited research to date that takes up this mandate in practice. Indeed, rarely are criminalized mothers encouraged to be decision makers within the research process, which leads to a lack of scholarly focus that considers mothers' strengths, resistance, and agency. We argue, therefore, that collaborative methodologies have great potential to expand and further develop understandings of these women's complex lives. Criminalized mothers' inclusion in the research process, from design to data collection to knowledge translation, could work to ensure the accessibility and validity of the process and outcomes, and can also aid in translating findings into concrete recommendations for improved organizational policies and programming towards reduced social exclusion. Participant-driven and collaborative frameworks could offer nuanced insight on the understandings of criminalized mothers' experiences and could present alternative discourses to more normative analyses.

Works Cited

Alexander, Leslie B., and Kenneth A. Richman. "Ethical Dilemmas in Evaluations Using Indigenous Research Workers." *American Journal of Evaluation*, vol. 29, no. 1, 2008, pp. 73-85.

Baldry, Eileen, et al. *Aboriginal Women with Dependent Children Leaving Prison Project: Needs Analysis Report*. Commissioned by Homelessness New South Wales, *Indigenous Justice*, 2008, www.indigenousjustice. gov.au/resources/aboriginal-women-with-dependent-children-leaving-prison-project-needs-analysis-report/. Accessed 11 May 2019.

Balfour, Gillian, and Elizabeth Comack. *Criminalizing Women: Gender and (In)justice in Neo-liberal Times*. Fernwood Publishing, 2006.

Belknap, Joanne. *The Invisible Woman: Gender, Crime, and Justice*. Wadsworth, 2001.

Bosworth, Mary. *Engendering Resistance: Agency and Power in Women's Prisons*. Ashgate, 1999.

Boyd, Susan C., and Lenora Marcellus. *Substance Use During Pregnancy, A Woman-Centred Approach.* Fernwood, 2006.

Bradbury-Huang, Hilary. *The SAGE Handbook of Action Research. 3rd ed.* SAGE Publications, 2015.

Brown, Leslie, and Susan Strega. *Research as Resistance: Critical, Indigenous, and Anti-oppressive Approaches.* Canadian Scholars' Press, 2005.

Brownlee, Jamie, and Kevin Walby. *Access to Information and Social Justice: Critical Research Strategies for Journalists, Scholars and Activists.* Arbeiter Ring Publishing Books, 2015.

Brydon-Miller, Mary, et al. "Why Action Research?" *Action Research, vol. 1, no. 1, 2003, pp. 9-28.*

Brydon-Miller, Mary et al. *Traveling Companions: Feminism, Teaching, and Action Research.* Praeger Publishers, 2004.

Campbell, Howard. "Drug Trafficking Stories: Everyday Forms of Narco-Folklore on the U.S.-Mexico Border." *International Journal of Drug Policy*, vol. 16, no. 5, 2005, pp. 326-33

Cancian, Francesca M. "Conflicts between Activist Research and Academic Success: Participatory Research and Alternative Strategies." *The American Sociologist*, vol. 24, no. 1, 1993, pp. 92-106.

Cancian, Francesca M. "Participatory Research and Alternative Strategies for Activist Sociology." *Feminism and Social Change: Bridging Theory and Practice*, edited by Heidi University of Illinois Press, 1996, pp. 187-205.

Cancian, Francesca M. "Feminist Science: Methodologies that Challenge Inequality." *Gender and Society*, vol. 6, no. 4, 1992, pp. 623-42.

Caplan, Paula J. *Don't Blame Mother: Mending the Mother-Daughter Relationship.* Harper and Row, 1989.

Carlen, Pat. *Women, Crime and Poverty.* Open University Press, 1988.

Carlen, Pat. "Why Study Women's Imprisonment? Or Anyone Else's? An Indefinite Article." *British Journal of Criminology*, vol. 34, 1994, pp. 131-40.

Carlton, Bree, and Marie Segrave. *Women Exiting Prison: Critical Essays on Gender, Post-Release Support, and Survival.* Routledge, 2013.

Chan, Wendy, and George S. Rigakos. "Risk, Crime, and Gender." *British Journal of Criminology*, vol. 42, no. 4, 2002, pp. 743-61.

Cook, Judith A. and Mary Margaret Fonow. "Knowledge and Women's Interests: Issues of Epistemology and Methodology in Feminist Sociological Research." Sociological Inquiry, vol. 56, no. 1, 1986, pp. 2-29.

Daly, Mary, and Chiara Saraceno. "Social Exclusion and Gender Relations." *Contested Concepts in Gender and Social Politics*, edited by Barbara Hobson, Jane Lewis, and Birte Siim, 2002, E. Elgar, 84.

Douglas, Susan J., and Meredith W. Michaels. *The Mommy Myth: The Idealization of Motherhood and How It Has Undermined All Women*. The Free Press, 2005.

Dupont, Ida. "Beyond Doing No Harm: A Call for Participatory Action Research with Marginalized Populations in Criminological Research." *Critical Criminology*, vol. 16, 2008, pp. 197-207.

Eljdupovic, Gordana, and Rebecca Jaremko Bromwich. *Incarcerated Mothers: Oppression and Resistance*. Demeter Press, 2013.

Enos, Sandra. *Mothering from the Inside: Parenting in a Women's Prison*. State University of New York Press, 2001.

Fine, Michelle, and Maria Elena Torre. "Intimate Details: Participatory Action Research in Prison." *Action Research*, vol. 4, no. 3, 2006, pp. 253-69.

Flicker, Sarah, et al. *Peer Research in Action III: Ethical Issues*. The Wellesley Institute, 2010.

Fox, Kathryn J. "The Politics of Prevention: Ethnographers Combat AIDS Among Drug Users." *Ethnography Unbound: Power and Resistance in the Modern Metropolis*, edited by Michael Buroway et al., University of California Press, 1991, pp. 227-49.

Friedersdorf, Conor. "Working Mom Arrested for Letting Her 9-Year-Old Play Alone at Park." *The Atlantic*, 15 Jul. 2014, www.theatlantic.com/national/archive/2014/07/arrested-for-letting-a-9-year-old-play-at-the-park-alone/374436/. Accessed 16 May 2019.

Friedman, May. *Mommyblogs and the Changing Face of Motherhood*. University of Toronto Press, 2013.

Goodman, Philip. "From 'Observation Dude' to 'An Observational Study': Gaining Access and Conducting Research Inside a

Paramilitary Organization." *Canadian Journal of Law and Society* vol. 26, no. 3, 2011, pp. 599-05.

Guta, Adrian, et al. *Peer Research in Action II: Management, Support and Supervision.* The Wellesley Institute, 2010.

Hannah-Moffatt, Kelly. "Criminological Cliques: Narrowing Dialogues, Institutional Protectionism, and the Next Generation." *What Is Criminology?,* edited by Mary Bosworth and Carolyn Hoyle, Oxford University Press, 2011, 440-55.

Hays, Sharon. *The Cultural Contradictions of Motherhood.* Yale University Press, 1996.

Horn, David. "This Norm Which Is Not One: Reading the Female Body in Lombroso's Anthropology." *Deviant Bodies,* edited by Jennifer Terry and Jacqueline L. Urla Bloomington, Indiana University Press, 1995, 19-48.

Kenny, Kathleen, and Amy Druker. "Ants Facing an Elephant: Mothers' Grief, Loss, and Work for Change Following the Placement of a Child in the Care of Child Protection Authorities," *Children of the Drug War: Perspectives on the Impact of Drug Policies on Young People,* edited by Damon Barrett, The International Debate Education Association, 2011, 151-70.

Kilgore, James. "Tackling Debtors' Prisons: Reflecting on the Death of Eileen DiNino." *Truthout,* 20 Jun. 2014, https://truthout.org/articles/tackling-debtors-prisons-reflecting-on-the-death-of-eileen-dinino/. Accessed 16 May 2019.

Kinser, Amber. "Mothering as Relational Consciousness." *Feminist Mothering.* Ed. Andrea O'Reilly, SUNY Press, 2008, pp, 123-42.

Laberge, Danielle. "Women's Criminality, Criminal Women, Criminalized Women? Questions in and for a Feminist Perspective." *The Journal of Human Justice,* vol. 2, no. 2, 1991, pp. 37-56.

Langan, Debra, and Mavis Morton. "Reflecting on Community/Academic 'Collaboration': The Challenge of 'Doing' Feminist Participatory Action Research." *Action Research,* vol. 7, 2009, pp. 165-84.

Larsen, Mike, and Kevin Walby. *Brokering Access: Power, Politics, and Freedom of Information Process in Canada.* University of British Columbia Press, 2012.

Maguire, Patricia. *Doing Participatory Research: A Feminist Approach.* Center for International Education, 1987.

Martel, Joane. "Policing Criminological Knowledge: The Hazards of Qualitative Research on Women and Prison." *Theoretical Criminology,* vol. 8, no. 2, 2004, pp. 157-89.

Elwood Martin, Ruth, et al. *Arresting Hope: Women Taking Action in Prison Inside Out.* Inanna Publications, 2014.

Maushart, Susan. *The Mask of Motherhood: How Becoming a Mother Changes Our Lives and Why We Never Talk About It.* Penguin, 2000.

Mopas, Michael S. and Sarah Turnbull. "Negotiating a Way In: A Special Collection of Essays on Accessing Information and Socio-legal Research." *Canadian Journal of Law and Society,* vol. 26, no. 3, 2011, pp. 585-90.

O'Neill, Maggie. "Cultural Criminology and Sex Work: Resisting Regulation through Radical Democracy and Participatory Action Research (PAR)." *Journal of Law and Society,* vol. 37, no. 1, 2010, pp. 210-32.

O'Reilly, Andrea. *Mother Outlaws: Theories and Practices of Empowered Mothering.* Women's Press, 2004.

Parnis, Deborah, et al. "Cooperation or Co-Optation?: Assessing the Methodological Benefits and Barriers Involved in Conducting Qualitative Research through Medical Institutional Settings." *Qualitative Health Research,* vol. 15, no. 5, 2005, pp. 686-97.

Razack, Sherene H. *Race, Space and the Law: Unmapping a White Settler Society.* Between the Lines, 2002.

Rebeiro, Karen L., et al. "Northern Initiative for Social Action: An Occupation-based Mental Health Program," *American Journal of Occupational Therapy,* vol. 55, no. 5, 2001, pp. 493-500.

Reid, Colleen, et al. "Finding the 'Action' in Feminist Participatory Action Research." *Action Research,* vol. 4, no. 3, 2006, pp. 315-32.

Ristock, Janice, and Joan Pennell. *Community Research as Empowerment: Feminist Links, Postmodern Interruptions.* Oxford University Press, 1996.

Roberts, Carol A. "Drug Use among Inner-city African American Women: The Process of Managing Loss." *Qualitative Health Research,* vol. 9, no. 5, 1999, pp. 620-38.

Roche, Brenda, et al. *Peer Research in Action I: Models of Practice.* The Wellesley Institute, 2010.

Shannon, Kate, et al. "Sexual and Drug-related Vulnerabilities for HIV Infection Among Women Engaged in Survival Sex Work in Vancouver, Canada." *Canadian Journal of Public Health*, vol. 98, no. 6, 2007, pp. 465-69.

Smirnova, Michelle, and Jennifer Gatewood Owens. "The New Mothers' Little Helpers: Medicalization, Victimization, and Criminalization of Motherhood Via Prescription Drugs." *Deviant Behavior*, 2018, pp. 1-14.

Sprague, Joey. *Feminist Methodologies for Critical Researchers: Bridging Differences.* Altamira Press, 2005.

Sudbury, Julia. *Global Lockdown: Race, Gender, and the Prison-Industrial Complex.* Routledge, 2005.

Thurer, Shari L. *The Myths of Motherhood: How Culture Reinvents the Good Mother.* Houghton Mifflin, 1994.

van der Meulen, Emily. "Action Research with Sex Workers: Dismantling Barriers and Building Bridges." *Action Research*, vol. 9, no. 4, 2011, pp. 370-84.

Watson Tara Marie and Emily van der Meulen. "Research in Carceral Contexts: Confronting Access Barriers and Engaging Former Prisoners." *Qualitative Research*, vol. 19, no. 2, 2019, pp. 182-198.

Watson, Tara Marie. "Research Access Barriers as Reputational Risk Management: A Case Study of Censorship in Corrections." *Canadian Journal of Criminology and Criminal Justice*, vol. 57, no. 3, 2015, pp. 330-62.

Winnicott, Donald Woods. *The Child, the Family, and the Outside World.* Perseus Publishing, 1973.

Yeager, Matthew G. "The Freedom of Information Act as a Methodological Tool: Suing the Government for Data." *Canadian Journal of Criminology and Criminal Justice*, vol. 48, no. 4, 2006, pp. 499-521.

Yeager, Matthew G. "Getting the Usual Treatment: Research Censorship and the Dangerous Offender." *Contemporary Justice Review*, vol. 11, no. 4, 2008 , pp. 413-25.

Chapter 7

Excluded from Good Motherhood and the Impact of Prison: Reflections of Mothers after Prison

Lucy Baldwin

In the Court, I could see them crying in the public gallery. From the minute I was sentenced to prison, I knew nothing would be the same ever again (Karen, forty-two, qtd. in Baldwin, "Motherhood Disrupted")

Social exclusion is a socially constructed concept, and it is inextricably linked to systematic discrimination and inequality. The inequalities of social exclusion lie in power relationships, as well as access to goods, services, rights, and resources, which reach across all personal arenas—social, political, economic, and, particularly relevant in this chapter, spiritual and emotional ones. To contextualize social exclusion for this chapter, it is important to establish what one can be excluded from. Throughout history women have been excluded from work, politics, education, independence, basic rights, and, fundamentally, gender equality. Clarice Feinman suggests that women are most often defined in relation to men; whether they are alike, different from, or complimentary to, the reference point remains men, masculinity, and male behaviour. She further suggests that women are defined in familial terms in relation to explicitly gendered categories—

as mothers, wives, and daughters. Men, in contrast, are not defined in relation to women but to a larger, public world where they operate as full and free citizens. Maria Black and Rosaline Coward argue that "Women are precisely defined. Never general representatives of humanity, of all people, but as specifically feminine, and frequently sexual categories.... Being a man is an entitlement not to masculine attributes, but a non-gendered subjectivity" (83). Or, in other words, as Feinman suggests, men represent the human and the universal, to which women are then the "other." This othering of women permeates all aspects of society and throughout all social and political thought. From this, a whole series of dichotomous categories are constructed around one (men) and the other (women).

Historically, motherhood has been, perhaps, the most significant means of excluding women and confining them to the home through time, although, paradoxically, it could be argued that motherhood also unites (some) women through a common bond. As Adrienne Rich has argued "Motherhood—unmentioned in the histories of conquest and serfdom, wars and treaties, exploration and imperialism—has a history, it has an ideology, it is more fundamental than tribalism or nationalism" (33). Rich suggests that "motherhood" is a term universally recognized as the institution surrounding mothering—the connotations of which are influenced by historical and societal landscapes—and is influenced to a greater or lesser extent by cultural- and time-related norms and values. Despite the contextual relevance of time and historical landscapes, there have always been constants in relation to mothering and motherhood, as in what is expected from mothers and how they are expected to behave (Baldwin "Mothering Justice"; O'Reilly, *21st Century Motherhood*). Mothers are expected to be good, kind, and nurturing, and to place themselves second to their children—thereby conforming to mothering ideals and expectations. Consequentially, it has become an accepted that motherhood and mothering are invariably associated with a plethora of emotions and judgements, both positive and negative, but rarely, if ever, ambiguous. Mothers falling outside the ideals and ideologies of motherhood find themselves excluded, judged, and, therefore, "othered." However, few are as completely socially excluded as the imprisoned mother.

Fear is often a relevant factor in relation to why people may become excluded, and Feinman suggests throughout history, fear of the nonconforming woman (i.e., the criminal woman) has always been high, but never more so than when that woman is also a mother (Zedner). Mothering, particularly good mothering, law breaking, and prison are deemed inherently incompatible, as Corston suggests, "Many women [in prison] still define themselves and are defined by others - by their role in the family. It is an important component in our self-identity and self-esteem. To become a prisoner is almost by definition to become a bad mother" (20). Becoming a prisoner magnifies the social exclusion most mothers entering custody have already felt through class, race, poverty, victimization, inequality, and judgment (Arditti et al.). Mothers in custody often deal with the pain of mothering from a physically excluded position while also managing the emotional fallout of already pain-filled lives (Carlen; Allen et al.; Baldwin, "Mothering Justice"). Being separated from their children and families, and managing the additional burdens of guilt, judgment, and social exclusion can feel overwhelming for these mothers (Sharpe; Baldwin, "Tainted Love").

How do mothers themselves experience such feelings? How does the judgment of others affect mothers in prison? How does it affect their view of themselves and of each other? Do they, as an already socially excluded group, then exclude others within prison walls, and if so why? Do mothers retain a sense of exclusion after release? This chapter seeks to address these questions—both from the literature available and from the author's own research. The chapter's research is primarily from a UK context but will also draw from international perspectives and findings. The chapter offers insight into the emotional experiences and sense of exclusion felt by both incarcerated mothers and mothers post-release. In addition, it will discuss the value of understanding more about incarcerated mothers lived experiences and offer recommendations in relation to working practices with such mothers. In this way, it will seek to minimize and compensate for the impact and effect of physical exclusion of mothers who go to prison. The effects of which are self-evident and eloquently described by one mother in the author's ongoing research: "I didn't just feel disconnected from my kids; I felt disconnected from everything—from the world even. I was so scared to come out of prison. I knew I'd have friends, and even family who wouldn't want to know me.... How can you feel part of something when you know you are not wanted?" (Kady,[1] twenty-eight,, qtd. Baldwin, "Motherhood Disrupted").

The Legacy of the Deviant Woman

Lucia Zedner puts forwards the view that prior to the mid-nineteenth century, approaches to female criminality were essentially moralistic; women were judged against what she calls "highly artificial" notions of the ideal woman being an exemplary being. Victorian notions of women as the weaker sex interacted heavily with over-medicalized beliefs that endured into the twentieth century. Interpretations for female criminality—namely biological and psychological ones—were suffused with a highly moral view of what constituted normality and, therefore, what constituted deviancy in women. In the exploration of early attitudes towards criminal women, it is impossible to ignore the influence of both patriarchy and religion, as to not "include or acknowledge the significance of their influence, legacy and relevance to current practice, would render such discussion incomplete" (Baldwin, *Mothering Justice* 142). Zedner argues that the ways in which women have been responded to historically in the criminal justice system reflects their position in wider society—a position fundamentally of inequality, in which women were subordinate to men. So-called deviant women were, therefore, "othered" and were excluded from wider society; they were viewed as lacking and somehow different to good, clean, and law-abiding women. Early reform in the nineteenth century was, thus, influenced by the need to "save souls" and to assist "fallen angels" in finding a pathway back to virtue, back to femininity, and back to civilized society (Zedner; Baldwin, *Mothering Justice*). Such attitudes pervaded and influenced the need to save all criminal women but especially those who were mothers because, as Zedner suggests, "in their role as mothers, they were identified as the biological source of crime and degeneracy" (327). Women, especially mothers, were viewed as the source of corruption and juvenile delinquency, and were perceived to be acting against their nature, righteousness, and femininity. Jelinger Symons, writing in 1849, suggests that "Female crime has a much worse effect on the morals of the young, and is therefore a more powerfully depraving character than crimes of men ... the influence and example of the mother are all powerful; and corruption if it be there, exists in the source and must taint the stream" (qtd. in Zedner 327). Such attitudes influenced, and arguably still do, the judiciary in relation to the oppressive and harsh sentencing of mothers (Minson; Carlen; Caddle and Crisp; Epstein). In the UK, for example, in 2011, Ursula—a young mother of two children under five, from whom she had never previously been separated, and with no previous convictions—was sentenced to five months in prison for accepting a pair of stolen shorts. The value of the shorts was less than ten English pounds. The shorts were stolen by her flatmate during riots that had swept her hometown the night before—riots that Ursula had played no part in. Ursula had tried on a pair of shorts and, as her legal counsel described, "foolishly and dishonestly" decided to keep them for herself. When the judge sentenced her, he said the following: "You are supposed to be a role model to your sons—you should have reported the goods stolen and the person who stole them.... You would expect decent people to speak up and say, 'no this is wrong, get that out of my house.' You are a role model to your sons, yet you decided to have a look at the goods and keep some for yourself" (sentencing judge's comments R vs Nevin 2011).

Was this young woman then punished so severely for her petty crime or for being, in the eyes of the judge, a less than "decent" mother and a less than perfect "role model" to her sons? This additional judgement delivered to and felt by mothers who experience prison has been previously documented (Baldwin, *Mothering Justice*; O'Malley and Devaney; Corston; Minson; Enos) and has been supported by mothers' own accounts in my research (Baldwin, *Motherhood Challenged*). The additional judgement, which for mothers proves they no longer belong in the category of good mother, is felt keenly from the moment they enter the prison space and stretches far beyond the prison walls after they are released (Baldwin, "Motherhood Disrupted," "Tainted Love"). Such a sentiment is illustrated painfully by one grandmother:

> All my life, all I'd done was be a mam ... my kids came before any man. We never had much, but we had love. I was a good mam; well I did my best ... when I went to prison, I felt like all that was wiped out; I'd failed.... Even worse because I'm a Nanna and a mam ... I'm meant to be respectable at my age.... I just looked around when I first went in [prison], and thought that's it ... I've let them all down ... look at this place ... how the fuck did I get to be here? (Maggi, fifty-five, qtd in Baldwin, "Motherhood Disrupted")

Exclusion from Good Motherhood: Mothers in and after Prison

Sandra Enos describes the challenge of retaining a good mother identity, particularly when faced with circumstances that only serve to challenge that perception of self. She argues that women's own inclusion of themselves into the good mother bracket is severely tested, particularly as the women are imprisoned because of their own criminal actions: "the very fact of imprisonment threatened claims to good motherhood because the women had committed offences that led to separation from the children in the first place" (102). Prison is, in fact, a space that cruelly serves only to repeat the inequalities, exclusion, and challenges faced by all women in wider society (Moore and Scraton; Sim; Scraton and McCulloch). For mothers, there are particular "pains of imprisonment" (Sykes)—specifically, those that relate to the physical separation of mother and child and the subsequent reduction in or removal of the mothering role (Baldwin, "Motherhood Disrupted," "Tainted Love"). Derek Layder suggests "we can't do relationships on our own" (77): furthermore, how people interact with others is greatly influenced by how they think they will be responded to by others. This is of particular significance for mothers in prison and for mothers who have left prison, since they already feel judged, shamed, and excluded. Imprisoned mothers have described how their relationships with each other and with prison staff would magnify their own sense of exclusion from good motherhood, and in fact, often from good citizenship: "The officers didn't care.... I wasn't a mother. I wasn't a grandmother who was feeling sad and in pain. I wasn't someone who had made a successful career and made one mistake—I was just a prisoner, the rest ... all gone" (Queenie, sixty-four, qtd. in Baldwin, "Motherhood Disrupted"). The mothers would absorb such messages and would internalize this feeling of being "less than" or 'imperfect' or "tainted" (Baldwin, "Tainted Love"). Such messages would serve only to add to the sense of failure they already felt—a sense that would result in mothers feeling different from other mothers outside of prison and also feeling separated from the moral righteousness of the assumed good mothers who were the officers.

Ervin Goffman argues that in a "total institution," such as a prison, the "social distance" between staff and prisoners is an inevitable consequence of the unequal relationship between, what he calls," the supervisory staff" and the "managed group" (18). The imprisoned mothers, however, did not see this condemnation of them as mothers as inevitable. It was frequent but not inevitable. Such a feeling is illustrated by a mother who experienced two different prisons during her sentence:

> In ... [name of prison] ... it felt like we [the mothers] were basically looked on as bad mothers, actually worse than that ... mothers who didn't deserve to have kids.... But in [name of second prison], it was different again. If a woman was new and had kids, they kept an eye on her, and they knew how important phone calls home and visits were to us mums. My officer even knew my kids' birthdays; in fact, she knew their names..., I was gobsmacked in my first week when she asked me how [son's name] was and how he was coping ... made me emotional her asking you to know, even thinking about it now does. I don't ever remember even being asked if I even had kids at the other place. I wasn't a mother there ... just a prisoner. (Rita, 35, qtd. in Baldwin, "Motherhood Disrupted")

Mothers described how the obvious emotional judgments of the officers (and sometimes the other mothers) would have an emotional impact on them and their identities as mothers. Rob Canton describes these emotions of punishment and judgement as "moral emotions" of "righteousness and retribution", (4). He suggests punishment takes many forms, but that a defining characteristic is censure. Jonathon Haidt suggests that a defining criterion of moral emotion is that "it is linked to the interests or welfare either of society as a whole or at least of persons other than the judge or agent: (853). Thus, women experiencing judgment from prison staff felt as though it was coming not only from the prison staff themselves but also from society in general, which was felt by the mothers as an additional and excluding punishment. They were criminal mothers; thus, they were bad mothers. This was simply put by one mother: "good mothers don't go to prison, do they?" (Maggi, fifty-five, qtd. in Baldwin, "Motherhood Disrupted").

One mother, in particular, demonstrated how such punitive and moralistic responses affected her, even when she was outside the prison walls. Her own guilt and damaged maternal identity resulted in her assuming she would be rejected and excluded, which led her to exclude herself before others could:

> It felt bad enough being a mother in prison and everyone knowing I was a bad mother, in fact telling me I was too ... but it's their job, so they have to deal with you anyway, but when I was out [of prison], I would avoid going to anything like play groups or nursery plays—anywhere where someone might ask me where I'd been.... why would I tell people that? Just so they could then ignore me and talk about me and my child behind our backs? Easier to stay away. (Sophie, twenty-one, qtd. in Baldwin, *Motherhood Challenged*)

Abigail Rowe reminds us that mothers in prison are not a homogenous group. Even among women who were all apparently "in the same boat" (i.e., imprisoned as mothers and separated from their children), research suggests that inclusive and exclusive groups will form. Enos found that mothers did, in fact, judge and exclude other mothers—particularly those who were "druggies," child molesters, or those that had hurt children. She found some mothers in her study would assert that certain crimes did not conflict with good mothering. In fact, mothers in her study would deem acquisitive crime often as a "way to do mothering" and that accessing additional resources, by whatever means, was part of their responsibility as caretakers. Enos quotes one mother who had committed property crime: "you can be a good mother and be involved in crime and shoplifting and stuff ... but drugs it's another thing" (118). In my study, mothers also described not wanting to associate with specific groups of prisoners, effectively excluding them to keep their own company. This was related specifically to mothers who had hurt children but was also extended to certain drug users, particularly users of opiates: "Because I had mental health issues I was on the vulnerable wing, so I was on with the child abusers and the ones who'd killed their kids—it made me furious. I was a good mum, and I didn't want to be lumped in with that lot. I kept away from them and asked them to stay away from me" (Annie, thirty-three, qtd. in Baldwin, *Motherhood Challenged*). One mother, who had fought hard to secure place on the mother and baby unit, herself an ex-drug user said the following:

I wouldn't mix with the ones who had hurt kids. I'd look at them and think, "I can't even see my kids and you hurt yours, what's that about?" ... Some of the druggies knocked me bad as well. I won't go near 'em. Don't get me wrong I'm no angel, and I know you get caught up in a cycle outside, it's not easy to get off and stay off. But to use smack [heroin] when your pregnant, well that's just wrong. What kind of mothers will they be if they can do that? (Kady, twenty-eight, qtd. in Baldwin, *Motherhood Challenged*)

Enos suggests that this "hierarchy of motherhood, drug use and criminality provide a notion of how these women constructed motherhood" (117). It is interesting that this perhaps reflects a similar hierarchy to that held by wider society.

The Reach of the Prison Walls

Aside from exclusion from good motherhood, the wider, multidimensional effects of imprisonment are well documented (Duff; Waquant). However, much of the published research related specifically to reintegration is either not gender specific or is related predominantly to male prisoners. In the UK, despite the fact that most women (over 80 percent) are imprisoned for nonviolent offences and that they serve relatively short sentences, (over 60 percent will be six months or less, many a matter of weeks), many women will have lost their homes and the care of their children by the time they are released (Prison Reform Trust; Baldwin and Epstein). Only 5 percent of children of imprisoned mothers remain in their own home; 14 percent go directly into the care of the local authority at the start or during their mother's sentence. Upon release, many prisoners, particularly criminal mothers, are returned directly to the multidimensional socially excluded position they were in prior to their incarceration, although often in a much worse position (Murray; Masson). Loïc Wacquant suggests that material and physical exclusion is compounded by reduced social capital as ex-prisoners. Goffman suggests that "blemishes of individual character" and "spoiled identities" translate to "stigma" for prisoners (4), which, as this chapter has illustrated, is especially keenly felt by prisoners and ex-prisoners who are mothers (Baldwin, *Mothering Justice*, "Tainted Love").

Baldwin suggests that Andrea O' Reilly's principles of matricentric feminism lend themselves well to criminology, thereby facilitating a mother focussed exploration of particular issues faced by imprisoned and post prison mothers, creating what Baldwin terms a 'matricentric feminist criminology' (Baldwin, "Motherhood Disrupted"). Released mothers must actively work to renegotiate their social identities as ex-prisoners and all that this entails for them, but, additionally, they must reestablish and, sometimes, reconstruct their roles and identities as mothers (Leverentz). For mothers who are to be reunited with their children on a full-time basis, this is perhaps obvious; however, those who have lost the care of their children, either temporarily or permanently, must also now renegotiate their maternal identity from an excluded or limited position. Several mothers in my study lost the care of their children to the local authority, but as one woman stated:

> Just because I don't live with my child and my child doesn't live with me doesn't mean I'm not a mother, I still feel like a mother; I think like a mother. I worry about the world he's growing up in, where he is, and what he's doing. I remember his birthday and think of him at school; in fact now I'm clean, even though I don't have him, I'm more of a mother than I was before. I was too chaotic to think of all that stuff then ... it's sad though that he doesn't get to see this mother. I'm an invisible mother now. (Nicola, forty-one, qtd. in Baldwin, *Motherhood Challenged*)

Visibility in their mothering, especially good mothering, was important to the women when they were in prison, and it remained so after their release. It was important to them that they could be seen as being good mothers in the act of mothering. Mothers talked about being aware they were being watched when in prison by other mothers as well as by staff, and also after their release. However, the mothers who commented on this did not feel this oversight was positive or supportive; rather, it was done in a suspicious way. Indeed, one mother commented that she struggled with this "lack of trust": "My mother refuses to trust me to have them, even though social services say I can have the kids. My mum keeps the two youngest; I see them every day, but she won't let me live with them, or them with me. She says if I kick off she will tell social services, so I have no choice ... that's the worst thing after prison: no one ever trusts you again" (Tamika twenty-six, qtd. in Baldwin, "Tainted Love").

Tamika's experience was not unique; two other grandmothers refused to allow children to return to their mothers, despite there being no formal restrictions against doing so. Many of the mothers described feeling shocked that things did not just return to normal; they said they now felt permanently excluded from good mothering, something they had not anticipated. Not all mothers leave prison and resume full-time care of their children; indeed, not all mothers would have had their children, or all their children, in their care before prison. However, most of the mothers felt their relationships—even with the children they had retained parental responsibility for—were forever changed. Whatever age their children had been when they were incarcerated, the mothers felt something had changed. For some mothers, reunification was more emotionally complex; some had lost their children to fostering, adoption, or alternative carers. One mother—who was sentenced to four months in custody when her baby was only three months old—felt she had completely lost her bond with her child because of her sentence. The baby had been taken into foster care after her mother was sentenced. The mother was pessimistic in her research interview about what this meant for their futures; she felt she now had nothing to live for, since her child no longer knew her and their contact was limited, supervised and fraught. This mother later took her own life, whilst still separated from her child. A grandmother and mother of adult children described how her relationship with her daughter (and mother of her grandchildren) was forever changed. Her daughter, whom she was previously close to, minimized contact with her following her release. She refused to visit her mother in her home town for fear that someone would find out that her mother had been to prison. For mothers, the ripple effects of being sent to prison have far-reaching and long-lasting consequences in terms of their mothering role and maternal identity (Arditti and Few; Baldwin, "Tainted Love").

Conclusion

This chapter highlights the exclusion felt by mothers who are imprisoned. This exclusion is often physical; these mothers are excluded from their children's lives, from opportunities, and from the benefits of being a free citizen. Most importantly; however, this chapter explains the ways in which women who are imprisoned as mothers feel excluded from the good mother identity and how their apparent failure to live up to the often unrealistic goals society places on them affects their emotions, relationships, and lived experience in and after prison. Indeed, uninformed and uncompassionate interactions with criminal justice staff, other incarcerated mothers, and the prison space can heavily impact the emotional and psychological wellbeing of mothers both as prisoners and beyond, which can contribute further to their social exclusion.

The chapter further highlights the struggle for reintegration of mothers who have been incarcerated and describes the relevance and importance of supporting women emotionally. Working with mothers and assisting them to maintain an active mothering role and a positive mother identity during their time in custody will prove beneficial in terms of maintaining relationships. Such an approach can assist with resettlement and, therefore, desistance, but failure to do so may negatively affect not only the mothers themselves but also their children for generations to come.

Endnote

1. All names from authors research are pseudonyms to preserve confidentiality and in line with ethical research principles.

Works Cited

Allen, Suzanne, et al. "Throwaway Moms: Maternal Incarceration and the Criminalization of Female Poverty." *Journal of Women and Social Work*, vol. 25, no. 2, 2010, pp. 160-72.

Arditti, Joyce, and April Few. "Maternal Distress and Women's Reentry into Family and Community Life." *Family Process* 47.3.2008: 303-21. Print.

Arditti, Joyce, et al. "Maternal Distress and Parenting in the Context of Cumulative Disadvantage." *Family Processes*, vol. 49, no. 2, 2010, 142-64.

Baldwin, Lucy. *Motherhood Challenged: A Study Exploring the Impact of Prison on Maternal Identity and Maternal Emotion*. Dissertation. Unpublished, De Montfort University, Leicester, Ongoing. Due for publication 2020.

Baldwin, Lucy. "Motherhood Disrupted: Reflections of Post-Prison Mothers." *Emotion, Space and Society*, 2017, pp. 1-8, wephren.tghn. org/site_media/media/articles/ESS_final_article__11orl7Z.pdf. Accessed 11 May 2019.

Baldwin, Lucy. *Mothering Justice: Working with Mothers in Criminal and Social Justice Settings.* Waterside Press, 2015.

Baldwin, Lucy. "Tainted Love: The Impact of Prison on Mothering Identity, Explored via Mothers Post Prison Reflections." *Prison Service Journal*, vol., 233, 2017, pp. 28-34.

Baldwin, Lucy, and Rona Epstein. *Short but Not Sweet: A Study of the Impact of Short Custodial Sentences on Mothers and Their Children.* De Montfort University, 2017.

Black, Maria, and Rosalind Coward. "Linguistic, Social and Sexual Relations: A Review of Dale Spender's Man-Made Language." *Society for Education in Film and Television*, vol. 39, 1981, pp 69-85.

Caddle, Diane, and Debbie Crisp. "Imprisoned Women and Mothers." *Home Office Research Study Number 162,* Home Office, 1997.

Canton, Rob. "Crime Punishment and the Moral Emotions: Righteous Minds and Their Attitudes Towards Punishment." *Punishment and Society*, vol. 17, no. 1, pp. 54-72.

Carlen, Pat. *Women's Imprisonment: A Study in Social Control.* Routledge and Kegan Paul, 1983.

Codd, Helen. *In the Shadow of Prison. Families, Imprisonment and Criminal Justice.* Willan Publishing. 2008.

Corston, Jean. *The Corston Report: A Report by Baroness Jean Corston of a Review of Women with Particular Vulnerabilities in the Criminal Justice System.* Home Office. 2007.

Duff, Antony. *Punishment, Communication, and Community.* Oxford University Press, 2001.

Enos, Sandra. *Mothering from the Inside: Parenting in a Women's Prison.* State University of New York Press. 2001,

Epstein, Rona. *Mothers in Prison: The Sentencing of Mothers and the Rights of the Child. Coventry Law Journal.* Special Issue, Research Report, 2012.

Feinman, Clarice. *Women in the Criminal Justice System*. ABC-CLIO, 1994.

Goffman, Ervin. *Asylums*. Penguin, 1961.

Haidt, Jonathon. "The Moral Emotions." *Handbook of Affective Sciences*, edited by Richard. J. Davidson, et al., Oxford University Press 2003, pp. 852-70

Layder, Derek. *Emotion in Social Life: The Lost Heart of Society*. Sage, 2004.

Leverentz, Annie. *The Ex-Prisoners Dilemma, How Women Negotiate Competing Narratives of Re-entry and desistance*. Rutgers University Press. 2014.

Masson, Isla. *The Long-Term Impact of Short Periods of Imprisonment on Mothers*. Dissertation. King's College London, 2014.

Minson, Shona. *Mitigating Motherhood: A Study of the Impact on Sentencing Decisions in England and Wales*. Howard League for Penal Reform. 2014.

Moore, Linda, and Phil Scraton. *The Incarceration of Women: Punishing Bodies, Breaking Spirits*. Palgrave, 2014.

Murray, Joseph. "The Cycle of Punishment: Social exclusion of Prisoners and their Children." *Criminology and Criminal Justice*, vol. 7, no. 1, 2007, pp. 55-81.

O'Malley, Sinead, and Carmel Devaney: "Maintaining the Mother-Child relationship within the Irish Prison System: The Practitioner Perspective." *Child Care in Practice*, 2015. 22 (1) pp. 1-15

O'Reilly, Andrea, editor. *21st Century Motherhood: Experience, Identity, Policy, Agency*. Columbia University Press. 2010.

O'Reilly, Andrea. *Matricentric Feminism, Theory, Activism and Practice*. Demeter Press, 2016.

Rich, Adrienne. *Of Woman Born: Motherhood as Experience and Institution*. Virago. 1986.

Rowe, Abigail. "Narratives of Self and Identity in Women's Prisons: Stigma and the Struggle for Self-Definition in Penal Regimes." *Punishment & Society*, vol.13, no. 5, 2011, pp. 571-91.

Scraton, Phil and Jude McCulloch, editors. *The Violence of Incarceration*. Routledge, 2009.

Sim, Joe. *Medical Power in Prisons.* Open University Press, 1990.

Sharpe, Gilly. "Precarious Identities: 'Young' Motherhood, Desistance and Stigma." *Criminology and Criminal Justice*, vol. 15, no. 4, 2015, pp. 407-22.

Sykes, G. M. The Society of Captives. Princeton, NJ: Princeton University Press, 1958.

Wacquant, Loïc. "Deadly Symbiosis: When Ghetto and Prison Meet and Mesh." *Punishment and Society*, vol. 3, no. 1, 2001, pp. 95-133.

Zedner, Lucia. "Women. Crime and Penal Responses. A Historical Account." *Crime and Justice,* vol. 14, 1991, pp. 307-62.

PART III

Disability, Care Work and Motherhood

Chapter 8

The Trouble with Engineering Inclusion: Disabled Mothering at the Limits of Enhancement Technology

Kelly Fritsch

In the months prior to my first daughter being born, I began to lose my ability to walk. As my life transitioned from "walkie" (Clare 359) to mobility scooter and electric wheelchair user, I began to encounter new barriers and exclusions in my everyday life. I have been disabled since birth—I've always had difficulty navigating stairs, always limped along slowly, and dreaded falling because getting up from the ground was so difficult. And because of my life-long limited physical capacities, I have always faced various barriers and forms of social exclusion. But new challenges arose as I increasingly became unable to independently walk more than a few steps beyond my apartment walls. How to buy and carry groceries without using a shopping cart? How to open heavy doors? How to get around town with limited accessible transit and taxi options, and no access to an accessible vehicle of my own? Figuring out the answers to these questions and others that have since emerged has taken years, numerous failures, and more than one instance of being completely stuck. But answering these questions became all the more complicated as I became a mother. If I had trouble navigating the world on my own, how would I navigate it with a child?

In the years that followed my first daughter's birth, one thing became clear: there are plenty of organizations, institutions, and individuals interested in engineering technological solutions to the so-called problem of being a physically disabled mother. Ideas and designs for adapted cribs, wheelchair strollers, "baby-lifters," altered highchairs and change tables abound. But such innovations, though often very useful and widely exalted, fail to sufficiently address and engage the ways in which disabled mothers are profoundly excluded from both mothering and community and social participation more generally.

Although I, like many disabled parents, face numerous barriers on a daily basis, it is not my physical limitations that exclude me from mothering as well as community and social participation. Rather, my limitations are social and relational: they are failures of my communities, even my disability communities, to address a lack of access to sustainable forms of disabled parenting and inclusion (Fritsch, "Contesting"). Nonetheless, it is difficult to specify how the individual physical limitations I face as a mother are not just mine and are not just an individual problem to solve but rather are embedded within broader social relations. This is in part due to the way in which the inclusion of disability within neoliberal economies makes systemic barriers out to be individual problems that can be solved and overcome through technological innovations that are embedded within neoliberal market logics.

This chapter focuses on the ways in which the dominant cultural discourses of disabled mothering re-enforce disability as located in an individual body in need of technological solutions. By charting out the extensive social barriers faced by disabled parents, I show how neoliberal processes of capacitating disabled people as parents sustain and celebrate disability as an individual problem that can be overcome by the technological advances of an inclusive society. Such engineered inclusion predominantly serves to benefit disabled mothers with newborns and young infants. These solutions largely do not aid disabled mothers with older children who face ongoing systemic barriers to participating in communities as mothers, nor do they challenge normative expectations of ideal mothering. Importantly, although some disabled mothers may benefit from certain kinds of technologies that enable more independent parenting, more substantial social changes are required, such as developing practices of interdependent care and collective access so as to radically address issues of social exclusion. In this relational model, disabled mothering marks the barriers some disabled parents face not as individual problems to be solved but as social relations in which all are implicated. I use this relational model to think through how disabled mothering emerges within and between bodies and its attendant political implications.

Disabled Parents, Social Exclusion, and Ideal Motherhood

Although nearly 15 percent of all parents have some type of disability (Parish et al. 51), disabled parents are overwhelmingly considered to lack the ability to parent (Parchomiuk). They are actively "discouraged from having children by their families, friends, and health care professionals and often face having their children removed from their care solely on the basis of their disability status" (Parish et al. 52). Some disabled women feel they are unable to become mothers because they view themselves as asexual, unattractive, unlikely to become lovers or wives, or unable to provide children with proper care (Parchomiuk; Walsh; Tarasoft). Ora Prilleltensky has found that disabled women do not believe they can live a life similar to their able-bodied peers and have doubts that they can fulfill their child's needs. This is due, in part, to the ways in which, as Lesley Tarasoft notes, "nondisabled women dominate the discourse and ideologies of femininity, body image, pregnancy, childbirth, and motherhood. For example, rarely when one imagines a mother do they picture a woman in a wheelchair" (90).

Disabled parents are also "frequently blamed for the interpersonal, behavioral, or developmental difficulties that their children experience" (Parish et al. 52). Indeed, much of the scholarly literature available on disabled parenting highlights the potential dangers of disabled parenting: the ways in which children may face "biological and psycho-social hazards" as a result of having disabled parents, the impact of specific impairments on such daily tasks as adequately dressing or feeding a child, and explorations of the social and economic barriers disabled parents face that leave their children at a disadvantage (Parchomiuk 232). Disabled parents, and mothers in particular, are often depicted as having an "upside-down" relationship with their child, as it is assumed that the child is burdened with the responsibility of caring for the parent (Malacrida 472; Prilleltensky). The notion of an "upside-down family" presumes that "disabled mothers not only fall short of ideal mothering, but that they depend on their children for care and services, exploiting these 'young carers' and robbing them of their childhood" (Malacrida 472). Because disability is so often associated with incompetency and lack, and because disabled mothers often require assistive devices or assistance to aid in their parenting, "the combination of cultural ideals of mothering as selfless devotion with visible indicators of attending to one's own needs and relying on institutional support increases the vulnerability of mothers with disabilities to the charge of bad parenting" (O'Donovan 94).

Rather than a reflection of bad parents and the individualized problem of disability, these risks and hazards are the result of social barriers and exclusion. Disabled parents are significantly constrained by increased levels of unemployment or underemployment, poverty, food insecurity, and inadequate and inaccessible housing, transportation, healthcare, and daycare (Kaiser et al; Parish et al; Through the Looking Glass; Evans and de Souza; Tarasoft). Disabled parents have limited ability to participate in public life and to access public places and leisure activities (Parchomiuk; Kaiser et al.). Systemic ableism leads to disabled parents as a group having less access to educational and occupational opportunities and heightens the chances of living in poverty, which, in turn, contributes to increased social marginalization and vulnerability, further exposing disabled parents to negative judgments about their capacities to parent. This context limits the ability of disabled parents to effectively parent.

Although disabled parents have varied experiences depending on such social factors as marital and socioeconomic status, geographical location, race, ethnicity, age, gender, sexuality, and access to social, cultural, and symbolic capital, according to Claudia Malacrida's research, racial, economic, and sexual difference intensifies the negative outcomes for disabled women. That is, while disabled women as a group are more likely to experience poverty, discrimination, and violence, it is disabled women who are also queer, living in rural isolation, or members of racial and ethnic minority groups that are particularly prone "to experience disability oppression that is complicated by their raced, classed, geographical, sexual and social locations" (Malacrida 473). Malacrida's findings are supported by other researchers who show the ways in which the intersection of race, disability, poverty, sexuality, and motherhood leads to experiences of multiple oppression and unique hardship (Parish et al. 53). Susan Parish et al. in their study of poor and racialized disabled mothers note the following:

> Challenges came from all levels of the system—policies, rules of the social welfare program, features of the neighborhood and community, concerns of the women's extended and immediate families, and the women's relationships with their children.... Chronic struggles to pay the bills, have sufficient food, clothe children, and afford school supplies were recounted by every focus-group participant, and several mothers reported having to choose between health care and other needs. Many of the mothers spoke about losing their basic household utilities or being evicted because of a chronic shortfall of resources. (56-58)

One study participant said, "It's too hard ... it's just to the point that even I can't even afford my medications ... it's like pick and choose. How much pain do I want to be in this month? ... do I want to be able to walk this month?" (qtd. in Parish et al. 58). Indeed, Lesley Tarasoft notes that disabled mothers may "delay seeking care or receive second-rate care" and that "inadequate financial supports together with social supports explain why some women with physical disabilities may not envision becoming mothers in the first place" (95).

If the normative relationship between motherhood and femininity is a "tightrope upon which to balance dependency and nurturance" for disabled women, this "tightrope" can be "particularly difficult to negotiate" because disabled mothers are more often embedded in relations of material and social dependency (Malacrida 469, 470). Malacrida's research on disabled mothering shows that disabled women "are more likely to experience dependency on institutional supports as a result of their unequal access to education, their difficulties in obtaining adequate employment and their higher likelihood of living in poverty" (Malacrida 471). If disabled mothers are employed, often the accessible transit service is "unreliable, inflexible and unsuited" to the responsibilities of working mothers (McKeever et al. 191), and many playgrounds, parent-and-tot groups, school buildings, and community recreational facilities are not accessible. And although physical access may not typically be a barrier to disabled mothers with cognitive impairments, "these women are more likely than others to be lone parents, living with poverty and unemployment" and facing higher levels of stigmatization, social isolation, and charges of incompetency (Malacrida 481). In their study of disabled mothers, Anita Kaiser et al. similarly find disabled mothers trying to negotiate this tightrope: "Mothers who have a physical disability say they are often regarded as being either superhuman, by performing child care tasks that others considered impossible for them to do because of their disability, or inadequate compared to their able-bodied counterparts" (124).

As disabled parents are often considered incompetent within this social context, they are frequently put under increased scrutiny and surveillance by doctors, social workers, nurses, and others that can lead to further social isolation, fear, and even the loss of child custody (Thomas). Disabled mothers in particular frequently face stigmatizing public perceptions, surveillance, and significant social barriers that serve to challenge and undermine their capacity to mother adequately (Track; Frederick; Malacrida; Blackford; Grue and Lærum). As Angela Frederick's research shows, many disabled mothers live in fear of being scrutinized by authorities and the public—highlighting the way in which members of the public frequently intervene when they see a disabled woman out with her children and report the family to child protective services out of concern for the welfare of the child. Too frequently "safety" is a guise used to question the abilities of disabled parents, and disability status ends up being used as a proxy for real evidence that the parent cannot adequately care for their children. Indeed, as Parish et al. highlight, "Nearly all the women reported an adversarial relationship with social services, and ongoing battles with caseworkers were the norm" (60). And as Frederick concludes, disabled mothers are "more likely to have their parental rights terminated, and when children are removed these families receive fewer supports for reunification" (35). That is, often when children are removed, "agencies offer disabled parents few supports to ease the effects of structural barriers such as lack of access to transportation and quality housing, and they rarely offer parents the opportunity to acquire adaptive training and equipment that might help them care for their children" (Frederick 34). For example, in Ontario in April 2012, Maricyl Palisoc gave birth to a baby named William. Palisoc and her partner Charles Wilton, who both are disabled, wanted to be parents and were thrilled to have William. However, soon after William's birth, the Children's Aid Society intervened and threatened to remove the child from Palisoc and Wilton's care unless they could show that baby William received full-time care from an able-bodied adult. Rather than inquiring what supports might be needed to help Palisoc and Wilton parent effectively or investigating what community supports might be available to help support them, the Children's Aid Society social worker charged that cerebral palsy made Palisoc and Wilton unfit parents and obtained a warrant to remove baby William from the home (Track 7). Only after significant media attention and help from various community organizations was William returned to the care of his parents.

Often the fear of surveillance, scrutiny, and loss of custody pushes disabled mothers to prove that "they are effective in realizing their parental role at any cost" (Parchomiuk 239). Monika Parchomiuk explains the following: "Mothers do not look for support outside, since it would imply their incompetence. As a result of these efforts and the sense of loneliness in managing on their own, they experience a decrease in emotional and physical wellbeing" (239). In their study of disabled mothers, Kaiser et al. note that "some informants felt a constant need to prove to others that they were capable parents, which drove them to be 'supermoms'" (127). Lars Grue and Kristin Laerum note that disabled mothers often feel that they need to "demonstrate a better than ideal performance of motherhood in order to pass as socially acceptable" and often monitor their gender performance in order to appear "as a mother in a way that makes them equal to other mothers" (678). Crucially, however, they point out that such attempts at "passing" are more difficult for disabled mothers who have speech impairments or difficulty maintaining their balance while walking, as these types of disabilities can appear as related to alcohol or drug consumption

Although the sum of all these findings draws attention to the precise barriers faced by disabled parents, what is missing from these studies is mapping out the ways in which disabled parents are included as parents, and how these forms of inclusion and many of the "solutions" purported to aid disabled parents may actually serve to reinforce neoliberal logics that individualize disability and care—capacitating some as the successful abled-disabled while leaving others to wither (Fritsch, "Contesting").

Technologies of Inclusion

Despite the multifaceted ways in which disability is a social relation rather than a medical problem that can be located in a singular body (Fritsch, "Blood"), disability is overwhelmingly treated as an individualized problem that can be overcome through techno-scientific innovations and interventions. For disabled parents, and disabled mothers in particular, these techno-scientific innovations and interventions sometimes are implemented through medical treatments or rehabilitating the impaired body itself, but more often they appear as assistive and adaptive devices, such as modified baby cribs and change tables, devices that lift a baby off the floor, modified slings and carriers for wheelchair users, car seats mounted to wheelchairs, and more. These assistive and adaptive devices are created by charities, nonprofit organizations specializing in disability assistance, engineering students and interns, hobbyists, disabled parents themselves, and companies specializing in adaptive equipment. They are designed to enable a disabled parent to independently take care of their child. Indeed, research has shown that the "use of aids and adaptations were central to parents' successful involvement in childcare" (Kaiser et al. 133). For example, modified baby cribs and change tables enable disabled mothers to move their child in and out of their crib, to change their diapers and get them dressed, whereas car seats mounted to wheelchairs enable these mothers to take their baby out for a walk or to the store. Other innovations, such as a car seat mounted on a portable luggage carrier, enable blind mothers who use white canes or have a guide dog to pull their child behind them with their free hand. Bells attached to clothing enable blind mothers to easily keep track of the movements of their child. In other cases, dressing a child in particular clothing, such as clothing without snaps or buttons, makes it easier to put on or remove clothes. In Kaiser et al.'s research one informant commented, "we'd dress him in those bib overalls where you can just lift him up by the straps and pick him up that way" (129). Slings, nursing pillows, and various kinds of wraps can be modified to carry babies and small toddlers on the laps of wheelchair users. Various tools have been developed to help mothers feed their children, do laundry and dishes, pick up toys, make beds, put on shoes, zip up coats, and give a child a bath. Kaiser et al. explain the following: "Parents find that childcare aids and adaptations make their lives much easier. Once the parents become accustomed to the aids and adaptations they become less focused on the task at hand and more focused on the interaction with their child" (124). Many of these innovations are developed by disabled people themselves and circulate on blogs, social media, and through organizations serving disabled people. These innovations also circulate through the media, where news stories abound to celebrate these technologies and the lease on life they bring. Celebratory headlines, such as "Teen Invents Wheelchair Stroller for Mom with Disability" (Khoo), serve to draw attention to assistive equipment that aid with independent parenting. "Aids and adaptations have consequently become an integral part of these parents' lives by enabling them to engage in tasks and childcare activities" (Kaiser et al. 124).

The Trouble with Engineering Inclusion

Stories of finding solutions are important and mark the creative means disabled people use in order to live their lives (NCD, "Rocking"). However, these stories do not fall outside of individualizing neoliberal logics, and it is crucial to attend to the ways by which disabled people are in/excluded within such troubling logics. These tools and technologies are important and enable many people to independently parent, especially babies and small children. However, these forms of inclusion and many of the solutions purported to aid disabled parents may actually reinforce the individualization of disability and care. That is, if you can afford these technologies, have a housing situation in which it is possible to make extensive and pricey modifications, have a disability that is common, predictable, and stable, have both the time and energy available to research, contact organizations, fill out forms, have the financial means to hire a nanny to help, or have a network of people who can build you things, you have an increased chance of flourishing as a mother. But, for example, as Maeve O'Donovan comments, when disabilities are not visible, or not always visible, disabled parents "may find themselves excluded from the community and support provided to those with [visible] physical disabilities" (96). Disabled parenting is governed by a normative understanding of disability that is dominated by visible forms of impairment and adaptive devices like that of the wheelchair (Fritsch "Neoliberal"), and disabled parenting is also governed by race, class, gender, and other structural factors, such as community accessibility and access to resources. Kaiser et al. found that disabled parents "worried about the affordability of aids and adaptations, claiming that they found them significantly more expensive than standard childcare products and they were disappointed with the lack of funding assistance" (131).

Even if one is able to access technologies that enable independent parenting in the home, many of these solutions do not enable accessibility outside of one's private home, which renders the ability to access schools, community centres, parks, playgrounds, swimming pools, and parent-and-tot groups out of reach. These technologies do not help with the ways in which disabled parents and their children may be excluded from birthday parties, playdates, and recreational opportunities due to inaccessible facilities and the ways in which disability is predominantly perceived as an individual problem rather than a set of social relations and practices. As Kaiser et al. found, although all their informants spoke of the "proper set-up of their home environment as being extremely important in enabling them to participate in childcare ... most informants described being the most distraught over their limitation in leisure activities with their child because of the decreased opportunity to bond and interact with them" (130).

For example, Heather Kuttai, a paraplegic mother, recounts a story of going swimming with her two year-old daughter. Her daughter asks Kuttai to take her down the waterslide at the pool. However, Kuttai tells her daughter that she is unable to go with her daughter up the stairs of the slide, leading her daughter to suggest that she needs "a walking person" to accompany her (99). In hearing her daughter voice this need, Kuttai feels like she is letting her daughter down. She comments: "I feel compelled to say, 'I'm sorry' a lot—to my husband, for costing us more money, to my children, when I cannot go to the places other moms go, to the earth, for making more pollution" (100). These feelings and expressions of sorrow, which are familiar to so many disabled people, are very much wrapped up within an individualistic logic of disability that is continually reaffirmed and reproduced within neoliberal relations. Such individualistic accountings of disability lead disabled parents to feel out of place in an ableist society (Fritsch, "Contesting"). Taking disability as a relational emergence contests individualizing understandings of disabled parenting and implicates us all in the exclusionary practices of ableism.

Collective Access and Inclusion: Towards a Relational Model of Disabled Parenting

As I have argued elsewhere, disability is a social-material relation of nature-culture (Fritsch, "Blood")—meaning that there are culturally specific ways of understanding and enacting disability as a set of possibilities and limitations that are both biologically and socially produced. Disability as a relation of nature-culture, for example, highlights the ways in which disability does not reside in an individual body that requires help to parent but rather marks the ways in which disability is embedded within social relations. Moving disability away from the individual body of the failed mother and emphasizing instead the macro and micro ways in which disability emerges within relations that have social, political, economic, and cultural consequences opens up room for reflection and concerted political action. Yet all too often the struggles of disabled people are individualized and seen as a problem to be solved within the realm of social services or are understood as a medical problem that resides outside of the collective social body.

Taking a relational approach to disability means fighting for increased accessibility in our communities. Not only does this mean ensuring ramps, elevators, and door openers are readily available in schools, community centres, and other places of social gathering but it also means ensuring neighbourhood playgrounds are designed for universal access, fighting for accessible and affordable transit and housing, and improving access to healthcare, attendant care, and education. It also means implementing practices of collective access, where access becomes not about accommodating an individual but rather imagining how to expand access for all in all aspects of our social, cultural, economic, and political lives. Finally, it means addressing accessibility and access as needing ongoing and continual attention, as the diverse needs of disabled people cannot be solved or met through any one particular design or policy. For example, universal design in practice tends to account for the most common form of access need (e.g., a wheelchair-accessible washroom). However, the standard guidelines for building a wheelchair-accessible washroom do not address the needs of disabled people who need a raised-height toilet, a lift to transfer onto the toilet, or a clean raised surface to lie down so as to remove and put back on clothing.

I do not want to be a good disabled mother if it means supporting neoliberal economies of technological capacitation that promise to enhance my individual difference within my particular household. The point is not to ignore inequitable social relations but to highlight how we are always already producing disability and how we can hold the state, our communities, and each other accountable for the kinds of production that rest on and reproduce inequitable social relations. This is to place the emphasis on what we can create together that does not re-inscribe individual accounts of overcoming disability or simply evoke creative individual solutions in the face of austerity. The goal is to mark and mobilize the relational emergences of disability as a way to hold ourselves accountable and work collectively to overcome the ways by which neoliberalism individualizes disability and leaves parents to rely on market-based solutions to achieve and celebrate independent mothering.

Works Cited

Blackford, Karen. "Erasing Mothers with Disabilities through Canadian Family-Related Policy." *Disability, Handicap & Society*, vol. 8, no. 3, 1993, pp. 281-94.

Clare, Eli. "Stolen Bodies, Reclaimed Bodies: Disability and Queerness." *Public Culture*, vol. 13, no. 3, 2001, pp. 359-65.

Evans, S., and L. de Souza. "Dealing with Chronic Pain: Giving Voice to the Experiences of Mothers with Chronic Pain and Their Children." *Qualitative Health Research*, vol. 18, no. 4, 2008, pp. 489-500.

Frederick, Angela. "Mothering while Disabled." *Contexts*, vol. 13, no. 4, 2014, pp. 30-35.

Fritsch, Kelly. "Blood Functions." *Journal of Literary and Cultural Disability Studies*, vol. 10, no. 3, 2016, pp. 341-56.

Fritsch, Kelly. "Contesting the Neoliberal Effects of Disabled Parenting: Towards a Relational Emergence of Disability." *Disabling Domesticity*, edited by Mike Rembis, Palgrave, 2017, pp. 243-68.

Fritsch, Kelly. "The Neoliberal Circulation of Affects: Happiness, accessibility and the capacitation of disability as wheelchair." *Health, Culture and Society*, vol. 5, no. 1, 2013, pp. 135-49.

Grue, Lars, and Kristin Tafjord Lærum. "'Doing Motherhood': Some Experiences of Mothers with Physical Disabilities." *Disability & Society*, vol. 17, no. 6, 2002, pp. 671-83.

Kaiser, Anita, et al. "Experiences of Parents with Spinal Cord Injury." *Sexuality and Disability*, vol. 30, no. 2, 2011, pp. 123-37.

Khoo, Isabelle. "Teen Invents Wheelchair Stroller for Mom with Disability." *The Huffington Post Canada*, 30 Sept. 2015, www.huffingtonpost.ca/2015/09/30/wheelchair-stroller_n_8220956.html. Accessed 11 May 2019.

Kuttai, Heather. *Maternity Rolls: Pregnancy, Childbirth and Disability.* Fernwood, 2010.

Malacrida, Claudia. "Negotiating the Dependency/Nurturance Tightrope: Dilemmas of Motherhood and Disability*." *Canadian Review of Sociology/Revue Canadienne De Sociologie*, vol. 44, no. 4, 2007, pp. 469-93.

McKeever, Patrick, et al. "'It's More of a Production': Accomplishing Mothering Using a Mobility Device." *Disability & Society*, vol. 18, no. 2, 2003, pp. 179-97.

National Council on Disability (NCD). *Rocking the Cradle: Ensuring the Rights of Parents with Disabilities and Their Children*, NCD, 2012, www.ncd.gov/publications/2012/Sep272012/. Accessed 11 May 2019.

O'Donovan, Maeve. "The Practical and Theoretical Challenges of Mothering with Disabilities: A Feminist Standpoint Analysis." *Philosophical Inquiries into Pregnancy, Childbirth, and Mother: Maternal Subjects*, edited by Sheila Lintott and Maureen Sander-Staudt, Routledge, 2012, pp. 93-106.

Parchomiuk, Monika. "Social Context of Disabled Parenting." *Sexuality and Disability*, vol. 32, no. 2, 2014, pp. 231-42.

Parish, Susan, et al. "It's Just That Much Harder: Multilayered Hardship Experiences of Low-Income Mothers with Disabilities." *Affilia*, vol. 23, no. 1, 2008, pp. 51-65.

Prilleltensky, Ora. "My Child Is Not My Carer: Mothers with Physical Disabilities and the Well-Being of Children." *Disability & Society*, vol. 19, no. 3, 2004, pp. 209-23.

Tarasoff, Lesley A. "Experiences of Women with Physical Disabilities During the Perinatal Period: a Review of the Literature and Recommendations to Improve Care." *Health Care for Women International*, vol. 36, no. 1, 2014, pp. 88-107.

Thomas, C. "The Baby and the Bath Water: Disabled Women and Motherhood in Social Context." *Sociology of Health and Illness*, vol. 19, 1997, pp. 622-43.

Through the Looking Glass. "Visible, Diverse, and United: A Report of the Bay Area Parents with Disabilities and Deaf Parents Task Force." *Through the Looking Glass*, 2006, www.lookingglass.org/announcements/67-news/100-report-task-force-on-bayarea-parents-with-disabilities-and-deaf-parents. Accessed 11 May 2019.

Track, Laura. *Able Mothers: The Intersection of Parenting, Disability and the Law*. West Coast Leaf, 2014.

Walsh, Samantha. "'Where Do Babies Come From?' Meeting Joanne and Kyle: A Reflection on Mothering, Disability and Identity." *Disabled Mothers: Stories and Scholarship by and about Mothers with Disabilities*, edited by Gloria Filax and Dena Taylor, Demeter Press, 2014, pp. 21-29.

Chapter 9

Exclusion, Constraint, and Motherhood: Conceptualizing the Construction of Motherhood and Mothering the Disabled Child

Karen Williams and Duncan Murray

Mohomed Jemni, speaking at a conference on deafness in 2013, stated, "The disability is not the problem; the accessibility is the problem." His statement resonates with mothers of disabled children, not only for their child but also for themselves. Mothers of disabled children face multiple issues of social accessibility due to their position. This chapter presents a theoretical framework to help provide further understanding of the types of exclusion experienced by mothers of disabled children. Although there has been work surrounding the severity of exclusion, the current field of social exclusion lacks a broad theoretical framework to explain the nature of exclusions faced by mothers of disabled children and their impact.

This study seeks to provide insight into the exclusions faced by mothers of disabled children via the use of constraint theory, which may be particularly applicable to the lives of mothers of disabled children. The theory helps identify subgroups of the population who face significantly higher levels of constraints and, thereby, face exclusion. We use the seminal work of Sara Ruddick as a reference point throughout this chapter. Although our work is located within a contemporary feminist ideology, one that contends feminism has yet to adequately embrace and address the uncomfortable relationship between itself and motherhood, Ruddick's classical work still has its relevance—particularly, identifying how mothers of disabled children experience, frame, and construct social exclusion. Ruddick provides a useful starting point to consider how constraint theory understands these exclusions and how they fit within the notion of the mother.

The Construction of the Mother and Exclusion

The mother

What does it mean to be the mother of a disabled child? How does it affect women who, for want of a better term, "fit" that label? Andrea O'Reilly reminds us that the category of mother is distinct from the category of women. Furthermore, Sara Ryan and Katherine Runswick-Cole argue that mothering a disabled child is distinct to the category of mothering a nondisabled child. Patriarchal ideals see mothers of disabled children as oppressed as mothers but also as women whose life course is not following the assumed normal or expected path. Or, as Gail Landsman articulates, it "has failed to follow the appropriate trajectory" (77).

Literature surrounding mothers of disabled children suggest they are subject to two dominant overlapping forms of stigma—Goffman's concept of courtesy stigma and that of mother-blame. Courtesy stigma is a particular form of stigma associated with disability, which is then "contracted" by mothers because of their relationship with their disabled child— a "stigmatized individual," as Goffman articulates. Mother-blame stems from the ideology of the good mother constructed around intensive mothering—a selfless, time, and labour intensive project (Hays). The rules associated with motherhood see the mother raise her children in accordance with the prescribed values and expectations of the dominant culture. These rules and values exist within a societal structure that holds a persuasive grip on the notion of a standardized child (A. James 102).

This adherence to the dominant social views on what constitutes a good mother is evident in Ruddick's work. Maternal work, as described by Ruddick, constitutes three demands: preservation, growth, and social acceptability (17). In addition to preserving the lives of children and fostering their growth, Ruddick highlights that "the primary social groups with which a mother is identified, whether by force, kinship, or choice, demand that she raise her children in a manner acceptable to them" (17). Social groups "require that mothers shape their children's growth in acceptable ways" and count "failure to meet their criteria of acceptability as her failure" (21). The standards of the group are then internalized by the mother. The influence of the gaze of others and its fear contribute to how the mother behaves and how she constructs what is good mothering, irrespective of whether or not she is authentic in that construction.

For the mother of a disabled child, the expectations of maternal care, and culpability, are intensified (Bumiller 968). Standards of social acceptance are typically set by those without disabilities and consequently the disabled are ranked upon these standards (Devine and Dattilo). Failure to meet or adhere to the dominant rules and standards of a culture may see the mother violate the construction of what is a "good" mother, and thus see the individual experience social exclusion.

Social exclusion

Social exclusion represents the barriers or mechanisms that detach individuals or groups from mainstream society (Giddens), and this detachment prevents full participation in the normal prescribed social activities (Silver). Social exclusion typically occurs when individuals or groups are considered to possess undesirable attributes and do not contribute to the group or violate its established rules (Baumeister and Tice). The consequences of social exclusion include not only exclusion but also other serious internal and external manifestations. For example, social exclusion has been linked to increasing levels of anxiety, aggressive behaviour, depression, low self-esteem, as well as a reduction in intelligent performance and prosocial behaviour (Baumeister and Tice; Baumeister et al.; Leary; Twenge et al.).

Constraint Theory

Originating in the leisure field, constraint theory seeks to understand and explain the factors that limit people's participation in desired volitional activities (Crawford and Godbey). Since the model outlines the factors constituting a constraint and how these constraints influence people's decision-making behaviour, this framework may have applications beyond leisure—particularly, identifying the types of social exclusion faced by mothers of disabled children. Specifically, three categories of constraints have been proposed by Crawford and Godbey: intrapersonal, interpersonal, and structural.

Intrapersonal constraints are distinct to an individual's own desires, feelings, and preferences, and they may include stress, anxiety, and prior experience (Crawford et al.). Interpersonal constraints focus on an individual's interactions with others, such as family commitments and public involvement (Murray and Howat). These kinds of constraints are often influenced by the behaviour of others and can be as extreme as physical abuse or as simple as not having a suitable partner to engage with in the activity. Structural constraints are intervening factors and logistical barriers, such as time, money, and transport (Crawford and Godbey). These constraints can also be the result of reference group attitudes that influence the availability and opportunity to participate in certain activities.

The different constraints are organized into a clear hierarchical sequence (Crawford et al.). This hierarchy suggests that intrapersonal constraints are the most proximal and affect an individual's preference for behaviour (Raymore et al.). They are also the strongest, most difficult to overcome, and they are thought to be the most significant predictor of behaviour. Structural constraints are the most distal constraints, are the easiest to negotiate, and are those that affect actual participation—meaning if these constraints can be overcome, there are no further barriers to participation (Raymore et al.). In essence, the implication is that those who experience higher levels of intrapersonal constraints are less likely to experience structural or interpersonal constraints. Their behaviour is already constrained prior to structural or interpersonal issues being a factor. Likewise, those who experience fewer intense intrapersonal constraints may then face subsequent interpersonal and structural constraints (Crawford et al.).

Accordingly, constraint theory provides a practical broad level model to understand and categorize the types of exclusions experienced by mothers of disabled children. Although the design of our study did not allow for testing of the hierarchical order of constraints, it is proposed that social exclusion for mothers of disabled children occurs at all three identified levels of constraint.

Our study identified two key research questions: 1. do mothers of disabled children experience unique social exclusions, and if so, what are they, and; 2. does constraint theory provide a framework to help understand and categorize the exclusions faced by mothers of children with disabilities?

Ruddick's construction of maternal thinking helps to understand how mothers interpret and experience social exclusion. Elizabeth Francis-Connolly suggests that motherhood is not restricted to the underage child; it exists across the life course. This idea is particularly relevant to mothers of disabled children and not only regarding the longevity of care but also its intensity. Francis-Connolly goes further and suggests that Ruddick's framework of maternal practice and thinking could assist in providing a framework that explores the lives of mothers who have disabled children (154). As such, this framework provides a useful conceptual reference point to understand exclusions and constraints that may be experienced by mothers of disabled children.

As discussed earlier, Ruddick's concept of maternal practice describes the work of mothers as the preservation, growth, and acceptability of the child, and is used as a tool to guide the findings. However, there are some potential concerns with using Ruddick's framework in such a way. Her work has been criticized for focusing predominantly on the experiences of white middle class mothers (Bailey). Although this is a potential limitation to be acknowledged, the sample described in this chapter represents a similar demographic (white middle-class mothers). Thus, Ruddick's maternal practice still remains applicable to use.

Research Design

In order to explore the research questions of the study, a qualitative approach, guided by Alfred Schutz's social phenomenology framework, was used. This approach allowed for the exploration of both the processes "by which people make sense of or interpret the phenomena of the everyday world" and an "understanding of 'ideal types' through which to interpret and describe the phenomenon under investigation" (Fereday and Muri-Cochrane 81).

Mothers interviewed for this study lived in a major city in southern Australia and were recruited through a snowball procedure (Goodman). The original point of contact was made by the first author of this chapter with other mothers whom she had previously interacted with. We utilized a nonprobability sampling method, informed by a purposive approach. Participants were required to be female, live within the metropolitan area where the study took place, and be the primary caregiver to a child of school age with a diagnosed physical or cognitive disability. To aid in consistency, the first author was the sole interviewer.

Thirteen mothers aged from thirty-six to forty-three years were interviewed. The age of the disabled child cared for ranged from eight to eleven. Of those interviewed, one was a single mother, one was in a de-facto relationship, and the remaining eleven were married. Regarding paid employment, none of the mothers were employed in full-time work. Seven did not engage in paid work, and six worked part-time. Of the six who worked part time, all except one worked during school hours or had the child's grandparents pick them up from school.

Interviews were transcribed in full. Pseudonyms were used to ensure that the identity of the participant, the names of children, and any other affiliations would be confidential. An inductive approach of thematic analysis to search for themes that emerged of the mothers' experience of social exclusion was then employed. We then entered a second stage of analysis that used the previously generated themes while employing the constraint theory framework of Duane Crawford and Geoffrey Godbey as a template.

Findings and Discussion

Next, we analyzed the types of social exclusion experienced by mothers through the constraint theory framework. The hierarchical order of constraints suggest that individuals will experience intrapersonal constraints first and move through the constraints as each is negotiated. We then discussed our findings with structural constraints. The reason for this was that although these are last to be encountered, they tend to be the most obvious and discussed.

Structural

Structural constraints were prominent in how mothers spent their own time and how they were able to engage in and perform the activities they had chosen to do with and for their children. Dominant constraints were time, money, and reference group attitudes, which limited availability.

An example of how structural constraints were heightened for mothers of disabled children was their ability to achieve financial independence or any form of mastery from paid work. Females earn less money than men and are also less likely to hold a position of status and authority (WGEA). In addition to this, there is an even greater pay gap between mothers and non-mothers (Crittenden 94). Furthermore, when compared to other mothers in Australia, mothers of disabled children are significantly less likely to be in paid work than are other mothers, and, if they are employed, it is considerably more likely to be on a part-time basis (AIHW). Mothers in this study mirrored this pattern of paid employment.

As described by Ruddick, mothers meet the needs of their children and foster their growth. The neoliberal expectation is that families will provide the necessary therapy and be responsible for all the care and ongoing support needed by the child—what Valerie Leiter coined the "therapeutic imperative" (837). This role is typically performed by mothers and was a dominant reason for the mothers in our study not being involved in paid labour. One participant named Jill said, "I couldn't possibly take Matthew to all the therapy and all the rest of it and work full time, there's no way," whereas another participant, Jessica, said, "Work is an issue for me because I kind of feel like I should be working and earning some more money for the family but still haven't figured out how I can fit it in with all the extra stuff I have to do for Jacob."

The time and financial constraints identified by mothers placed them in a double jeopardy situation. In essence, the time, therapy, and care required for their children meant they were unable to work or only work a low-paying, part-time job while also bearing the additional costs. Issues such as the affordability of housing were prominent, particularly surrounding the security of being able to enter or maintain a position in the housing market. Even for mothers who had experience or qualifications, such as Jessica, who had a PhD and eight years of study and research, the glass ceiling was not even encountered as an issue; they had hit the maternal wall at full speed, and it was made of reinforced concrete. Furthermore, even when mothers were offered the opportunity to increase their participation in paid employment, their limited access to resources often restricted their ability to do so. One woman named Elise said the following: "I got asked to do four days [at work] ... in a normal situation you'd just go yeah no worries I'll book him to afterschool care but ... they don't have it at the special school."

The lack of opportunity to return to paid work and increase their disposable income was also driven and reflected by typical gender-role expectations that the mothers were expected to take on. Performing this role saw mothers' time limited by what Nicky James describes as different kinds of care. One woman named Jane said the following: "For me to keep the family dynamics the way they are you know how there's one person that's always the glue and I was the glue that kept it all together ... I found that going back to work and not having the time to do all the things I had to do was really hard."

Mothers who lived with or engaged in the neoliberal version of the idealized heteronormative family—living with a male partner—found themselves often needing to perform gender roles associated with both the "man of the house" and the domestic and care performing female. In such heteronormative families, the breadwinning male was often found to work away, long hours or two jobs, as income earning appeared to become his main function. Mothers then became responsible not only for the additional needs of their child but also for household labour even that typically associated with men. This was highlighted by the following comments: "I look after the home, but my husband works away, and so I clean the gutters, mow the lawn" (Mandy); "I'm the one that does all the housework and the garden and the stuff for the kids and just the main person that does all of that, and he earns the money that keeps all of that going" (Jane); and "[If] the car breaks down, I fix it. I service my own car. I play builder, lawn mower man; carburettor decides it's going to blow up, I pull it apart and fix it" (Diana).

In addition to the roles performed by idealized families, since the rapid deinstitutionalization that occurred in the 1970s, there has been an assumption "that parents', especially mothers', involvement in care equates to responsibility for it" (Breen 18). This assumption suggests that institutionalization still exists; however, now that institution is the family. Lauren Breen also highlights how when services are offered, their delivery often reinforces exclusion rather than reducing it. The types of constraints discussed by Breen were evident in the structural constraints identified by mothers in this study:

> Once he was diagnosed with autism the [hospital] kicked him out. They don't have the funding for autism that goes through [autism support agency]; everything gets outsourced. As soon as the autism word came up, that was it, out. So then that was the case of finding the occupational therapist, new speech therapist, new physiotherapist, new everything. (Diana)

> Being unable to work and because therapy goes term on, term off. Even if I were to say I can work two days a week and try and find school hours two days a week, that would change the following term when occupational therapy runs on a Monday. But next term, you might be doing speech or whatever and that will now be on a Thursday. So for every twelve weeks your days would change and that doesn't give you any form of stability; it's frustrating, very frustrating, no matter where you go you hit a brick wall. (Diana)

The wall hit by mothers was evident not only in the constraints of motherhood but also their ability to mother. In addition to the availability of childcare, reference-group attitudes regarding the appropriateness and availability of an activity were also prominent. Mothers talked about constantly being told, sorry we can't cater for your child because they do not fit within the standardized mechanisms available. Diana said, "[Her son] couldn't do scouts because they don't have the mechanism to deal with [him]," whereas Tracey noted, "There's no sport around for kids [with disabilities]. I've looked into it. He wants to play basketball; he always asks. Well not surprisingly everyone else in the family plays it, but I can't find anything." Although mothers often understood this rationale, it still produced a constraint. The barriers that excluded their children were not necessarily produced by the deficiency of their child; they were rather reflective of the structural and attitudinal barriers present.

Interpersonal

The issue of paid employment was a prominent one and a contentious one for mothers in this study. Mothers' engagement in paid employment was constrained by the expectations of others who often took the constant availability of mothers for granted. Underlying this assumption was a tacit expectation that mother's maternal roles can be called upon at any time. This expectation was particularly prominent when a child's behaviour did not conform to normal school requirements:

> It used to be not too bad, but now they have a new principal and now they wouldn't even give him five minutes; last year, I nearly lost my job. They'd be ringing me ... and I would try and stay and do my shift, but that whole time he would be sitting in the office crying and it shouldn't have got to that situation anyway. When you see him about to have a meltdown, that's when you take a proactive approach. (Jill)

The time and constant availability of the mother was just assumed. The understanding or willingness to accommodate a child that failed to meet the social norms was immediately put back on the mother and expressed to her as "the" role they were expected to perform.

Moving away from paid work, a prominent theme that emerged as an interpersonal constraint was reflective of what Ruddick describes as "the gaze of others." For mothers of disabled children, this gaze was insidious and pervasive. About this gaze, Tracey said, "Oh all the time, that's my life; I could write a list," whereas Chris added, "Everyone looks at you different ... more than a normal child, because I've got two normal children." For mothers, this gaze acted as a form of surveillance that exercised normalizing judgment. Whilst mothers were often comfortable with their child's behaviour in their own homes, the gaze of others saw them reflect Ruddick's concept of inauthenticity— "When she thinks inauthentically a mother valorises the judgment of others" (113). Jessica and Elsie discussed taking their children to the informal activity of the playground and the more formal activity of play-group:

> I've had people in playgrounds where they might be throwing sand or something ... other parents would come over and yell at

them and your trying to explain ... but yeah I just don't take them to playgrounds anymore. (Jessica)

I'm thinking about having a term off at the YMCA ... I'm a bit conscious of the looks from the other mothers of all the other typically developing kids, doing the right stuff. (Elise)

Both mothers expressed either a desire to leave or not return to a situation they might have otherwise found enjoyable. The motivation to attend either the informal activity of the playground or the formal activity of the YMCA included possible social benefits for the mother but was primarily around the social and physical benefits for their children, particularly those of play. In most cultures, it is generally accepted that childhood is a time for play and that learning and development occurs through play. Although play allows children to negotiate the social minefield of interaction, the approved standards of play in playgrounds and play groups need meet a level of uniformity and functional predictability to be viewed as acceptable. Regardless of whether one agrees or disagrees with there being an appropriate standard of child play, the outcome remains the same—the mother of the child becomes excluded.

Mothers were not ignorant of the difference between their children and those of their peers. A consequence of this was that mothers often felt there was an assumed superiority demonstrated by mothers of children without impairments, which resulted in some mothers feeling as though their actions or abilities as a mother were being questioned based around an assumption of what appropriate mothering should encompass. This ability was not limited to the public arena; mothers often felt this expression of perceived superiority within their own social circles. They felt as though the behaviour of their child gave others, and often mothers of children without impairments, good reason to question their approach to parenting:

They just don't get the behaviour issues and "the have you tried this" or "have you tried this" and just having no idea they're barking up the wrong tree and they're looking at you this way because if it was [their] kid they wouldn't do it. (Diana)

[An acquaintance thought] we put too much emphasis on the fact that Simon had a disability and that we made allowances for that—things like if we'd leave the park early she felt that we should have pushed him and made him stay and do different things. (Jane)

The result of such questioning saw mothers often end long-term friendships:

They [friends] just didn't get it, and you know life has changed dramatically. I've basically told all my friends to get lost, and it's easier to deal with it that way. One by one, I have told them all where to go because they haven't got it and they have opened their mouths one too many times—just not getting the whole picture. (Diana)

Mothers felt as though there was a hierarchy in relation to where mothers sat within the social order. There was a subtle, covert level of social exclusion, whereby some mothers were viewed as "in" due to their adherence to societal mothering norms. Other mothers were "out" based on their inability to adopt rightful mothering practices.

As seen above, mothers consistently removed themselves from a previously freely chosen activity. Nancy described the following situation: "Someone had made a comment about, 'you need to be stricter with her, she is just being too naughty' and they just don't get it. I don't like to be treated like that as a parent so we just left." The deviation by the child from the socially ascribed forms of play or behaviour mirrors what Ruddick describes as mothers "relinquish[ing] control to others [and] los[ing] confidence in their own values" (111). The exclusion felt was produced by the gaze of others and the mothers' awareness that their children violated many of the socially approved standards of behaviour.

Beyond the gaze, these interpersonal constraints were also experienced directly and overtly. For Sandra, her son "got told not to go back to kinder-gym." And Nancy shared the following story about her child:

She had pretty major surgery ... I didn't really know if she was in pain or if she was just frightened.... She couldn't communicate very well.... And was just crying and the nurse came in because she could hear her down at the nurse's station and she asked us how long we were supposed to be staying at the hospital, and I said oh two nights and she said well ... "I will be speaking to your doctor to make sure you go home tomorrow"... She just made you feel awful, made you feel like you shouldn't be there, and this was at the children's hospital.

The final prominent interpersonal constraint was the lack of opportunity to form social relationships. Whereas the behaviour of the child resulted in mothers leaving a situation or being told they were no longer welcome, the exclusion of the child from peer relationships also had an effect on the mother. Mandy shared the following: "Usually kids make friends at school so the mums get close ... so with him sometimes not being included ... I don't know anybody."

Interpersonal constraints through the behaviour of others influenced the participation of mothers (Crawford and Godbey). Furthermore, as discussed in the following section, the exclusion fashioned by others often produced an internal form of exclusion within the mothers themselves.

Intrapersonal

Ruddick's concept of the "fear of the gaze of others" (112) was evident throughout the interviews. The fear of gaze created high levels of stress and anxiety among mothers and also reduced their own self-belief in being able to achieve particular tasks. The mothers also engaged in much of what has been described as emotional labour and emotional management (Hochschild).

The internalized anxiety of how people may react, rather than the direct behaviour of others, often reduced participants' preference for participating in activities, such as work, family activities, and their own leisure. This anxiety caused stress when about to engage in an activity, such as going to dinner, reduced their enjoyment when participating, and also prevented them participating entirely. Conformity to social standards often minimizes anxiety by "keeping one within the group's norms and standards" (Baumeister and Tice 168). Any event or behaviour that is contradictory to these standards is thought to be a trigger of anxiety (168). The stress and anxiety felt by mothers was evident in such statements as: "You get in the car, and you're stressing cos you're thinking it's not going to go well" (Chis). This anxiety was often so strong that the exclusion of mothers was often self-imposed: "I wouldn't take him to certain places cos I think what are they going to think of him, so I just won't take him" (Emily).

This constraint has strong ties to self-efficacy and the individual's own judgment of their ability to perform a specific task within a given situation (Bandura). Self-efficacy, thus, acted in a manner that presented a constraint which was internalized and interpreted by mothers' own view of their situation. This type of constraint was highlighted by Jane who stated, "I don't think it's like I'm excluded in ways like I'm rolling up and someone saying you shouldn't be here, it's more thinking it through yourself and thinking it's going to be too hard to try and pull it off."

Often for mothers, it became a culmination of experiences that wore them out. Although this may have been in part due to the specific needs of their child and the more overt exclusions that they faced, mothers also appeared to have reached a point where they could no longer tolerate being told how to be a good mother: "Even say when if we go to people's houses and they go oh why is he doing that and you think I can't be bothered explaining it over again, oh is he still doing that ... we just make excuses you know, can't make it or whatever but you know what it is it's that stigma" (Emily).

Anxiety causes people to shift their attention away from the possible benefits, directing their attention towards possible threats (MacLeod et al.). This anxiety was found to drive other forms of social exclusion in mothers' lives, such as leaving their child to spend time with their partner. For example, Tammy stated, "We haven't left him ... you don't know how he'll go; you know what it is, it's this fear thing ... I can't see us leaving him with somebody." Although in many cases this fear had been triggered by witnessing previous attempts by friends and family to look after their child, the fear had now been internalized, preventing further attempts. Anxiety was also found to constrict their opportunities to re-enter the paid workforce, which was reflected in such statements as, "I'm trying to find a job that's ten to two because there's no way I'm going to leave him ... I couldn't do it, no, no, no" (Jill).

As mentioned above, the previous experience of mothers was also a trigger for them to feel uncomfortable about attending an otherwise enjoyable activity. Having to manage their emotions regarding how they felt they were being viewed became a kind of emotional labour they no longer wanted to perform. As Emily stated, "We avoid going to certain friends' places because it's too stressful for us knowing that their thinking we don't discipline our children." In addition to how they felt they were being viewed as a mother, previous experience also saw them exclude themselves after how they had previously witnessed their child being treated. Amy offered the following story about her child: "Even like an indoor play centre, Michelle's been teased before because she's got a nappy on or why aren't you talking and I just haven't gone back since then; it's like I'm in a little cocoon."

Summary

Although the qualitative methodology employed and the small sample size (n=13) limit the generalizability of the results, our findings suggest that the exclusions experienced by mothers of disabled children fit comfortably within the three levels of constraints proposed by Crawford and Godbey. Employing constraint theory highlights the need to attend to more than structural issues such as time, money, and access. Although structural constraints remain critically important, it is also vital to address lower level constraints.

Lower levels of constraints suggest that dealing with the pervasive standardized and normalized approaches to motherhood became a threat to the participants' own value as a mother. This covert social exclusion based on the constant opinions of others made it increasingly difficult or uncomfortable for mothers, and created feelings of being unwelcome. Mothers in this study perceived they were being judged, rated, and measured as a parent due to their child's behaviour. This evaluation of their parenting prowess subtly excluded them from a role as a good or caring mother (Ruddick).

Moreover, the higher-end constraints (interpersonal and structural) created intrapersonal constraints. The ongoing and insidious nature of social exclusion resulted in several mothers in this study internalizing issues and developing self-exclusionary practices. Rather than moving forwards through the negation process to achieve inclusion, mothers sometimes went backwards and began internalizing their exclusion, which is of particular importance, as intrapersonal constraints are considered the most difficult constraints to negotiate.

Although the framework offered an understanding of the nature of exclusions faced by mothers of disabled children, the scope and design of the study did not necessarily determine or explicitly test whether constraints were faced in accordance to the hierarchy of the theory. What was found and not reported here was the negotiation tactics employed by mothers to negotiate many of the constraints they encountered (Williams and Murray). Indeed, Ruddick (116) affirms that the negotiation of exclusions and constraints may well exist, even in a prescribed environment that determines the good mother's behaviour, as she states, "Alternative conceptions of acceptability are sometimes present and almost always latent in maternal practice" (116). To conclude, although the fear of others and fear of gaze may well exist, Ruddick's acknowledges that negotiation of the constraints mothers face, substantial as they may be, may indeed be an integral part of the process mothers of disabled children must navigate.

Works Cited

Australian Institute of Health and Welfare (AIHW). "Children with Disabilities in Australia." *AIHW*, cat. no. DIS 38. 2004, www.aihw. gov.au. Accessed 13 May 2019.

Bailey, Alison. "Mothering, Diversity, and Peace Politics." *Hypatia*, vol. 9, no. 2, 1994, pp. 188-98.

Bandura, Albert. "Self-Efficacy: Toward a Unifying Theory of Behavioral Change." *Psychological Review*, vol. 84, no. 2, 1977, pp. 191-215.

Baumeister, Roy F., et al. "Social Exclusion Impairs Self-Regulation." *Journal of Personality and Social Psychology*, vol. 88, no. 4, 2005, pp. 589-604.

Baumeister, Roy F., and Dianne M. Tice. "Point-Counterpoints: Anxiety and Social Exclusion." *Journal of Social and Clinical Psychology*, vol. 9, no. 2, 1990, p. 165-195.

Breen, Lauren J. "Early Childhood Service Delivery for Families Living with Childhood Disability: Disabling Families through Problematic Implicit Ideology." *Australasian Journal of Early Childhood*, vol. 34, no. 4, 2009, pp. 14-21.

Bumiller, Kristin. "Quirky Citizens: Autism, Gender, and Reimagining Disability." *Signs*, vol. 33, no. 4, 2008, pp. 967-91.

Crawford, Duane, W., and Geoffrey Godbey. "Reconceptualizing Barriers to Family Leisure." *Leisure Sciences*, vol. 9, no. 2, 1987, pp. 119-27.

Crawford, Duane, W., et al. "A Hierarchical Model of Leisure Constraints." *Leisure Sciences*, vol. 13, no. 4, 1991, pp. 309-20.

Crittenden, Ann. *The Price of Motherhood: Why the Most Important Job in the World Is Still the Least Valued*. Macmillan, 2002.

Devine, Mary Ann, and John Dattilo. "Social Acceptance and Leisure Lifestyles of People with Disabilities." *Therapeutic Recreation Journal*, vol. 34, no. 4, 2000, pp. 306-22.

Fereday, Jennifer, and Eimear Muir-Cochrane. "Demonstrating Rigor Using Thematic Analysis: A Hybrid Approach of Inductive and Deductive Coding and Theme Development." *International Journal of Qualitative Methods*, vol. 5, no. 1, 2006, pp. 80-92.

Francis-Connolly, Elizabeth. "It Never Ends: Mothering as a Lifetime Occupation." *Scandinavian Journal of Occupational Therapy*, vol. 5, no. 3, 1998, pp. 149-55.

Giddens, Anthony. *The Third Way*. Polity 1999.

Goffman, E. *Stigma*. Aronson, 1963.

Goodman, Leo A. "Snowball Sampling." *The Annals of Mathematical Statistics*, vol. 32, 1961, pp. 148-70.

Hays, Sharon. *The Cultural Contradictions of Motherhood*. Yale University Press, 1996.

Hochschild, Arlie, R. *The Managed Heart*. University of California Press, 1983.

James, Allison. "The Standardized Child: Issues of Openness, Objectivity and Agency in Promoting Childhood Health." *Anthropological Journal on European Cultures*, vol. 13, 2004, pp. 93-110.

James, Nicky. "Care= Organisation+ Physical Labour+ Emotional Labour." *Sociology of Health and Illness*, vol. 14, no. 4, 1992, pp. 488-509.

Jemni, Mohamed. "Breaking the Silence of Deafness: Mohamed Jemni at TED2013." *blog.ted.com*, 2016, blog.ted.com/breaking-the-silence-of-deafness-mohamed-jemni-at-ted2013/. Accessed 13 May 2019.

Landsman, Gail H. "Reconstructing Motherhood in the Age of 'Perfect' Babies: Mothers of Infants and Toddlers with Disabilities." *Signs*, vol. 24, no. 1, 1998, pp. 69-99.

Leary, Mark R. "Responses to Social Exclusion: Social Anxiety, Jealousy, Loneliness, Depression, and Low Self-Esteem." *Journal of Social and Clinical Psychology*, vol. 9, no. 2, 1990, pp. 221-29.

Leiter, Valerie. "Dilemmas in Sharing Care: Maternal Provision of Professionally Driven Therapy for Children with Disabilities." *Social Science and Medicine*, vol. 58, no. 4, 2004, pp. 837-49.

MacLeod, Colin, et al. "Attentional Bias in Emotional Disorders." *Journal of Abnormal Psychology*, vol. 95, no. 1, 1986, pp. 15-20.

Murray, Duncan, and Gary Howat. "The 'Enrichment Hypothesis' as an Explanation of Women's Participation in Rugby." *Annals of Leisure Research*, vol. 12, no. 1, 2009, pp. 65-82.

O'Reilly, Andrea. *Matricentric Feminism: Theory, Activism, and Practice.* Demeter Press, 2016.

Raymore, Leslie, et al. "Nature and Process of Leisure Constraints: An Empirical Test." *Leisure Sciences*, vol. 15, no. 2, 1993, pp. 99-113.

Ruddick, Sara. Maternal Thinking: Toward a Politics of Peace; with a New Preface. Beacon Press, 2002.

Ryan, Sara, and Katherine Runswick-Cole. "Repositioning Mothers: Mothers, Disabled Children and Disability Studies." *Disability and Society*, vol. 23, no. 3, 2008, pp. 199-210.

Silver, Hilary. "The Process of Social Exclusion: The Dynamics of an Evolving Concept." *SSRN*, 2007, papers.ssrn.com/sol3/papers.cfm?abstract_id=1087789. Accessed 13 May 2019.

Twenge, Jean M, et al. "Social Exclusion Decreases Prosocial Behavior." *Journal of Personality and Social Psychology*, vol. 92, no. 1, 2007, pp. 56-66.

Williams, Karen J, and Duncan W Murray. "Negotiating the Normative: The Other Normal for Mothers of Disabled Children." *Journal of Family Studies*, vol. 21, no. 3, 2015, pp. 324-40.

Workplace Gender Equality Agency (WGEA). "Parenting, Work and the Gender Pay Gap Perspective Paper." *WGEA*, 2016, www.wgea.gov.au. Accessed 13 May 2019.

Chapter 10

Learning with Difference: The Experience and Identity of Asian Immigrant Mothers with Children with ASDs in Canada

Yidan Zhu and Romee Lee

Introduction

Autism spectrum disorders (ASDs) affect between one in two hundred and one in three hundred people in Canada, and there has been a dramatic increase in the number of children receiving this diagnosis (CIHR). ASDs are characterized by three main areas: social relatedness, verbal and nonverbal communication, and extremely restricted behaviours and interests (Grewal). Since many children with ASDs are high functioning, they may seem just like other children. The diagnosis and treatment process poses unique challenges for families, particularly for the parents (Altiere and von Kluge), which distinguishes this type of disability from others due to the prevailing vagueness about its cause, diagnosis, and treatment. Indeed, there are studies examining the parents of children with ASDs regarding how they suffer from these uncertainties (Cassidy et al.; Lee, Harrington, Louie, and Newschaffer).

Since some children with ASDs are from immigrant families, a number of scholars have explored how the parents of these children encounter the challenges that concern them (Grewal; Kediye et al.; King et al.). Immigrant parents are often placed in difficult situations, as they are often asked to make decisions about diagnosis and treatment when they are not yet settled in the host society (Lai and Ishiyama). Despite the literature available, little is known about Asian immigrant mothers' experiences of diagnosis, treatment, and accessing of social support systems for children with ASDs. As a result of the paucity of research, Asian immigrant mothers with children with ASDs often become invisible in local schools as well as in treatment or parenting programs, which leads to isolation and social exclusion from their parenting practice in their new society.

This chapter examines the experiences of Asian immigrant mothers with children diagnosed with ASDs, and it discusses the politics of difference and social exclusion in their learning of mothering practice. We explore two major research questions. First, how do these mothers experience differentiation and exclusion, if any, in their mothering experience? Second, how do these mothers (re)construct their identity and produce their own knowledge and skills for their children? Through in-depth interviews with seven Asian immigrant mothers in Vancouver, we find that Asian immigrant mothers with children diagnosed with ASDs are affected by unequal social and power relations, which interact with their identity construction and knowledge production.

The chapter comprises three parts. It begins with a review of the literature pertaining to the current medical and social welfare systems for children with ASDs and their families in British Columbia (BC), the province where the research was conducted. The second part examines the current debates on difference and mothering—in particular, how these concepts are perceived and treated by mainstream Canadian schools, settlement organizations, and healthcare institutions. The third section outlines our research on Asian (more specifically, Chinese and Korean) immigrant mothers with children diagnosed with ASDs in Vancouver, BC; we explore how they experience the differentiation and social exclusion in their everyday lives and how they learn to become mothers with these differing experiences. We also review the meaning of mothering and discuss how to understand mothering through Asian immigrant mothers' knowledge production and identity construction. In conclusion, we suggest ways that the diagnosis and treatment process can better accommodate and create social justice for these immigrant mothers and their children.

BC's Formal Supports for Children with ASDs

The government of BC provides services including diagnosis and treatment as well as funding for children with ASDs. The British Columbia Autism Assessment Network (BCAAN) provides diagnostic assessments for children up to nineteen years of age. After the parents receive the diagnosis from BCAAN, they are asked to bring the forms and related documents to the local Ministry of Children and Family Development (MCFD) office. Social workers from the office help parents to apply for government funding for their children, which varies according to age. Children under six years of age can receive up to $22,000 per year, whereas children over the age of six receive only $6,000 per year. After receiving the funding, the parents must then find service providers and start their child's applied behaviour analysis (ABA) treatment. A comprehensive ABA program includes several professionals, including behaviour consultants and analysts, speech language pathologists, occupational therapists, physiotherapists, and social workers. Parents are expected to build a cooperative relationship with them to implement the treatment programs they create, outside of structured therapy sessions.

Among our research participants, some of the families have received the government funding for treatment, but some have not. For example, one of the mothers is still waiting for the funding but has already started the treatment for her son with the family's own money, since early intervention is generally believed to be beneficial.[1] Some of the mothers lack the needed English language skills and consequently do not receive or fully understand the information needed for them to implement their child's program or understand the diagnosis. One of the mothers did not even know how to apply for the funding. Given the barriers that newcomers experience as they try to make a new life for themselves in Canada, understanding their experience and identity construction process could provide a new lens through which to review and improve policies and programs in BC's medical system and social services in order to create greater cultural sensitivity.

Politics of Difference and Social Exclusion in Motherhood Learning

This chapter adopts a critical feminist framework when examining the theoretical debates about difference and social exclusion. It explores how closely the factors of difference and social exclusion are related, perceived, and practiced in Asian immigrant mothers' motherhood learning practice through their experience of diagnosis, treatment, and everyday caring for their children with ASDs. Motherhood learning refers to the immigrant mothers' experience of learning about their role as a mother with ASD children.

The ideas of difference and social exclusion are widely explored in feminist studies (Bakan; Bannerji; Barrett). Scholars have related the concept of "social exclusion" to social inequalities, such as unequal race, gender, and class relations, which often originate in the perceived differences of people from the mainstream (Bannerji). These unequal power relations bring, in turn, a socially constructed notion of "difference" as established processes of social conflicts and products of a capitalist society, within which human actors reproduce these social relations (Bakan). In order to understand the motherhood learning experiences of Asian immigrant mothers with children with ASDs and the social exclusion that they face, we conceptualize the notion of difference in three ways: difference as experience, difference as social relations, and difference as praxis.

First, difference as experience means that the concept of difference is coordinated by people's experience of their everyday practice. In this way, the concept of difference is constructed as "common sense" and is frequently utilized to distinguish dichotomies, such as man and woman, West and non-West, or civilized and non-civilized. In understanding difference through individuals' everyday experience, we find that the meaning of difference is challenged. Difference is a framework for us to explore how individuals with different experiences interact with the social world while simultaneously shaping and being shaped by social institutions. This framework provides possibilities for the investigation of social institutions from the standpoint of individuals who are often labelled as different.

Second, we understand that difference is shaped by the inter-connections between people's everyday activities and their relations to social institutions. Difference as social relations, in a dialectical sense, reminds us that difference is socially organized, which happens in interactions between actual everyday life and social institutions. This dialectical thinking of difference also leads to the understanding that difference is socially constructed and allows us to consider how we could use it as an inquiry to problematize social institutions and the everyday world.

Finally, difference as praxis understands difference as a constitution between theory and practice. The concept of difference is constantly changing and is developed by the interactions between ideas and reality, theories and facts, and thinking and doing. Bertell Ollman points out that our society as a vehicle is moving and changing, and proposes several philosophical questions. Where is it travelling? Who is driving it and controlling its speed and direction? How could we drive it? In locating difference as praxis in a dynamic society, we find that it provides opportunities to become the "drivers" of the society (Ollman). Studying the concept of difference as praxis through a critical feminist theoretical framework, we find the study of Asian immigrant mothers' experiences to be valuable learning that is vital to the needed social change.

Whereas the concept of "difference" as experience, social relations, and praxis helps us understand the relationship between the individual and the institution, the notion of "social exclusion" helps us to understand how the politics of difference has been practiced and how people construct identities through the reproduction of difference. We frame social exclusion based on shared identities by applying the arguments provided by Himani Bannerji and Iris Marion Young. Bannerji examines identity, which as understood as a "historical and social subjectivity and agency (26)," is produced from the notion of difference. She further examines how social difference has been reproduced within capitalism and argues that difference is socially constructed through certain social relations. Being a woman does not necessarily mean a common and fixed group identity but instead represents a serial collectivity in which various groups of women in relation to their collective social structures and histories can be discussed without normalizing one group while excluding others.

We do not necessarily locate Asian mothers with children diagnosed with ASDs as a group with a particular identity per se. Instead, we define them as diverse people who exist as a serial collective with intersecting voices of race, gender, class, culture, and disability.

The Research

This research was conducted between late 2015 and early 2016. We interviewed seven Asian immigrant mothers with children diagnosed with ASDs in Vancouver. Semi-structured interviews, designed to explore the mothers' experiences, lasted from one hour to three hours. During the interviews, we mainly explored how they experienced the diagnosis and treatment of their children, how they learned the skills necessary to parent and best help their children, and how they constructed their identities and produced their knowledge of mothering throughout the learning that happened within this process.

Demographic information

The sample included five Chinese and two Korean mothers whose kids had been diagnosed with ASD in BC. Most of the mothers immigrated to Vancouver between 2008 and 2011. Most were college educated in their home countries or in Canada. The diagnosed children were all boys.

The profile of participants is as follows (Table 1). The names were changed to pseudonyms to protect their privacy.

Table 1. Participant Demographics

No.	Name (pseudonyms)	Year of Immigration	Education Level	Child's Name	Child's Age (Age at diagnosis)	Country of Origin
1	Maggie	2011	Bachelor	Kevin	4 (2)	China
2	Ann	2008	High School	Bowen	3 (2)	China
3	Crystal	2011	Bachelor	Jim	6 (4)	China
4	Emily	2011	PhD	David	4 (2)	China
5	Hannah	2009	Bachelor	Robert	8 (4)	Hong Kong, China
6	Kate	2008	Bachelor	Kevin	18(9)	Korea
7	Dana	2003	Bachelor	Andrew	21(12)	Korea

Results

Despite BC having a relatively strong social welfare system and providing funding for these children and their families, the mothers reported challenging experiences in learning about their role as mothers to their special children and remained excluded and differentiated in either the Canadian school system or their local community. Many immigrant mothers with ASD children still suffer in providing supportive treatment programs, finding a safe learning and living environment, and being recognized in local social, political, and economic society. Three main themes of Asian immigrant mothers' experiences of raising kids with ASDs were derived: (a) the social construction of their identity; (b) cultural difficulties in conducting mothering; and (c) production of knowledge and skills through learning.

Identity Construction of Asian Immigrant Mothers with Children with ASDs as Sociocultural Process

We found that the mothers who participated identified as immigrant parents with disabled children, both of which interact with their everyday learning of mothering practice. We argue that the mothering practices of Asian immigrant mothers are often misunderstood or labelled in multiple ways. Once they had struggled with the conception of disability and the fear of possible misunderstanding or mislabelling of their children by the general public, their mothering experience was also shaped by unequal social relations including race, gender, class, and, most importantly, disability.

The participant mothers experienced a sense of being labelled as a different kind of group of mothers with race, gender, class, and disabilities as noticeable differences. Not long after the diagnosis of their children, they realized that ASD is a vague category that became convoluted with their immigrant identity, mostly in negative ways. Emily struggled because she was not sure what being autistic meant to her son and her family. The hardest part was the labelling because she came to understand that people "create an image of autistic children in a wrong way." Hannah also shared her fear of labelling her kid, which started when her son Robert was diagnosed four years ago: "I often feel a great pressure from people who think that my kid is 'not normal'

[and] therefore [is] 'doing something wrong' just because he is diagnosed. What if he will be okay in the future but this label will stay with him forever?" She then compared her decision to that made by one of her friends who is also an immigrant from China: "She insisted that her son was not autistic. I think she is strong enough to make this decision. After hearing this mom's story, I couldn't fall asleep for several days and asked myself what if I have [made] the wrong decision for sending him to be labelled [to get the diagnosis and treatment].

On the one hand, many mothers with young kids talked about the difficulties they experienced when they had to accept the diagnosis. They were concerned that since their children were too young, there would be a possible misdiagnosis due to any cultural influences on the screening. They also found that the diagnostic tests were based on English, which is not their mother tongue, and they hardly used it at home. Yet Kate and Dana, whose children are now eighteen and twenty-one years old, respectively, explained how they embraced and came to terms with their sons' diagnoses, which were done relatively late in their teenage years. They had watched their children's difficulties and isolation from peers when their kids were in kindergarten and primary school in Korea before their immigration to Canada. They thought their sons needed some support to counter their apparent lack of social skills, even more so in this new society, a new land they had to settle in as a minority. Despite this wish for their sons, both they and their husbands struggled to find work to survive as new immigrants and could not afford much professional support for their sons.

For these mothers, "labelling" functioned as an emotional support, too. Both of them were somehow relieved in thinking that their sons would now have more people, other than parents, who understood them as disabled in schools and communities. For example, Dana's son was not diagnosed as having an ASD initially but was the second time around, after he had experienced many instances of bullying and misunderstanding of his behaviours in the early years of immigration. Dana described how she felt when she heard that he had an ASD: "I felt rather relieved that he's now finally labelled, thinking that he and I would now be a little bit free from finger-pointing and blame, at least. After the diagnosis, I could say 'Sorry, he has an ASD.'" Likewise, labelling felt different among the participant mothers according to the age at diagnosis, but it was overall related to their immigrant, and therefore, minority identity.

Immigrant identity affects their parenting, too. The often invisibility of their children's disabilities often caused misunderstanding about the mothers and their parenting style, which was often labelled as "being Asian" or "not Canadian" or even "bad." Ann shared her experience when she encountered a form of prejudice about her parenting:

> In the playground, I watch him carefully to protect him from dangerous behaviours since he does not have any ideas about safety. One day, a mother came to me and said, "Your kid is spoiled. Please let him do what he likes." I think she wanted to say that "Asian mothers always prevent their children from doing things." I was very angry.

The stories of the participant mothers showed that they were labelled on the basis of race, gender, class, and disability. There were certain assumptions or stereotypes of Asian immigrant mothers' practice of mothering, which socially constructed them through the imagination of their mothering activities. This process was fluid and changing throughout their experience of mothering their children.

Cultural Difficulties in Mothering Children with ASDs

In our study, we found that the linguistic and cultural barriers in the Asian immigrant mothers' settlement experience as well as their mothering practice shaped their diasporic and hybrid identities. First of all, language barriers were immensely difficult in that they interfered with their ability to freely communicate with doctors, teachers, and therapists in the diagnosis and treatment process. For example, Ann found that her language barrier made it extremely challenging for her to support her child: "I often get frustrated when people tell me important matters for my son's treatment, such as different kinds of treatment. One day, they talked about ABA or IBI. I was totally confused and scared I would commit any mistake that would cause any damage to my son." Maggie also felt helpless, not knowing how to search for help: "At the beginning, I couldn't find any social worker for help. Some mothers told me that I could search for help but I didn't even know how to search. I still don't have resources for my kid. Language is a major challenge for my mothering."

They were also challenged due to cultural differences when they tried to interact with healthcare professionals more closely for their children. Kate shared an experience of serious misunderstanding of the Korean culture regarding discipline that happened in the middle of her son's screening process. When a group of specialists interviewed him, they repeatedly asked him in the first place if there had been any inappropriate parenting in the family. When Kevin spoke in English, which was not at all fluent at that time, about his parents having spanked him a couple of times, they became cold to her. She recalled that she was just a step away from being charged with child abuse due to a huge misunderstanding:

> They are good people who had good intention to help my son. But they stereotyped me, saying that they know the Korean way of parenting well in that it often includes hitting their children to discipline them, and this is never allowed here in Canada. I became humiliated and lonely by being misunderstood as a bad mother who treats her child badly since he does not come up to her expectations. This was devastating, but all I had to do at that moment was try my best to make them understand what really happened, because they are important people to my son.

In the treatment process as well, the participant mothers were often differentiated and excluded from either an immigrant mothers' group or a group of mothers of children with ASDs, and sometimes from both. They sometimes felt that they were accepted neither in the disability (ASDs) group nor in their ethnic and larger immigrant communities, both of which they believed they should belong to. For example, Emily participated in a parenting program for new immigrant mothers with a settlement organization. She experienced great confusion, as most of the curriculum, course materials, and discussions did not fit into her knowledge of and experiences with parenting her child. She was told in the settlement parenting program that although her child had had conflict with other children, she should not interfere in her child's relationship with others. However, as a mother with a child with ASDs, she thought she should intervene in her child's behaviour.

Kate, another participant, shared similar feelings about a parenting program for mothers of children with ASDs. Immediately following her child's diagnosis, she registered her son in a group treatment program and signed herself up for parenting programs; however, she was soon disappointed due to the programs' minimal consideration of her culture. She found that she was very isolated in the parenting groups and she could not find enough support in sharing her experience as a Korean immigrant with ASD children in Canada.

In addition, many mothers reported that they are often excluded and differentiated in their children's schools in society. For example, Crystal offered one of the most disheartening reflections regarding "othering" attitudes in her son's school. Ever since she first received the diagnosis, she hoped that her son would grow to be a happy boy who knew how to communicate with people, which is much more modest than her initial hopes she had for him. She thought her hope for her son would be fulfilled by his school owing to the cooperation of teachers and special assistance teachers. However, she soon realized that her son's school hardly cared about this and tried to shift responsibility for her son to the special education teacher.

> His teacher hardly cares [about] him because she understands that Jim is supposed to be cared [for] by another teacher of special education who is hired to take care of these "unique" children in school. I feel alienated when I find she does not know anything [about] him, and the assistance teachers are too busy to take care of him. I often see she talks about lots of things regarding others, I mean, other kids and their parents. But she hardly says anything about my son to me. There were often times that he was even beaten by the kids in the class due to the misunderstanding of his autistic behaviour. In these unhappy incidents, his teacher was hardly helpful. I often visit his school and talk to the principal and the teachers but same disappointment happens every time. They don't tell you that they treat you differently, but they actually treat you differently.

Emily shared a similar story about how differentiation started to happen in her son's daily routine in his daycare, which was not at all helpful to her family:

> When we first introduced us as new immigrants, the people in his daycare were really nice to us and warmly accepted my son.

Since David received diagnosis, however, everything seems to be changed. I no longer feel that we are treated as the same way we were treated warmly before. I will tell you one. They deliver monthly newsletters in which they provide pictures of children who have birthdays on the month and celebrating comments. I saw the names and the pictures of the children in the daycare who were born in July, except my son. I do not know if this is a simple mistake or not, but this hurt me and my husband deeply.

The participant mothers also addressed how their daily parenting practices were challenged. On the one hand, they needed to learn how to best parent their child as a student with special needs and help to improve their behaviors; on the other, they tried to help their children to fit into the daycare or school with other children. Their identities were shaped through negotiating their mothering practice with the parenting programs, the supportive programs for parents and children with ASDs, and the schools. There are unequal power relations between these mothers and the institutions. Their knowledge of mothering has been differentiated and excluded. With these adjustments of parenting and reconstructing identities, their mothering was sometimes misrecognized or differentiated in ways they did not expect, which, therefore, produced exclusion and/or isolation.

Production of Knowledge and Skills through Learning

Participant mothers shared their learning experiences; these ranged from tangible knowledge and skills to critical reflections and/or communities of practice that appropriately fit their mothering in their everyday space of living. We found that their learning was initially conventional but moved on to more experimental and culturally appropriate types of learning, which contained an extensive amount of self-directed learning, either individually or collectively. As outcomes of learning, they grew and started to interact with healthcare professionals with increased strength and self-confidence.

Participant mothers reported that they first learned mothering strategies through mainstream healthcare sectors. For example, Crystal learned a modelling method and became accustomed to applying the scenarios to her everyday interactions with her son; this helped to manage most of his aggressive behaviours. Most of the participant mothers also searched for new knowledge and skills, alternative treatments, as well as culturally appropriate approaches that were linked to the uniqueness of this disability and their immigrant identity. For example, Maggie talked about how she started learning about food and nutrition therapy for those with ASDs that had not been scientifically approved by mainstream, Western medicine. She started reading books in English and created Chinese-style recipes based on her learning. She described how much this learning process was empowering through being with other Chinese mothers:

We [the Chinese mothers with children with ASDs] organized a support group and have shared new information like what I learned about nutrition and other medical and alternative therapeutic development. Then we have created a lot of activities to learn from each other. This works for me, and I will say other mothers too would feel the same way.

Kate put an end to her child's year-long conventional speech therapy and moved instead to individual counselling therapy with a Korean-Canadian counsellor. She attributed the improved outcomes to this counsellor's focus on social relations with family and classmates, since the weekly counselling benefited not only her son but also Kate and the entire family, which became a whole support team for Kevin:

His Korean counsellor takes care of not only Kevin but also his brother, me and my husband. Now we are all better and happier by understanding how we can support him as family. It makes us feel great. I am particularly glad that my husband's relationship with him is very improved since now he understands how to connect [with] his autistic son who is Korean, Canadian, and Korean-Canadian.

However, Kate also shared that she has struggled but failed to combine this treatment, which she feels is culturally appropriate for Kevin, with his schooling. For example, she mentioned that her son's school refused to include the Korean-Canadian counsellor in the meetings for Kevin at school. She found it was difficult for her to communicate with the local, English-speaking counsellor, which would make it more difficult to provide Kevin with good treatment at school.

Dana talked about her attempts to seek inclusion in the community with the neighbourhood mothers whose children have ASDs, which were hardly successful due to linguistic and cultural barriers. Now she understands that what she has wanted throughout her son's childhood was to form friendships with Korean mothers with children diagnosed with ASDs for mutual support.

Despite these difficulties, the participants' increased knowledge and skills, which reflected their identities as immigrant mothers, enriched the mainstream healthcare sector, their children's schools, and their communities because of their increased participation. They reported that they now regularly communicate with healthcare workers, share their learning needs with them, arrange various spaces for their children, and even occasionally plan learning occasions together.

Conclusion

This chapter examines the identity construction, knowledge production, and motherhood learning experiences of Asian immigrant mothers with children diagnosed with ASDs, and discusses the politics of difference and social exclusion in their learning of mothering practice. We argue that these Asian immigrant mothers live under immensely unequal social and power relations that interact with their identity construction and knowledge production.

In our research, we interviewed seven Asian immigrant mothers with children diagnosed with ASDs in Vancouver. We have three major findings. First, these mothers are socially constructed as a unique group of mothers. This categorizing process shapes their identity and their experience of unequal social relations. They and their children are frequently misunderstood and even labelled, and their mothering experience has been differentiated and socially excluded, which makes them reflect on who they are and how they can adjust their mothering practice to fit into the society in which they are situated. Second, these Asian mothers experience linguistic and cultural barriers. They have many difficulties in terms of receiving their children's diagnosis, getting access to social services and government welfare, and communicating with professionals, including doctors, behaviour interventionists, and school teachers. We argue that these barriers greatly shape their identity as hybrid and diasporic, which marginalizes them as a group of women with experiences that are regarded as different from those in mainstream Canadian healthcare practice. Third, we find that Asian immigrant mothers' learning experiences come with social and cultural practice, which provides us with a different lens to understand the meaning of motherhood and the knowledge of mothering for these children.

Andrea O'Reilly points out that the notion of motherhood needs to be redefined, given that it has been challenged from different standpoints, and she argues that mothering is a practice. This definition enables scholars to examine the experiences and practices of mothering as "distinct and separate from the identity of mother" (5), and O'Reilly further points out that the word "mother" is not a monolithic identity, since mothering is not a singular practice (Chandler; O'Reilly).

Similarly, our study examines Asian immigrant mothers' identity construction and challenging experiences, and their unique knowledge production with their children. We found that difference and social exclusion are reproduced through immigrant mothers' settlement process and learning for their children. We suggest that healthcare providers, government administrators, social workers, and school teachers need to pay more attention to these mothers' identity construction, knowledge production, and individual as well as collective struggles to embrace them as a legitimate part of a mosaic society.

Endnote

1. Research shows that early intervention makes a big difference to the child's overall development (Koegel and LaZebnik).

Works Cited

Altiere, Matthew J., and Silvia von Kluge. "Family Functioning and Coping Behaviors in Parents of Children with Autism." *Journal of Child and Family Studies*, vol. 18, no. 1, 2009, pp. 83-92.

Bakan, Abigail. "Marxism and Antiracisms: Rethinking the Politics of Difference." *Rethinking Marxism: A Journal of Economics, Culture & Society*, vol. 20, no. 2, 2007, pp. 238-56.

Bannerji, Himani. *Thinking Through: Essays on Feminism, Marxism, and Anti-Racism*. Women's Press, 1995.

Barret, Michele. "The Concept of Difference." *Feminist Review*, vol. 26, 1987, pp. 29-41.

Canadian Institutes of Health Research (CIHR). "Fact Sheet–Autism Spectrum Disorders." *Canadian Institutes of Health Research*. CIHR Press. 2012.

Cassidy, A., McConkey, R., Truesdale-Kennedy, M., & Slevin, E., Roy Mcconkey, Maria Truesdale-Kennedy, Eamonn Slevin. "Pre-schoolers with Autism Spectrum Disorders: The Impact on Families and the Supports Available to Them." *Early Child Development and Care*, vol. 178, no. 2, 2008, pp. 115-28.

Chandler, Mielle. "Emancipated Subjectivities and the Subjugation of Mothering Practices." *Maternal Theory: Essential Readings*, edited by Andrea O'Reilly, Demeter Press, 2007, pp. 529-41.

Grewal, Sophia. "Diagnosis and Treatment Barriers Faced by South Asian Families in Canada Who Have Children Diagnosed with an Autism Spectrum Disorder." Dissertation. School of Professional Psychology, Pacific University, 2010.

Kediye, Fatima, et al. "Somali-Canadian Mothers' Experiences in Parenting a Child with Autism Spectrum Disorder." *Journal of the Association for Research on Mothering*, vol. 11, no. 1, 2009, pp. 211-23.

King, Gillian, et al. "Barriers to Health Service Utilization by Immigrant Families Raising a Disabled Child: Unmet Needs and the Role of Discrimination." *Pathways to Prosperity: Canada*. Pathways to Prosperity Partnership. 2011.

Koegel, Lynn Kern, and Claire LaZebnik. *Overcoming Autism: Finding the Answers, Strategies, and Hope That Can Transform a Child's Life*. Penguin, 2014.

Lai, Yuan, and F. Ishu Ishiyama. "Involvement of Immigrant Chinese Canadian Mothers of Children With Disabilities." *Exceptional Children*, vol. 71, no. 1, 2004, pp. 97-108.

Lee, L. C., Harrington, R. A., Louie, B. B., & Newschaffer, C. J., Li-Ching Lee, Rebecca A. Harrington, Brian B Louie, Craig J Newschaffer. "Children with Autism: Quality of Life and Parental Concerns." *Journal of Autism Developmental Disorder*, vol. 38, 2008, pp. 1147-60.

Ollman, Bertell. *Dance of Dialectic: Steps in Marx's Method.* Urbana and Chicago: University of Illinois Press, 2003. Print.

O'Reilly, Andrea, editor. *Twenty-First Century Motherhood: Experience, Identity, Policy, Agency.* Columbia University Press, 2010.

Young, Iris Marion. *Intersecting Voices: Dilemmas of Gender, Political Philosophy, and Policy.* Princeton University Press, 1997.

Chapter 11

Daughters Who Mother Their Mothers: An Exploration of the Social Exclusion of Unpaid Intergenerational Home Care Workers

Krystal Kehoe MacLeod

"Aging in place" has become a popular catchphrase with both Canadian policymakers and the growing population of seniors aged sixty-five and older. Aging in place policies restructure health and social services to help seniors live in their family homes for as long as they choose (Federal/Provincial/Territorial Ministers 2). Although it is not explicitly stated, a fundamental assumption of this policy initiative is that seniors have family members who are willing and able to make a significant investment in time, work, and money to support them in their choice to age in place. This chapter explores the implications of the push for seniors to age in place from the perspective of the family members who provide the bulk of the supports and services seniors require to do so. Drawing on the experiences of adult daughters, this chapter looks at the personal and social aspects of social exclusion connected to the unpaid work daughters perform to care for their elderly mothers. It also pays attention to the complex power relations contextualizing this kind of intergenerational care work and looks for promising practices in integrated homecare programs that help daughters cope with the social exclusion related challenges they encounter when caring for their mothers who wish to age in place.

To understand why daughters play such an important role in caring for their aging mothers, we must consider the broader contextual factors influencing the aging in place movement. As the priorities of citizens and governments continue to be shaped by preferences for individualism, independence, privacy, choice, and personal control, neoliberal-inspired discourses dominate policy and program development around the issue of healthy aging. Seniors are embracing the "choice" to live in their domestic homes until the end of their lives, even if they need help caring for themselves. At the same time, public policies continue to focus on shifting both the costs of elder care from publicly funded institutions to private homes and the responsibility to provide care from the state to the individual as a means of achieving cost savings to the public purse. These trends have contributed to the "relocation of care" from a public service provided by the state to the private responsibility of families—transferring the duty to care from the paid to the unpaid workforce (Armstrong 537).

Homecare is characterized by a gendered division of labour where women undertake the majority of the care work necessarily for seniors to age at home (Keefe 110; Cranswick and Dosman; Sinha 10; Williams 122). Gender also shapes the intensity and type of care work done by family carers (Lero and Joseph 15), as women are more likely than their male counterparts to spend more time per week on caregiving tasks and twice as likely to provide personal care, including bathing, toileting, and dressing (Sinha 11). Although the uptake of the caregiving role by women has been extensively discussed and theorized in the literature (Aronson; Benoit and Hallgrimsdottir; England and Dyck; Finch and Groves; Grant et al.; Kahana et al.; Martin-Matthews and Phillips; Power; Ryan et al.), research has disproportionately focused on the health and experiences of spousal caregivers (Bastawrous et al. 1528). However, adult children are increasingly becoming primary caregivers to their aging parents (Bastawrous et al. 1528; Sinha 5), and adult daughters are three times more likely than sons to provide care (Stein 126). It is within this context that this chapter focuses on women's experiences as daughters providing homecare to their mothers as they age in place.

However, studying the individual experiences of daughters involved in intergenerational care in the home should move beyond discussing what caregiving tasks daughters perform for their mothers to a discussion of two important related issues: first, how this type of unpaid care work is connected to caregivers' experiences of social exclusion; and second, if, and how, integrated care programs are addressing this aspect of caregiver burden. Literature exists on the individual experiences of daughters providing homecare for their mothers (Arber and Venn; Bull and Jervis; Holroyd) and also on how policies and programs are being used to address issues of social exclusion (Bell and Menec; Forbes et al.; Scharlach and Lehning; van Malderen et al.). This chapter, however, merges these two units of analysis to use the individual experiences of caregiving daughters to shed light on promising practices in integrated homecare.

Hilary Graham suggests that caregiving in the home blurs the conceptual distinction between "caring for" (task-oriented, physical labour) and "caring about" (relational, therapeutic, and emotional labour) (13). Although homecare policies and programs in a neoliberal climate typically make an empirical distinction between these, Julia Twigg argues that the actual practices of body work and the social practice of caregiving overlap in ways that cannot be separated (427). In the literature, the term "caregiver" is often used to refer to individuals who help an elderly person with activities of daily living (ADLs) (Katz et al. 915) and instrumental activities of daily living (IADLs) (Sims-Gould et al. 69). ADLs include feeding, bathing, dressing, toileting, and help with medication, whereas IADLs include transportation, shopping, running errands, laundry, household chores, meal preparation, home maintenance, shovelling, yard work, banking and financial management, and organizing appointments with paid service providers. However, many types of "caring about" work do not fit easily into these traditional categories. Care work such as monitoring a client's health and wellbeing, attending medical appointments, making care decisions on behalf of a client, figuring out how to navigate the system of health and social care services, advocating on a client's behalf, paying out of pocket for material items and care services needed by the client, and providing emotional support are less visible than ADLs or IADLs, but they still require a significant amount of an unpaid care worker's time, effort, and financial resources. This chapter considers all manifestations of care work as equally valid and, thus, defines a caregiver or carer interchangeably as an individual who assists an elderly person with any, many, or all of the above listed tasks.

In the same way that distinguishing between the various kinds of caregiving work is problematic, there is also a tendency to draw artificial lines between "medical-health" care and "custodial-social" care, which has resulted in inconsistencies in state ownership and funding of different types of care. Reliance on the biomedical model to socially construct healthcare as more important than social care has led to the increasing commodification of care normalizing the private sector as the provider of social care services and the state as the provider of healthcare services, which reinforces the tendency to think about healthcare and social care in separate siloes. Yet empirical evidence rooted in the social determinants of health literature show that a combination of both types of care are prerequisites for healthy aging (Evans and Stoddard; Raphael). Although the concept of integrated care was developed predominantly as a means of achieving neoliberal policy objectives, such as improved efficiency and effectiveness, it proposed to do so by offering an alternative to the traditional siloed approach to care provision. Integrated care programs were designed to use a multidisciplinary team to offer a basket of both healthcare and social care services to clients and family carers (Gröne and Garcia-Barbero 7; Kodner and Spreeuwenberg 3; Leutz 77-78). This chapter reflects on the successes of integrated care programs in supporting caregiving daughters in ways that address their experiences of social exclusion.

In order to assess the social integration of unpaid carers, specifically daughters who care for their elderly mothers, the term "social exclusion" will be used to "focus on relational issues: in other words, inadequate social participation, lack of social integration and lack of power" (Room 243). Drawing on Benjamin Gray et al.'s categorization of the four types of social exclusion (personal, social, service, and financial) experienced by caregivers of persons with mental illness (478), this chapter focuses on the personal and social aspects of exclusion as experienced by daughters caring for their elderly mothers. Personal exclusions refer to perceptions rooted in assumptions about caring work as naturally women's work (Armstrong and Banerjee 15;

Finch and Groves 5), which leads daughters to feel that the challenges they experience as unpaid carers are best kept quiet and dealt with privately. The social aspect of social exclusion refers to feelings of isolation stemming from a narrowing of social networks, the overwhelming time commitment of unpaid caregiving, and the restrictions in employment and leisure resulting from caregiving. Given the unique context in which daughters provide care to their mothers, this chapter pays particular attention to the delicate balance of power required to engage in intergenerational care by looking at how the inversion of the caregiving relationship introduces additional complexities into daughters' experiences of social exclusion and the strategies available to them to help deal with this issue.

A study of five integrated care programs across Canada was undertaken to uncover the promising practices of using integrated care to provide homecare services to elderly clients (Kehoe MacLeod). Purposive samples of program administrators, paid care workers, unpaid care workers, and clients were recruited in collaboration with integrated care programs: Aging in Place (Ottawa, Ontario), Seniors Managing Independent Living Easily (SMILE) (Kingston-Trenton region, Ontario), Carefirst (Scarborough, Ontario), Capital Care's Comprehensive Home Option for Integrated Care for the Elderly (CHOICE) program (Edmonton, Alberta), and Fraser Health's Home Health program (Hope, British Columbia). Fourteen of the carers who took part in this study were daughters doing unpaid care work for their elderly mothers, and their experiences are the data analyzed in this chapter. Each participant took part in one semi-structured interview between 2012 and 2013 where they spoke about a range of aspects relating to their role as unpaid carers and their perceptions of, and experiences with, the integrated care program in which their mother was enrolled. With the participants' permission, their interviews were audiotaped and transcribed. In addition, detailed notes of field observations were kept. These interview transcripts and field notes form the basis of this analysis.

In their interviews, all of the daughters described experiences with personal aspects of social exclusion; they shared their feelings that there was an unspoken expectation for them to be able to deal privately with the difficult aspects of caring for their mothers. Pat Armstrong explains that this "private notion of care" is rooted in the argument that care is an "individual, family and female responsibility rather than a collective one" (539). Daughters experienced increased stress as a result of being expected to care for their mother alone, and this was often connected to feelings of guilt, anger, being overwhelmed, and panic. In some cases, these emotions led to outbursts in the form of crying or yelling. A daughter in Hope described her daily emotional turmoil saying, "every once and awhile I just burst, and it's hard because I love her [mother], you know? And I don't want her to go in a home, and I want to keep her with me as long as I can. And I feel like a real ogre, a real bitch. I hate me at the point in time, you know?" Other daughters, like this one from Carefirst, reported repressing their emotions leading to feelings of perpetual exhaustion: "I feel so tired and then always so angry; [I have] a lot of anger towards them [parents]."

A shared perception among daughters was that the integrated care programs their mothers belonged to did not offer them as unpaid carers access to formalized mechanisms through which to share their difficulties in participating in this type of care work. In fact, several highlighted that even the paid care workers did not have access to subsidized counselling or an employee assistance program to help them deal with the emotional labour of care work, so it was unsurprising to the unpaid carers that there were no supports in place for them either. In the absence of access to counselling for unpaid carers at the program level, the daughters relied on the informal emotional support offered by their mothers' paid care workers. Whereas one daughter was an outlier in explaining that she did not want to "burden" the paid workers by sharing her own feelings, paid carers were the primary source of emotional support for the other thirteen daughters. Daughters cited the paid carers' shared understanding of the challenges inherent in providing elder care stemming from their extensive work experience in this area as the primary reason they had become informal counsellors. As a daughter with Carefirst explained, "They understand my situation. They will give me a lot of ideas. [They say:] 'You need to relax yourself. Don't hold everything in your hands.' ... I will talk to them because I understand that they've taken care of a lot of seniors. They have a lot of experience." Paid carers were highly valued by daughters as their trusted confidants and emotional supports.

Homecare programs that prioritized continuity of care, in particular keeping the same worker with the same family for an extended period of time, were the most successful at facilitating the kind of trusting relationship between carers required for daughters to feel comfortable seeking out this type of emotional support from the paid workers. A daughter with the SMILE program described the bond she had developed with her mother's worker saying, "She has been [doing] a bit of counselling, you know. She's been a sounding board; I can call her any time." The funding mechanism used in the SMILE program, wherein they provide clients with the funds to hire a worker of their choice, was especially promising for promoting continuity of care. In contrast to other programs where clients reported (with significant frustration) having numerous different paid care workers, SMILE clients typically had the same worker for the duration of their time in the program, sometimes up to five years. This facilitated the development of a strong bond between the client, the unpaid carer, and the paid carer. One daughter described her SMILE funded carer as "like family ... better than family," and numerous clients and paid carers involved in the SMILE program echoed this sentiment.

In response to their identification of service gaps in the area of supporting unpaid carers in their provision of emotional labour, many daughters suggested that having some way to share their struggles with others who were going through the same thing would be beneficial. Whereas one daughter advocated for access to professional counselling, several others suggested that program-facilitated peer support groups or networks could be feasible solution. In particular, they expressed the desire for a forum in which they could share their difficulties accepting the changing dynamics of their relationship with their mothers and collaborate on coping strategies. One daughter in Hope summarized the challenges she was struggling with as a result of the shifting power relations inherent in intergenerational care provision:

It's going from having your baby to having your parent, but it's harder, and I think why it's harder is because you had a mother who was very strong. She was an incredible mother; she did lots and was incredible right up until a year ago...part and parcel of the issue too is to get your mind wrapped around the fact that your mother [now] is not really who your mother was...sometimes

I treat her like a child and she says "You're treating me like a child," and it's like, "Yeah, I am, and I kinda have to."

A daughter with Carefirst shared a similar experience: "Sometimes I feel so angry with mother. Why do you don't take care of yourself? She so takes care of the family, especially my father ... but find something for herself? She says: 'I don't know.'...So, I am so angry, you know?" Daughters explained that caring for their mothers as they age is similar in some respects to caring for their own children "but there's a big difference. So there's a lot...of emotional stress." They suggested that sharing their experiences with one another could be used as a coping strategy to deal with feelings of social exclusion and would allow them to challenge the perception that they should keep their experiences a secret. They asked for integrated homecare programs to take a lead in coordinating support groups for the caregiving daughters of the elderly women enrolled in their programs. Additionally, several daughters explained that they found it difficult to leave their houses because of their mothers' need for constant monitoring. They suggested the programs create virtual or telephone networks they could access. The daughters felt these networks would give them "somebody to talk to," provide them with easier access to information on available services, and offer an avenue through which they could solicit advice from other unpaid care providers in similar situations without the "stress of having to leave home." At the time of the study, none of the programs offered any formal counselling or support services for the unpaid carers of their clients. Facilitating a peer support network for unpaid carers would be a welcome step in supporting daughters in their caring work.

Social isolation was a persistent theme emerging from the experiential accounts of daughters caring for their elderly mothers as they age in place. Feeling a lack of social integration with friends, families, and communities was often discussed in relation to daughters' struggle to cope with the time intensive nature of caregiving work. In their interviews, daughters discussed how their unpaid care work affected their family relationships and leisure time, their opportunities to participate in paid employment, as well as their desire and ability to maintain their social networks. Although a few daughters shared the caregiving work with their partners (this was more often the case for daughters who were related to the mother by marriage as opposed to by birth), most daughters reported being solely responsible for providing their mothers' unpaid care. When mothers and daughters were not living in the same residence, daughters reported visiting their mothers daily or even twice daily. When considering the intensity of this care work in combination with their other caregiving responsibilities—for example caring for children, partners or other relatives—daughters expressed such feelings as they were caregiving "24/7." As one daughter explained, "Right now, my life is wrapped around caring for three people. Not me. So right now, I don't, most of the time, I don't do anything for me per se, other than when I'm in my car by myself—that's nice." Reduced leisure time as a result of participating in unpaid care work is a common theme in the literature (Gahagan 49; Ory et al. 184; Schuz et al. 231). Data from this study support this finding and draw attention to carers' feelings that the intense nature of their unpaid care work leaves them feeling "trapped in their home" and wanting to "escape." One daughter explained that the intensity of her unpaid care work has made her "go a bit strange," saying that "You want to get out." The feeling of being "tied down" because of their responsibility to care for their mother was shared among all daughters interviewed. They reported that keeping up with all of the daily tasks required to care for their mothers was "stressful" and "overwhelming." One daughter recounted her efforts to explain to her mother the impact of her decision to age in place on the daughter's own emotional state: "So I said, 'Well mom, you can stay in your own apartment ... but you have to have a little bit more support—I just can't be doing this.' And I'd like to just visit and have a visit, not always [be] thinking of everything else I need to do for her [Sigh]. Not that I mind doing some things, but it's very emotionally exhausting." Another participant explained that although she found the intimate nature of the everyday caring tasks difficult, it was the prospect of having to continue this unpaid care work for her mother-in-law into the unforeseeable future that she found particularly distressing.

> I'd been the one cleaning bums ... it got very hard on me, and I made my own mistake ... I was kind of thinking a little bit more finite about how long this whole thing would go on. This sounds really cold; I'm not trying to be cold [crying]; I didn't think it was going to be five, ten years or I, if I had known that at the start, there is no way I [would have signed up for this].

In addition to compromising their time for leisure and self-care, daughters also reported that caring for their mother put a strain on their relationship with their partner and/or children. One daughter with the SMILE program explained that she and her husband were unable to take their children out for dinner or to family social events in the evenings because their elderly mother lived with them and could not be left alone. She also felt she was missing out on family time after the children got home from school and her husband from work because she often had to use this time to catch up on her own paid work after she put her mother to bed. In addition to unpaid care work affecting present family relations, some daughters suggested that the burden of this care work had future implications as well. For example, one daughter explained that she and her partner had decided to put off having children—partly because they felt that the care required by their mother was so overwhelming that they could not see adding to their caregiving burden and partly because they were fighting so much about the division of care work that they had no desire to participate in the intimate relations required to conceive. This was a source of extraordinary anguish for the daughter, as she desperately wanted her own children and resented her mother for jeopardizing this.

Few daughters saw a renegotiation of how the care work is shared among unpaid carers as being a viable option for reducing the intensity of their caregiving responsibilities. Instead, seeking out publicly subsidized and/or privately paid for help from paid workers was their primary coping mechanism. Reporting that "It's a relief to have her [paid carer] in" and "it does take a weight off you," daughters relied on paid carers to assist them with a variety of traditional caregiving tasks, for instance, housekeeping, bathing, and food preparation. They also helped with some less traditional tasks as well, such as helping with the transportation of their mothers to and from appointments or adult day programs. Once daughters were able to share the burden of caring with someone else, they felt less alone, less stressed out, and more able to cope. As a daughter with the SMILE program explained, "Suddenly we were getting some order in the house and I was starting to feel like, 'Oh, I can address this now.' Instead of just keeping up, I was able to get a little bit ahead." Even daughters whose male partners helped with aspects of caregiving reported benefiting from paid help. Most of the paid care workers coming into the home were women who were prepared to help with the personal care tasks that up to this point had been relegated to the daughter as the primary female care provider. Daughters reported that bringing in paid carers gave them some relief from the physical strain of bathing and lifting the client and allowed them to share the responsibility for their mothers' social and emotional support.

One theme apparent from the interviews was that daughters felt significant pressure to ensure adequate social engagement of their mothers. Most were keenly aware that they were their mothers' primary source of social interaction and often their only remaining connection to their community. For instance, a daughter in Hope reported feeling pressured to take her mother grocery shopping even though she was pressed for time and it would certainly have been faster to do this task alone, yet she recognized that this was the only time her mother got out of the house each week. Many daughters struggled balancing "caring for" and "caring about," given the time pressure under which they were working. Daughters frequently described feeling that they should be "visiting" or "socializing" more with their mother because if they were not doing this, no one else would be either. Yet they found it difficult to prioritize talking with their mothers when there were so many other tasks to be done. The impetus for one daughter to seek out help from the SMILE program was when she began "thinking that we needed to get somebody in to do all of the stuff that I was coming here and doing because I wasn't spending any time stimulating my mother or visiting; I was cleaning their house and all of that." Some daughters used paid carers to help with physical care tasks freeing them up to do the more emotional care work themselves, whereas others preferred to share the responsibility for clients' social inclusion with paid workers by having them spend time socializing with clients or taking them on social excursions outside the home. As a daughter with the SMILE program shared, "I think it's wonderful that she [the paid worker] sits and talks with [her mother] because I think that's such an integral part of the program, just that socializing, that visit so that it's not all on the family, on me."

Sharing the burden of the physical and emotional care with paid carers gave daughters "more time" and "less work." Daughters reported using this time away from caring for their mothers to complete their other chores—for example, cleaning the house or performing caregiving duties for other family members—or to participate in paid employment. Although it was not leisure time per se, the daughters explained that simply being able to leave the house to go grocery shopping, take their children to activities, or go to work helped them combat the feelings of social exclusion that came with unpaid caregiving in the home. A daughter involved with the SMILE program explained, "Just the fact that [the paid worker] was here, I would go. Just being able to get in the car and make some excuse, 'I have to drop this off at [work]' and then just take longer ... you know. And not having to feel guilty." Many daughters echoed these feelings suggesting that help from paid workers gave them both freedom and peace of mind.

Help from paid carers also offered daughters much needed respite from their caregiving tasks. However, it was clear from the interviews that the levels of paid support that daughters were able to access through publicly funded home support programs were insufficient to enable them to maintain their social networks. As one daughter explained, "When I come home, and I'm a senior citizen myself, I just don't have the energy to do anything. I just need to veg out!" At the end of the day, daughters reported not having the energy left to socialize with friends or family as much as they wished they could. Specifically, daughters identified a pressing need for a larger number, and more appropriate, respite care options. The daughters were looking for a larger allocation of publicly subsidized respite hours, as most felt that their respite entitlement was "very low." One caregiver explained that respite care was an area of the publicly funded system where policymakers had got it "very wrong." For instance, a daughter in Hope resented the lack of respite because it restricted her ability to visit her grandchildren: "You have no time. So I think what they need to do is open up more respite rooms ... there's getting to be more of us baby boomers that are keeping their family at home." In addition to offering more respite, some daughters suggested that the process of organizing respite should be less complicated; they felt it was "very stressful and exhausting" to arrange. Finally, daughters emphasized that respite care should be more client centred so that it betters meets the needs of clients who are used to being in a home-like environment. A daughter with a Cantonese-speaking mother living in the Scarborough area stressed the "severe lack of organizations in the

Chinese community for respite services"; she said there were "huge" waitlists for cultural-specific respite and all the other respite options were "all English-speaking" and that "I [could] use those for mom but she won't be happy." Many daughters stressed that they did not feel comfortable leaving their mother in respite care unless they were certain she was comfortable.

Daughters suggested that they would like to see both short stay respite in an institutional setting—such as a long-term residential care home for clients following acute episodes (e.g. falls, pneumonia, hospital stays)—as well as in-home respite care options. The CHOICE program demonstrated promising practices in respite care for seniors living at home by operating ten care beds at their program site, which was housed in a wing of a residential long-term care facility. CHOICE used these beds to offer short-term respite for participants of their homecare program at $40 per night so family members could go out of town. The program also used the care beds to help clients make the transition from hospital to home; there was no cost to clients in this case. As one daughter explained:

> They [the hospital] were going to send [my mother] home after one day in the hospital and then have a nurse come in and do the dressing changes. But the staff here [at CHOICE] said, "No. You bring her to us and we can monitor. We can do the dressing changes; we can respond immediately if there is any kind of infection or concerns." So she was here for two weeks until she was healed. And so, you know, I'd come and visit her here. That way I wasn't concerned that I was missing something because I don't have a medical background.

The CHOICE program offers its participants a more familiar respite option with the care beds being located at the main program site where all clients come for their medical and social care appointments and attend the adult day program at least once a week. The respite care is provided by the same program staff during the day and staff from the residential care home at night. Offering respite care in a familiar environment—surrounded by the client's usual care providers who are knowledgeable about their personality, health status, and preferences—is a very promising practice. Although daughters explained that they would still prefer to have the option for in-home respite care, both mothers and daughters agreed that CHOICE's care beds were the next best thing.

By drawing attention to the personal and social aspects of adult daughters' experiences of social exclusion, this chapter has highlighted how intergenerational care affects caregivers' time, opportunities, resources, and relationships. The promising practices of integrated homecare programs in Ontario, Alberta, and British Columbia has showed how these programs are working to address some of aspects of social exclusion highlighted by unpaid carers. In particular, this chapter has drawn attention to the importance of paid carers as supports for unpaid carers and has emphasized the benefit of programs that prioritize continuity of care as well as the importance of increasing access to respite care that has been customized for clients who are used to living at home. However, there is still more work for integrated homecare programs to do. This chapter recommends that homecare programs should facilitate peer support networks for the unpaid carers of their program participants. Programs should also make an effort to offer access to in-home respite care that many clients and unpaid carers consider being the preferred option for keeping clients comfortable while giving caregivers both a break and peace of mind. It is clear that adult daughters connect their experiences caring for their aging mothers at home with feelings of being socially excluded. Integrated homecare programs offer some promising practices, but more can be done to support daughters in coping with the social exclusion they encounter when doing the essential work of caring for their aging mothers.

Works Cited

Arber, Sara and Susan Venn. "Caregiving at Night: Understanding the Impact on Carers." *Journal of Aging Studies*, vol. 25, 2011, p. 155-65.

Armstrong, Pat. "Relocating care: Home care in Ontario." *Women's Health in Canada: Critical Perspectives on Theory and Policy,* edited by M. Morrow, et al., University of Toronto Press, 2007, pp. 528-53.

Armstrong, Pat and Albert Banerjee. "Challenging Questions: Designing Long-term Residential Care with Women in Mind." *A Place to Call Home: Long-term Care in Canada*, edited by P. Armstrong, et al, Fernwood Publishing Inc., 2009, pp. 10-28.

Aronson, Jane. "Elderly People's Accounts of Home Care Rationing: Missing Voices in Long-term Care Policy Debates." *Ageing and Society*, vol. 22, 2002, p. 399-418.

Bastawrous, Marina, et al. "Daughters Providing Poststroke Care: Perspectives on the Parent–Child Relationship and Well-Being." *Qualitative Health Research*, vol. 24, no. 11, 2014, pp. 1527-39.

Bell, Sheri, and Verena Menec. "'You Don't Want to Ask for the Help' The Imperative of Independence: Is It Related to Social Exclusion?" *Journal of Applied Gerontology*, vol. 34, no. 3, 2015, pp. NP1-NP21.

Benoit, Cecilia, and Helga Hallgrimsdottir, editors. *Valuing Care Work Comparative Perspectives*. University of Toronto Press, 2010.

Bull, Margaret, and Lori Jervis. "Strategies Used by Chronically Ill Older Women and Their Caregiving Daughters in Managing Posthospital Care." *Journal of Advanced Nursing*, vol. 25, 1997, pp. 541-47.

Canada, Federal/Provincial/Territorial Ministers Responsible for Seniors Forum. *Thinking About Aging in Place*. Development Canada, 2012, www.seniors.gc.ca/eng/working/fptf/pdf/place.pdf. Accessed 14 May 2019.

Cranswick, Kelly, and Donna Dosman. *Eldercare: What we Know Today.* Canadian Social Trends, *Statistics Canada*, 2008. Catalogue no. 11-008-X, No. 86. www.statcan.gc.ca/pub/11-008-x/2008002/article/10689-eng.htm . Accessed 14 May 2019.

England, Kim and Isabel Dyck. "Managing the Body Work of Home Care." *Sociology of Health and Illness*, vol. 33, no. 2, 2011, pp. 206-19.

Evans, Robert, and Gregory Stoddart. "Producing Health, Consuming Health Care," *Social Science and Medicine*, vol. 31, no. 12, 1990, pp. 1347-63.

Finch, Janet, and Dulcie Groves, editors. *A Labour of Love: Women, Work and Caring*. Routledge and Kegan Paul, 1983.

Forbes, Dorothy et al. "'Her World Gets Smaller and Smaller with Nothing to Look Forward to': Dimensions of Social Inclusion and Exclusion among Rural Dementia Care Networks." *Online Journal of Rural Nursing and Health Care*, vol. 11, no. 2, 2011, pp. 27-42.

Gahagan, Jacqueline. "Far as I Get is the Clothesline: The Impact of Leisure on Women's Health and Unpaid Caregiving Experiences in

Nova Scotia, Canada." *Health Care for Women International*, vol. 28, no.1, 2007, pp. 47-68.

Graham, Hilary. "Caring: A Labour of Love." *A Labour of Love Women, Work and Caring*, edited by J. Finch and D. Groves, Routledge and Kegan Paul, 1983, pp. 13-30.

Grant, Karen, et al., editors. *Caring For/ Caring About Women, Home Care and Unpaid Caregiving*. Garamond Press, 2004.

Gray, Benjamin, et al. "Patterns of Exclusion of Carers for People with Mental Health Problems—the Perspectives of Professionals." *Journal of Social Work Practice*, vol. 41, no. 4, 2010, pp.475-492.

Gröne, Oliver, and Mila Garcia-Barbero. "Integrated Care: A Position Paper of the WHO European Office for Integrated Health Services." *International Journal of Integrated Care*, vol. 1, no. 2, 2001, pp. 1-10.

Holroyd, Eleanor. "Hong Kong Chinese Daughters' Intergenerational Caregiving Obligations: A Cultural Model Approach." *Social Science and Medicine*, vol. 53, 2001, pp. 1125-34.

Kahana, Eva, et al. *Family Caregiving Across the Lifespan*. SAGE Publications Inc., 1994.

Katz, Sidney, et al. "Studies of Illness in the Aged. The Index of ADL: A Standardized Measure of Biological and Psychological Function." *Journal of the American Medical Association*, vol. 185, 1963, pp. 914-19.

Keefe, Janice. "Home and Community Care." *Continuing the Care: The Issues and Challenges for Long-term Care*, edited by M. Stephenson and E. Sawyer, CHA Press, 2002, pp. 109-41.

Kehoe MacLeod, Krystal. "Integrated Care Programs for the Delivery of Home Health and Social Care to the Vulnerable Elderly: A Study of Promising Practices." Dissertation. Carleton University, 2017.

Kodner, Dennis, and Cor Spreeuwenberg. "Integrated Care: Meaning, Logic, Applications, and Implications—A Discussion Paper." *International Journal of Integrated Care*, vol. 2, no.4, 2002, pp. 1-6.

Lero, Donna, and Gillian Joseph. *A Systematic Review of the Literature on Combining Work and Eldercare in Canada*. University of Guelph, 2007, www.worklifecanada.ca/cms/resources/files/256/Workand Elder carepaperSEPT19-FinalsenttoHomewood-1.pdf . Accessed 14 May 2019.

Leutz, Walter. "Five Laws for Integrating Medical and Social services: Lessons from the United States and the United Kingdom." *The Milbank Quarterly*, vol. 77, no. 1, 1999, pp. 77-110.

Martin-Matthews, Anne, and Judith Phillips, editors. *Aging and Caring at the Intersection of Work and Home Life,* Psychology Press, Taylor and Francis Group, 2008.

Ory, Marcia, et al. "Prevalence and Impact of Caregiving: A Detailed Comparison between Dementia and Nondementia Caregivers." *The Gerontologist*, vol. 39, 1999, pp. 177-85.

Power, Andrew. *Landscapes of Care: Comparative Perspectives on Family Caregiving.* Ashgate Publishing Limited, 2010.

Raphael, Dennis. *Social Determinants of Health.* Canadian Scholars Press, 2009.

Room, Graham. *Beyond the Threshold: The Measurement and Analysis of Social Exclusion.* The Policy Press, 1995.

Ryan, Assumpta, et al. "Issues in Caregiving for Older People with Intellectual Disabilities and Their Ageing Family Carers: A Review and Commentary." *International Journal of Older People Nursing*, 2013, pp. 217-226.

Scharlach, Andrew, and Amanda Lehning. "Ageing-friendly Communities and Social Inclusion in the United States of America." *Ageing and Society*, vol. 33, 2013, pp. 110-36.

Schuz, Benjamin, et al. "Leisure Time Activities and Mental Health in Informal Dementia Caregivers." *Applied Psychology: Health and Well-being*, vol. 7, no.2, 2015, pp. 230-248.

Sims-Gould, Joanie, et al. "Family Caregiving and Helping at the Intersection of Gender and Kinship: Social Dynamics in the Provision of Care to Older Adults in Canada." *Aging and Caring at the Intersection of Work and Home Life*, edited by A. Martin-Matthews and J. Phillips, Taylor and Francis Group, 2008, pp. 65-83.

Sinha, Maire. *Portrait of Caregivers. Statistics Canada*, 2012. www.statcan.gc.ca/pub/89-652-x/89-652-x2013001-eng.htm . Accessed 14 May 2019.

Stein, Catherine. "'I Owe it to Them': Understanding Felt Obligation toward Parents in Adulthood." *How Caregiving Affects Development: Psychological Implications for Child, Adolescent, and Adult Caregivers,* edited by K. Shifren, American Psychological Association, 2009, pp. 119-45.

Twigg, Julia. "The Body in Social Policy: Mapping a Territory." *Journal of Social Policy,* vol. 31, no. 3, 2002, 421-40.

van Malderen, Lien et al. "The Active Ageing Concept Translated to Residential Long-term Care." *Quality of Life Research,* vol. 22, 2013, pp.929-37.

Williams, Allison. "The Welfare State in Retreat: The Impact of Home-care Restructuring on Women's Labour." *The Commodity of Care: Home Care Reform in Ontario,* edited by P. Leduc Browne, Canadian Centre for Policy Alternatives, 2003, pp. 121-146.

PART IV

Personal Narratives

Chapter 12

The Process of (Un)Deservingness: Gestational Surrogacy and Mental Health

Nancy Sinclair

Introduction

My story, like that of many women in Canada, starts with the strong, irrevocable desire to be a mother, be that a consequence of the motherhood imperative, personal desire, or something in between. Like many, I then became a patient in the world of artificial reproductive technology (ART). It is my experiences as an ART patient—the deep, difficult emotions, and barriers to treatment I have battled within that context— that have motivated me to examine the sociopolitical dynamics influencing my experiences. The following is an examination of my journey through ART as a patient—that is, a service user who fought for some level of autonomy in that treatment while seeking gestational surrogacy.

In 2010, my partner and I entered into the world of ART with the vague label of "unexplained infertility." In retrospect, it was an easy introduction to ART, although it did not seem so at the time; I became pregnant immediately through intrauterine insemination (IUI) and gave birth in 2011. Expecting similar results, we returned to our reproductive specialist (RS) for a sibling journey in 2012. After many failed cycles of treatment, we tried in vitro fertilization (IVF), a more invasive and costly procedure. Though more emotionally and physiologically challenging, I was finally pregnant again—this time with twins! In joy and fear, we gleefully entered an anticipatory world of minivans and tandem nursing. But when I was fifteen weeks pregnant, the trajectory of my pregnancy, our family, and my mental health all changed. Rare complications took hold of the pregnancy; the babies were alive and growing, but the outlook was bleak. Despite the unlikelihood of reaching viability in the pregnancy (twenty-four weeks), we developed a plan of expectant management; I needed to give the babies a chance at life. An imperative act of parenting for me, I chose to protect my children as long as I could. I needed to fight for them. I needed to know them. And I needed to be able to say that I did everything that I could, no matter how the story ended.

The babies, Maggie and Patrick, were born at twenty-five weeks gestation—two beautiful little people who fought this battle with me. Despite medical interventions, a few hours after birth, Maggie died in my arms, enveloped in my love for her. Patrick, luckily, was healthy. He wiggled in his isolette and enjoyed drops of my breast milk. When he was four days old, snuggled up in the warmth of my chest, as I tried to give him a lifetime of love in the short moments we had together, he too died.

Reeling from our losses and anxiety-ridden, we returned to the world of ART seeking bigger and better interventions. What are the ART solutions for a woman with unexplained infertility, high risk pregnancies, and overwhelming grief and anxiety? My solution was gestational surrogacy, which I will discuss below, but the RS refused to support this. The following discussion is an autoethnography centred on my experience in seeking gestational surrogacy as a fertility treatment subsequent to a history of infertility, the neonatal deaths of my twins, the risk of further loss, and the impact on my mental health such a pregnancy and loss may have.

The account of my experience with Ontario-based fertility treatment clinics is the starting point for a critical examination of the process of deservingness and entitlement. Although some fertility treatments are becoming (theoretically) universally available, other treatments continue to be at the discretion of the treating RS. I will propose that the determination of my (un)deservingness was an act of social exclusion. In order to contextualize my discussion, I will first provide an overview of relevant policy and research, before returning to my story and experiences in this system.

It seems imperative to acknowledge my privilege and situate myself as a white, cisgender, heterosexual woman, with access to financial means—all of which influence my access to, and experience within ART, as well as my ability for self-advocacy in that system. Although I believe that the following theoretical and policy discussion has implications for many ART patients, I seek only to represent my own experiences. Other ART patients face different, interlocking challenges and oppressions by nature of their identities and statuses, which while beyond the scope of the current discussion is an important area for further research.

The Motherhood Mandate and Fertility Treatment for Women

The far-reaching and diverse discussions about the motherhood mandate situate motherhood as an essential part of a woman's identity. It is culturally pervasive, and is found in media, arts, and policy (Gotlib; Remennick). Becoming a mother is framed "as something that is essentially in their own best interests as women" (Gotlib 331). We raise women in a culture that emphasizes and promotes the importance of motherhood to the self-actualization of women (Arendell; Gardner; Gotlib; Russo).

The motherhood mandate is essential in a conversation about access to fertility treatment and deservingness because it is the sociopolitical framework within which the decision to seek treatment and the treatment experience exist. When we understand that motherhood is synonymous with womanhood and identity, we can begin to appreciate the importance of successful fertility treatment for women relying on ART. For instance, despite the source of infertility being shared fairly evenly between men and women (McDaniel et al. 171), the onus of fertility tends to be placed on women, both in terms of physical treatments as well as psychological responsibility (Remennick 823). Rosario Cebello et al. note that women feel grief, a sense of dysfunction, and shame regarding their failure to reproduce naturally (499). Arthur Greil identifies themes relating to feelings of defectiveness, alienation from the fertile norm, frustration, hopelessness, and anger, whereas Julia McQuillan et al. found that psychological distress persisted over time among women, seemingly in support of the relevancy of one's identity. These findings demonstrate the importance of infertility for women in particular; it is deeply personal, identity driven, and can cause lasting emotional struggles.

Gestational Surrogacy in Canada

Gestational surrogacy in Canada is regulated by the Assisted Human Reproduction Act (AHRA), which is currently under review. According to this legislation, a woman may consent to carry a pregnancy for the purpose of giving the child to an intended parent (IP) at birth. It should be noted that gestational surrogacy involves carrying a pregnancy in which the fetus is biologically unrelated to the pregnant woman. Despite inclusion in law, surrogacy policies vary between clinics. These policies establish RSs as ultimate gatekeepers, who engage in judgments of deservingness, to which I will return below.

In practice, when an IP and potential gestational surrogate (GS) want to proceed with treatment, the treating clinic will likely require psychological assessment, physiological testing, and independent legal counsel for all involved. Despite surrogacy being altruistic in Canada, the process is costly for the IPs, who typically pay treatment and pregnancy-related expenses. One third-party agency estimates this to cost between $30,000 and $76,000 (Surrogacy in Canada).

Unfortunately, surrogacy is often the topic of sensational news coverage, promoting culturally based assumptions wherein GSs necessarily suffer emotional complications post-pregnancy. Elly Teman astutely contextualizes these assumptions as reflective of the motherhood mandate and good mother imperative; it is assumed and promoted that women should want to produce and parent children, gestational surrogacy contradicts this assumption. This incongruence is questioned in layperson's conversations as well as in research (Teman). Despite assumptions of harm and unnaturalness, research consistently finds that GSs were healthy, assertive, and realistic women who were happy with their decisions to be a GS and felt fulfilled in relinquishing the baby to the IPs. In fact, contrary to what the general public may assume, it is the relationship with the IPs that is most likely to create a negative experience for the GS; the relationship can be a difficult one to navigate, and when it has not been healthy, GSs were more likely to report having had a negative surrogacy experience.

Provider-Patient Power Dynamics and Deservingness

It is pertinent to consider the provider-patient relationship and to pay particular attention to the experience of female patients in the healthcare system. It is widely acknowledged that the provider-patient relationship is necessarily characterized by a power imbalance, wherein the provider is an expert and gatekeeper and the patient is less informed and follows direction (Dickerson and Brennan 196). Suzanne Dickerson and Patricia Brennan identify the following social structures: professional licensing, prescription privileges, and the patriarchal structure of healthcare institutions, which is paired with the authority and prestige that these embody, all of which serve to actualize physicians' power.

By way of exercising power, RSs are engaged in a process of deservingness judgment. This is necessarily reflective of power, as they are in a position to "frame and define the problem, [and have the] power to decide the policies to address it" (Cousins 1252). In examining deservingness, N. T. Feather and Sarah S. Willen each differentiate universal healthcare from personalized healthcare. In the context of universal healthcare, entitlement and universal access to care are presumptions, as determined by policy. The case of personalized healthcare, in contrast, involves the assessment of what an individual has earned or deserves. Susann Huschke observed deservingness in humanitarian healthcare, wherein physicians expected patients to appear, behave, and fill a particular image, and when they did not, they were less likely to receive treatment in the future. In this deservingness-based healthcare system, the power of the medical specialist is pronounced, as their role may include not only the traditional privileges of gatekeeper, policymaker, and care deliverer, but also the power to judge one's deservingness. In addition to the imbalanced relationship in the provider-patient dyad, women are in a specifically precarious position within healthcare (and specifically in the field of obstetrics and gynecology). Gender bias has been documented in the provider-patient relationship, biomedical research, pharmaceutical testing, diagnosis and treatment, and access to care (Andrist; Munsch). Moreover, studies have found that women's complaints are taken less seriously—and are more often attributed to psychological distress—and that women are left waiting in emergency care settings longer than men (Ruiz and Verbrugge). Teresa Ruiz and Lois Verbrugge note that despite the vast evidence of gender bias in medicine, individual practitioners do not believe they enact gender-biased treatment.

The above discussion provides insight into the context within which women, including myself, access treatment through ART clinics. Women are culturally pressured to pursue motherhood and may feel a deep, desperate desire to bear children. In Ontario, at the time in which I was a patient, fertility treatment remained a generally privatized service, in a province wherein most other medical treatments are publically funded. This situation creates a confusing setting that patients must navigate, as it seems reasonable to assume they do not anticipate any other barriers to service. Yet treatments like surrogacy remain difficult to access, as they are made available based upon each ART clinic's and RS's preferences, which brings to light the power dynamics at play when seeking ART in personalized healthcare models. The RSs have the power to establish policies regarding types of treatment and inclusion while also judging patients as deserving of them or not. This power, though problematic for patients, is unsurprising given the history of the provider-patient relationship, particularly in the case of women. It stands to reason, then, that women as patients of ART are in a vulnerable position, as they are without power and are at the risk of difficult emotional experiences; moreover, they must demonstrate their deservingness to the RS and will likely have a history of being overlooked in the system by virtue of their gender.

Autobiography

There are no words to sufficiently describe my grief following the deaths of Maggie and Patrick. It was raw. It was overwhelming. It nearly broke me. Maybe it did break me; I am still unsure. It did break my spirit in that I lost hope. We wanted more children, but I knew that I could not face another death; if the death of another child did not physically kill me, I was unsure that I would not do it myself. It was in this grief and hopelessness that I decided that surrogacy was my only solution, but my plan was atypical. I was looking for a GS who would agree to carry a pregnancy for us, while I tried the same. I imagined this as an experiment with my body as we tested the high risk nature of a pregnancy, with hope housed externally. I simply knew that I could not face the anxiety of experimenting with my body in pregnancy, and the potential loss, without someone else offering tangible hope. I needed the promise of a happier ending.

My surrogate and I were shocked when the ART clinic denied me surrogacy treatment. I reminded them of our difficult history. I explained that I needed this. It was explained to me that I did not qualify for surrogacy; our reasons did not suffice. The clinic had strict surrogacy guidelines within which I did not fall. They argued that the GS must be protected from the potential harms of surrogacy and that in my case, these risks did not outweigh my needs. Did I not deserve surrogacy as a fertility treatment? What were they implying about the GS and me, and our abilities to make decisions about our bodies?

Deservingness, Power Imbalances, and Stigma in Action

As noted above, Ontario ART clinics offer services in a confusing space between a universal healthcare system and one in which most patients must pay for services required. The clinic and its clinicians maintain the decision-making role about who can access surrogacy as a treatment, among many other powers affecting patients, which creates a difficult system for patients to navigate. I wondered if it was strategically unwise to self-advocate and risk being judged as undeserving. There is a fine line to walk between being seen as a deserving and passive patient, and an autonomous service user capable of self-advocacy, who may be judged as less deserving. How do I best represent myself and my body, and please the gatekeeper? When I contacted the ART clinic, I presumed that I would be treated as requested. I believed that since I had experienced infertility and undue hardship, and faced the possibility of a repeated loss, that I must be deserving of gestational surrogacy treatment. Why, then, was I denied this treatment? What was influencing the RSs in their policymaking?

Returning to the theme of power imbalance, it is important to consider that two women (I and the woman who agreed to be a GS) were proposing a treatment using our bodies. This was being done within a system that disadvantages women historically, as women's concerns have historically been overlooked and their ability to make decisions about their bodies dismissed (Munsch; Ruiz and Verburgee). The RSs' actions reveal their belief that they know better than a woman herself, about her body and abilities, which is a quintessential example of paternalism within a patriarchal system. She, the GS, was protected from herself. Liezl van Zyl and Anton van Neikerk note that prohibition of surrogacy is tantamount to the violation of a woman's right to self-determination and reinforces the misconception that women "are incapable of full rational agency" (404). The argument can be made that the RS's decision regarding when a GS and IP deserve such treatment may be serving to reinforce provider-patient power dynamics (Cousins; Willen).

If not a conscious gender bias, then what motivates the RS to deny the treatment? The motherhood mandate may provide some insight. Consider the implications of a woman agreeing to be a GS; it is unnatural and incongruent with the assumptions of the motherhood mandate. Women are expected to want to be pregnant, to give birth, and to love and parent the child birthed. To be separated from the child is framed as a tragedy. If a woman agrees to be a surrogate, she is seen as naïve for not understanding how she will grieve or as uncaring because she does not want the child. The inherent assumption that the ART clinic made regarding emotional risk of a GS is reflective of the motherhood mandate. However, as Teman emphasizes, numerous studies have concluded that women have positive experiences bearing children for others. The ART clinic seems to have an outdated and a biased view of women, leading to misinformed policies geared to protect women (from themselves). If the policies actually reflected the research, as Teman suggests, then the clinics may focus on the IP-GS relationship to increase the likelihood of a positive experience for the GS instead.

There also seems to be a double-edged sword with the motherhood mandate. If the GS needs protection, is she being protected only from herself or also from the IPs? The rhetoric of exploitation of GSs is strong in conversations about surrogacy, which vilifies the IP as the exploiters. Here, the IP is desperate for a child as she seeks to confirm her identity as a woman through motherhood. The motherhood mandate is used to frame the IP as a desperate villain and the GS as either naïve or coldhearted, but certainly unnatural.

Outside of the paternalistic arguments presented by the clinic, our case simply did not qualify for its program. My body's ability to carry a pregnancy was not poor enough to risk the wellbeing of a GS. My plight was twofold: risk of complications reoccurring and my mental health. I do not intend to explore the medical literature relating to risk of reoccurrence here; there was a fundamental disagreement in terms of tolerance of risk levels between the RS and me. Beyond my risk levels, I wanted a surrogate for my mental health. I believed that my grief and anxiety were too overwhelming to manage a pregnancy on my own, and there was a woman in my life who agreed and was willing to support me as a GS. Not unlike the argument above about gender bias, I suggest that the clinic's decision to dismiss this argument was reflective of stigma relating to mental illness. The Mental Health Commission of Canada and the Canadian Alliance on Mental Illnesses and Mental Health note that mental health is highly stigmatized, and that the stigma is often worse than the illness itself. This begs the question: how was my own mental health interpreted by the RS? I would argue that mental health is not considered a real illness in the same way infertility is, and, as such, it was judged to be undeserving of treatment. That is to say, that despite my emotional distress, I was refused surrogacy treatment because I did not fit the criteria of illness the clinic had established. The criteria exclusively identified physical reasons for surrogacy. The failure to consider mental health as a reason for surrogacy treatment speaks to the invisibility of mental health and emotional suffering; they are insufficient and undeserving reasons to access treatment. The exclusion from treatment is the enactment of RSs' power as policymakers to maintain social structures and to exclude certain groups of people from treatment. Working within a system that allows for such paternalism, the RSs decided that my measurement of emotional suffering was neither accurate nor worth exploration and treatment. Yet the (mis)understanding of mental health may have led to the consideration that if I am suffering so much that I require surrogacy treatment, then perhaps my capacity to parent must be questioned altogether. Regardless of their specific reason, the RSs, as professionals, thought they knew what was best for me, as a woman and patient, and determined me undeserving—a decision inherently shaped by their own biases and privileges.

Conclusions: Social Exclusion and a Way Forwards

I have examined my experience of being denied surrogacy at a fertility treatment in the context of universal-individualized healthcare and the inherent provider-patient power dynamics that exist therein. These dynamics manifest themselves in the practices and policies of patriarchy and paternalism, which are deeply rooted in archaic notions of women framed by the motherhood mandate. Through denying me treatment, the ART clinic was engaged in an act of social exclusion. My journey in infertility and parenting has occurred within a cultural system that strongly encourages women to have children and offers fertility treatment to achieve this goal. Indeed, in 2015, Ontario became the only Canadian province to provide publically funded fertility treatments (Blackwell), while other provinces had cancelled similar programs or were providing support through taxes.

For me, though, RSs found that I was undeserving; they found me wanting and perhaps a villain. And I was left emotionally unwell without the opportunity to continue with a fertility treatment plan with which I was comfortable. Although the ART clinic assessed risk based upon uninformed notions of women and surrogacy, they ignored the emotional risk to me as a patient. Not only do I want to suggest that this was a form of social exclusion from motherhood itself, but it was also an act of structural social exclusion on the basis of mental illness. It is an example of mental illness being overlooked and undervalued.

Although ART clinicians likely work with the best of intentions, I would suggest that there are opportunities for improvement. Surrogacy is a legal and supported means of having children in Ontario, and the level of deservingness judgment must be challenged; the system, one that affects women disproportionately, must be transformed. One can hope that the inclusion of fertility treatments, including surrogacy, in the public healthcare system may serve to do just this, as this inclusion positions fertility treatment in the world of publically funded and medically necessary treatments, rather than that of individual choice and elective procedures. This has the potential to shift power in provider-patient relationships, remove barriers to treatment, and provide support in childbearing for women. Regardless of new health policy changes, the power imbalances that allow RSs to judge deservingness and that maintain problematic social structures will take time to change. Linda Andrist has provided a feminist model for women's healthcare, which is also applicable to fertility centres. The model highlights symmetry in the provider-patient relationship as its first tenet, and it suggests changes in the use of space, time, records, language, and personal titles to challenge traditionally hierarchal relationships. It is paramount that RSs recognize their power in contrast to the vulnerability (emotionally and physically) of female patients and that they direct their practice in such a way as to promote the patients' empowerment. The hierarchy must be challenged and women's stories and emotions must become part of the treatment model. Fertility clinics, of all places, must begin to trust that the women they serve know their bodies and know their limits.

The GS and I knew our bodies, our capacities, and our needs. Eventually, we found a clinic that respected us. In March 2015, we welcomed two new children into our family, one carried by me and the other by the GS. Our GS-born daughter, in part, bears the name Hope, a testament to our journey and futures.

Works Cited

Andrist, Linda. "A Feminist Model for Women's Health Care." *Nursing Inquiry*, vol. 4, no. 4, 1997, pp. 268-74.

Arendell, Terry. "Conceiving and Investigating Motherhood: The Decade's Scholarship." *Journal of Marriage and Family*, vol. 62, no. 4, 2000, pp. 1192-1207.

Blackwell, Tom. "Huge Demand for IVF Treatment in Ontario— Where It's Funded —Has Wait Lists Stretching to 2018." *National Post*, 20 May 2015, nationalpost.com/health/huge-demand-for-ivf-treatment-in-ontario-where-its-fully-funded-has-wait-lists-stretching-to-2018. Accessed 14 May 2019.

Cebello, Rosario, et al. "Silent and Infertile: An Intersectional Analysis of the Experiences of Socioeconomically Diverse African American Women with Infertility." *Psychology of Women Quarterly*, vol. 39, no. 4, 2015, pp. 497-511.

Cousins, Linwood. "Deservingness, Children in Poverty, and Collective Well Being." *Children and Youth Services Review*, vol. 35, no. 8, 2013, 1252-59.

Dickerson, Suzanne Steffan, and Patricia Flatley Brennan. "The Internet as a Catalyst for Shifting Power in Provider-Patient Relationships." *Nursing Outlook*, vol. 50, no. 5, pp. 195-203.

Feather, N. T. "Deservingness and Emotions: Applying the Structural Model of Deservingness to the Analysis of Affective Reactions to Outcomes." *European Review of Social Psychology*, vol. 17, no. 1, 2006, pp. 38-73.

Gardner, Renee. "Subverting Patriarchy with Vulnerability: Dismantling the Motherhood Mandate in Toni Morrison's *Beloved*." *Women's Studies*, no. 45, no. 3, 2016, pp. 203-14.

Gotlib, Anna. "But You Would Be the Best Mother", Unwomen, Counterstories, and the Motherhood Mandate." *Bioethical Inquiry*, vol. 13, no. 2, 2016, pp. 327-47.

Greil, Arthur. "Infertility and Psychological Distress: A Critical Review of the Literature." *Social Science & Medicine*, vol. 45, no. 11, 1997, pp. 1679-1704.

Huschke, Susann. "Performing Deservingness: Humanitarian Health Care Provision for Migrants in Germany." *Social Science & Medicine*, vol. 120, 2014, pp. 352-59.

McDaniel, Susan, et al. *Medical Family Therapy and Integrated Care.* American Psychological Association, 2014.

Mental Health Commission of Canada. "Stigma and Discrimination." *Mental Health Commission of Canada*, 2016, www.mentalhealth commission.ca/English/what-we-do/stigma-and-discrimination. Accessed 14 May 2019.

McQuillan, Julia, et al. "Frustrated Fertility: Infertility and Psychological Distress among Women." *Journal of Marriage and Family*, vol. 65, no. 4, 2003, pp. 1007-18.

Munch, Shari. "The Women's Health Movement: Making Policy 1970-1995." *Social Work in Health Care*, vol. 43, no. 1, 2006, pp. 17-32.

Remennick, Larissa. "Childless in the Land of Imperative Motherhood: Stigma and Coping Among Infertile Israeli Women." *Sex Roles*, vol. 43, no. 11, 2000, pp. 821-41.

Ruiz, M. Teresa, and Lois M Verbrugge. "A Two Way View of Gender Bias in Medicine." *Journal of Epidemiology and Community Health*, vol. 51, 1997, pp. 106-19.

Russo, Nancy F. "Overview: Sex Roles, Fertility and the Motherhood Mandate." *Psychology of Women Quarterly*, vol. 4, no. 1, 1979, pp. 7-15.

Surrogacy in Canada Online (SCO). "Cost of Surrogacy." *Surrogacy in Canada Online*, surrogacy.ca/intended-parents/cost-of-surrogacy. html. Accessed 14 May 2019.

Teman, Elly. "The Social Construction of Surrogacy Research: An Anthropological Critique of the Psychosocial Scholarship on Surrogate Motherhood." *Social Science and Medicine*, vol. 67, no. 7, 2008, pp. 1104-12.

Willen, Sarah S. "How Is Health-Related "Deservingness" Reckoned? Perspectives From Un-authorized Immigrants in Tel Aviv." *Social Science & Medicine*, vol 74, 2012, pp. 812-21.

van Zyl, Liezl, and Anton van Niekerk. "Interpretations, Perspectives and Intentions in Surrogate Motherhood." *Journal of Medical Ethics*, vol. 26, 2000, 404-09.

Chapter 13

Multiple Jeopardies and Liminality in Low-Income Lone Mothering: Experiencing and Resisting Social Exclusion

Amber Gazso and Jason Webb

Lone mothers with low income experience the daily challenges of achieving and maintaining instrumental (e.g., food, shelter, and clothing) and expressive (e.g., affection and intimacy) support for themselves and their dependents in order to survive. They perform mothering amid other personal, social, and structural barriers—or "multiple jeopardies"—such as poor health, unaffordable daycare, limited job prospects, social stigma, and race-based discrimination. As well, they mother in liminal states or spaces of being—that is, mothering with low income is often a transient and ambiguous social status. It is performed in between complete destitution and income security, or homelessness and adequate housing, or poor health and good health.

These everyday realities exacerbate mothers' feelings of social exclusion, as they often feel disconnected from others who have greater economic and social means, their communities, and even society (Sen). Our chapter investigates whether or not this is the case. Drawing on qualitative interviews with thirty lone and racially diverse mothers,[1] we unpack the relationship between social support, multiple barriers, and liminality. We critically explore whether and how mothers' social exclusion is created by multiple jeopardies and their experience of simultaneous liminal states and spaces. We are particularly curious about whether mothers' social support networks can mitigate the perception of social exclusion.

Our analytic approach in this chapter is to juxtapose our theorizing of low-income mothers' social exclusion with mothers' own experiences, or their stories about their lives. We weave mothers' voices into our theoretical musings and, for reasons of space, highlight the voices of only select mothers to illustrate the common themes across their stories.[2] In essence, we seek to establish the coherence, or lack thereof, that materializes between theorizing about mothers' lives as socially excluded and examining mothers' stories about their lives as actually lived. Through our analysis, we conclude that lone mothers' burden of creating social support networks—and, therefore, their family's social inclusion—is severely constrained, especially among racialized mothers, despite the presence of social supports,

Multiple Jeopardies, Liminality, and Social Exclusion

In Canada, lone mother families are the most impoverished of all families (Statistics Canada, "National Household Survey"). According to data from the Canadian income survey, lone mother families had the lowest income after tax in 2013. In the same year, 16.5 percent of Canadian children under the age of seventeen lived in low-income households; 12.8 percent of children in two-parent families lived in low-income households compared to 42.6 percent of children in lone-mother families (Statistics Canada, "Canadian Income Survey").[3] Among lone mother families, poverty is not equally experienced. Racialized, immigrant, and Indigenous mothers are more likely to experience greater poverty than Caucasian mothers (2). Meta research supports this; some mothers may experience a higher degree of economic vulnerability, including Somali, Haitian, Latin American, and Southeast Asian mothers and mothers from various Indigenous groups (38). Immigrant women experience low income to a greater extent than immigrant men, and racialized immigrant women are among the poorest of the poor (National Council of Welfare).

Lone mothers' poverty stems from and is exacerbated by multiple jeopardies. In Black feminist thought, the notion of jeopardies captures how Black women experience both racism and sexism in society (double jeopardy), which can additionally interlock with other oppressions in multiplicative relationships (King 46-47). Although race is usually emphasized, the notion of jeopardies has been extended in feminist sociology more broadly to capture a plethora of oppressions. For example, the concept of double jeopardy has been used to capture women's experiences of low income and low social support (Fingerman et al. 860) and to highlight racialized children's experiences of racism and victimization (Widom et al. 43). Multiple jeopardies continue to inform research that ranges in emphasis—from how Indigenous women experience multiple jeopardies on the basis of race, ethnicity (identity as an Indigenous woman), and gender (Gerber, 122) to how mental health intersects with race, class, and gender to produce mental health inequalities (Rosenfield, 1791).

In our study, lone mothers working for low wages or on social assistance, and especially those racialized or Indigenous, are in a position of "multiple jeopardy." Of the thirty mothers, twenty-three were on Ontario Works[4] (hereafter OW); six were working but for just above poverty-level wages, and one was undocumented and had no source of income. Mothers in our study experienced two marginal statuses: they were women and in a position of low income. Lone mothers who do not have the human capital (i.e., education, work experience, and skills) to garner a job with reasonable pay and benefits and do not have the support of the other parent of their children[5] are at a disadvantage. Indeed, Diana Pearce coined the term the "feminization of poverty" to capture women's unequal experiences of low income comparative to men's. When asked if she had enough to live, Hope's[6] (age twenty-six, two children, Caucasian) response was common across all mothers receiving OW.

> Hope: No. I struggle, I go to food banks. I do. It's usually the food banks or my grandma will help me out here and there, if I need ... the food bank that I go to has a church thing that has clothes, kids' clothes, and stuff, so I usually check through there.

Perhaps the most telling example of the economic constraints lone mothers may face is in terms of housing. Not all mothers received subsidized housing, so many had to pay full market rent. In such cases, their monthly allowance from OW went directly to rent, and all other household and everyday life costs (e.g., bills, groceries, and clothing) were paid for through the support they received from Child Benefits. These amounts, however, were deducted from the total amount mothers received in OW—thus, maintaining mothers' receipt of poverty-level incomes. Paying full market rent put lone mothers on OW at an extreme economic disadvantage, as there is no money left over for those activities that can create self-fulfillment or feelings of inclusion for mothers or their children, such as recreation and leisure time.

When the feminization of poverty concept was further unpacked in our study, it became obvious that there were racial differences in mothers' poverty (see also Gazso and Waldron 133-34). Mothers in our study were Indigenous, Caucasian, or were additionally diverse in their racial and ethnic backgrounds (i.e., Black Caribbean mothers, Chinese mothers, and mixed-race mothers). Notably, of the thirty mothers interviewed, only nine were Caucasian.

Indigenous mothers experienced struggling each month in the same manner as other non-Indigenous mothers. Alyssa (age twenty-five, one child, Indigenous) explained that although OW can cover rent and that Child Benefits are necessary, there were still needs she could not meet:

> They don't give you, now they don't give you any money for your children; they just give you money for yourself.... I think it should be a little bit more cause it's hard to even like eat healthy cause like ... we really want fresh fruits and stuff, but in that time period where you don't have any money, you can't like get like your fresh vegetables and stuff like that.

However, the income insecurity experienced by Indigenous lone mothers is further textured by histories of cultural genocide (e.g. residential schools) and ongoing colonization and racial injustice. For example, all seven Indigenous mothers interviewed maintained strong ties with their nations and the reserve land upon which they grew up. The geographic displacement of Indigenous peoples through colonial racism has had a lasting impact on their contemporary family relations. Efforts to preserve cultural identities and social belonging can create mothers' greater economic marginalization because of the sheer cost of traveling back and forth to the reserve, sometimes hundreds of kilometers away. Barb (age fifty-four, two children, Indigenous), like Alyssa and others, explained how the combination of OW and Child Benefits was simply not enough to raise her two children under age twelve. She additionally discussed how a family member's emergency on reserve meant that she had to make sacrifices that exacerbated her already compromised financial situation:

> Like financially, yes, of course ... like if emergency up north, like my, ah, my aunt who raised me, I had to go back and forth up north.... And I had to find somebody here to come and stay here ... stay with Jason and while I had to go up north to cause she was dying of cancer. Yeah, there was a really, going back and forth like Greyhound and car rentals. Yeah, it was, really stressful ... so that's where you know the most stressful time and things would happen yeah.... I always have to borrow during the month. There's my aunt I just borrow, and then their dad that I have to borrow money from all the time, and sometimes my friends and yeah in the city, and yeah, cousins.

Health challenges can also jeopardize the financial and social wellbeing of lone mothers. The cost of prescription drugs to treat physical or mental health conditions is expensive and more than likely not covered under OW. Many lone mothers and even their children will face risks of greater health problems in the future simply because they cannot afford treatment. Margaret was living with her twenty-year-old daughter, who was also a lone mother, when she was interviewed. She was forty-six, Caucasian, and was working part time stocking shelves at a local department store. Her lone mother status and her low income intersected to create a situation in which she could not afford her required medication:

> Yeah, like right, so I just had to go see a specialist ... so now he's telling me so they found three different things so I have to make an appointment and go back in, and he knows I have to take this cocktail of stuff. And I'm like, how the hell am I going to? Like this is interesting; let's see what happens now, you know. Like I don't know how to do it, and I don't think OW helps you with ... just a drug card.... Yeah, so it's cost.

Although her daughter lived with her and helped out with rent, this did little to change her situation. Referencing making ends meet, Margaret further illustrated how the financial impact of intersecting jeopardies can be prolonged:

Yeah, she gives me $200 a month, and then I asked her like if there's any times where, you know, she feels like she can have a little extra or something, cause ... that might cover one bill or something right, cause I pay all the utilities and everything here. So, as for ends meeting, they haven't met in years. They forget what each other looks like.

The health conditions of children can also place lone mothers in a deeper position of economic marginalization. Cadence's (thirty-three, three children, mixed-race) eighteen-month old daughter had a serious health condition for which she could not afford to treat on her monthly income from the state. As she imagined her future, she speculated she would see little relief in financially providing for her daughter's health, especially given her likelihood of only qualifying for insecure, low-wage work:

Prescriptions ... And this isn't covered by welfare and this isn't covered. And you know, and it's not like every job has benefits. And you have to actually go find a job that has benefits so I can maintain my daughter's health. And that's not, I'm not happy with that ... I use whatever money I have.... Yeah, I have no choice.

Mothers' experiences of multiple jeopardies—which are experiences of several oppressions that interlock with their low-income status—connect to their experiences of social exclusion. Amartya Sen argues that poverty engenders multiple, intersecting deprivations that fundamentally diminish citizens' capacity to be active political subjects in civil society and instead promotes their social exclusion (5). In his understanding, social exclusion can be caused by material deprivation, in which those with low income lack not only the necessary resources to sustain a household but also the means to achieve upward financial mobility (3). Clearly, these stories of lone mothers demonstrate how their experiences of multiple jeopardies inhibit their accumulation of financial resources and, thus, contribute to their being socially excluded.

Sen also defines relational deprivation as a subtle yet endemic characteristic of social exclusion; low-income persons can be excluded from normative social relations, either within their own community or segments of civil society (7). They may experience an eroded "status in the public realm and feeling of public worthiness" (Caragata 167). Specific examples of relational deprivation are apparent in popular "poor-bashing" rhetoric, such as the public's vitriol towards racialized single mothers on income assistance programs (Swanson 23, 90-91). More than this, stigmatizing rhetoric towards racialized lone mothers is an example of how mothers' multiple minority statuses are perceived by others. Multiple jeopardies are further linked to relational deprivation through mothers' past, current, or future participation in the labour market. Of the six mothers engaged in paid work, all had low-wage jobs. For such mothers as Cadence, who anticipate future work, they will enter into a labour market characterized by unequal hiring and pay for women, especially racialized women (Galabuzi 100-103, 109-114). For Sen, material and relational dimensions of social exclusion function in concert to produce capability deprivation (8). That multiple jeopardies create capability deprivation is illustrated by the limits on choice inherent in mothers' experiences on OW. As Cadence explained, she has limited capability to afford her child's medication. Her choice was to pay for the medication by whatever means she had, including becoming indebted to others or creating personal debt via credit. Thus, the social consequences of poverty compromise an individuals' capacity to fully actualize a meaningful life vis-à-vis their embedded position within private and civil networks.

In our view, an understanding of lone mothers' experiences of multiple jeopardies and their linkages to deprivation—and thus social exclusion—can be further buttressed by the concept of liminality. Liminality, an anthropological concept developed by Victor Turner, refers to the period of transition from one status to another (97). Turner defines liminality as a space or moment or "statelessness" in which people reside in the interstices of civil society during which time they wait—or take decisive action— until they can be integrated back into a community. For Turner, "liminal entities are neither here nor there; they are betwixt and between the positions assigned and arrayed by law, custom, convention, and ceremonial" (95). Liminal individuals are those who have their social status removed and exist outside and beyond normative communities and are, therefore, susceptible to external coercion from authoritative actors. Kim Hopper further explains the core features of liminality: "suspension of the rule of the commonplace; intermingling with unfamiliar others in strange settings, often mobile circumstances; and a heightened sense of uncertainty, of things being unfinished and in process" (20). Moreover, liminality relates to the relationship between the political and social transformations in a national political economy that contextualizes the life chances for low-income and otherwise marginalized women in Canadian society (Leginski 1-3). The transition from one social and political order to another is not delineated in an evident fashion; instead, societal transformation occurs in a continuous state of transitionality.

Considering the lone mothers in our study, we understand them as occupying several transitory, ambiguous, or liminal states and/or spaces. We see mothers' experiences of one or more jeopardies as placing them in transitionary phases (on the verge of self-transformation) and requiring their negotiation of their identities in "borderlands." Specifically, mothers are in between complete destitution and income security, homelessness and adequate housing, or poor health and good health. We extend this conceptualization of liminality to additionally consider mothers' subjective perceptions of liminal existence. In essence, we see mothers' liminality as inviting societal stigma and self-stigmatization or internalized oppression.

Mothers told stories of social policy rules and regulations that created their transitory states of being. By their very placement in social policy eligibility categories (e.g., "sponsored" via immigration policy; "persons with multiple barriers" [and so unemployable] via OW), mothers' liminal states were created by policy. Jayla—who is a Black and from the Caribbean and is an eighteen-year-old mother of an infant son—was sponsored to Canada by her father. Immigration policy welcomed her to Canada but conditionally, as she was prohibited from drawing additional support (i.e., social assistance) for raising her child. As she explained it, "No, I can't go on welfare because my dad sponsored me here. So if I do, he would have to pay back the money." Jayla's social rights of citizenship, including belonging, were not denied, but they did not equal those of other mothers in her situation either. The circumvention of her rights to support while experiencing low income illustrates that she has become a liminal person in the discourse of immigration policy. As a racialized lone mother, Jayla's need for OW would be further suspect because of public suspicion about racialized immigrant women's dependence on the state (Carrier and Mitchell).

Cadence, whom we introduced earlier, discussed how being on OW places mothers in a position of conditional entitlement; some supports were covered and others were not. Her experience of "borders" drawn around her social rights while on OW was a common one with other mothers too. Such policy regulation of social rights maintains their poverty and keeps them far away from a reasonable standard of living. Sheila—who was thirty-one, with three children, and had immigrated to Canada from Iran— described policy rules and, implicitly, how such liminal space was created:

> Sheila: The caseworker is just a worker, and she follows the rules, I know the rule is there; she is a nice lady, but the rule is there. Do you understand what I mean?
>
> Interviewer: Yes, I do.
>
> Sheila: That's what I mean. I liked her a lot, but she said "you cannot go over $850" [in monthly allowance from OW]. And I said, "I'm sorry that's the rule." So I don't have a problem with her. The problem was the rules.

Darlene immigrated to Canada from Ecuador with her parents when she was a child. She was thirty-one, with three children. She further explained how the effects of the liminal spaces circumscribed by policy were felt by her: "When you are on that [OW], you are only qualified until a certain time. Like, there's a level of things that you can qualify for. You know what I mean? And the other things, "oh no, you can't because you're in here [on OW]." You can't, you know what I mean?"

Some lone mothers interviewed experienced a physical space of liminality between their own home and the street or a shelter. These mothers lived in subsidized housing that was received conditional on their participation in a community rehousing program. In order to qualify for the program, mothers had to have experienced domestic violence and be referred through the family shelter system. Beyond housing, the program provided access to OW, education, and other programs to support daily living, with the goal of helping women exit OW and enter into paid work. In this liminal place, these mothers could feel highly scrutinized and their past choices subject to stigma. Kyla, who was twenty-five, Caucasian, and with one child, discussed how her liminal existence was linked to current and future relational deprivation and, thus, social exclusion.

> Kyla: But unfortunately with all of that I got good support but they're going to be ending because I'm turning twenty-five.
>
> Interviewer: And then what happens when you turn twenty-five? You are almost excluded from a lot of the supports aren't you?
>
> Kyla: Its ... my arm is cut. The umbilical court is cut. That's it! Cut! Like I can still contact the worker and people that I do know down there, but they really can't. Like I can't go in the establishments. I can't enter. I'm beyond the age.

To summarize, lone mothers' experiences are suggestive of how multiple jeopardies and liminality are connected to their social exclusion, whether they spoke of this directly or it can be inferred from their stories. Poverty intersected with racialization and other oppressions to shape lone mothers' economic and social experiences of their communities in ways different from those who earn reasonable middle-class incomes. Social policies, including OW and immigration policy, have the potential to draw mothers into liminal spaces that limit their autonomy and, therefore, create opportunities for them to be socially excluded.

Other research, however, shows that lone mothers experiencing low income develop multiple coping strategies to meet their children's food, shelter, and clothing needs. Reciprocal exchanges of instrumental (e.g., physical aid, financial assistance, and material goods) and expressive support (e.g., guidance and affection) from the state or community organizations is common (Gazso, Waldron and McDaniel, 9; Gazso and McDaniel 392). The extent to which these social supports can mitigate social exclusion and suggest inclusion is the focus of our next section.

Social Support Networks: Mitigating Social Exclusion?

The lone mothers we interviewed gave and received supports from family and friends, which included the following: caregiving, entertainment, or recreation for their children; emotional affection; material items such as clothing, furniture, or money; child support payments; and translation. From community agencies, mothers received the same kinds of support with the exclusion of child support payments, but they did receive reciprocate support in the form of their volunteering. Finally, in terms of formal, government support, mothers could receive emotional support from caseworkers as well as instrumental (e.g., financial) support facilitated through social policies, such as social assistance, Child Benefits, and housing subsidies (Gazso et al. 9). The degree to which each lone mother accessed all of these supports, however, was an important question. Ecomaps[7] for each lone mother revealed that not all shared the same sources of support or considered supports to be strong or plentiful in the same way. Here, we refer to the support mothers received, which we have already introduced, and further integrate new examples where appropriate.

Lone mothers' receipt and/or exchange of support can invite their feelings of belonging and thus, their feelings of being socially included. Indeed, mothers are not just recipients of instrumental support; they can also give time and energy back to their respective communities. Darlene, for example, volunteered at a local organization in support of immigrant families. She provided English to Spanish language translation assistance to non-English speaking persons. Among other mothers, childcare was commonly exchanged among friends and family.

The size of the mothers' support networks did not seem to easily connect to their experiences of inclusion or exclusion. That is, it was not commonly the case that a large network facilitated inclusion. Margaret's Ecomap, for example, revealed a network comprised of ten friends and family, four sources of community support, and two sources of government support. But in her words, "I'm a real loner, like I'm a loner to a fault, like it's not good; I'm alone too much. Like I'm alone, if I'm not at work, I'm at home, and probably if I'm home, I'm in my room. I don't know where I developed this habit. I just hibernate. So I spend like all my time alone.

For Jayla and Sheila, the available supports in their communities and from the state could not replace the support they left behind when they immigrated to Canada. As a young woman being sponsored by her father in Canada, Jayla had to decide to leave her mother. It is not surprising that Jayla felt the loss of her mothers' emotional and instrumental support: "My biggest challenge was moving here to Canada without my mom. It was even harder when I had to move out of my sister's house cause I'm not used to staying on my own, but my brothers try to come visit me if I can't go to Brampton to visit them. So it's a lot better now." Sheila participated in the same community rehousing program as Kyla. She, too, occupied that liminal space between a home and a shelter or the street. And when asked about the family or friends that make up her network, she responded: "I have family friends, no extended family, just my two daughters. Me and my two daughters."

For some lone mothers, support relations with the fathers of their children could invite further social exclusion. Support from the fathers of their children was often unpredictable, unreliable, or even undesired. Georgia, who was twenty-five, with three children, from the Caribbean, said the following:

> He's not like you know, there's no set time; sometimes he'll take him for four visits in a row. And then [say] "I'm going to come for him and like not next weekend, the weekend after." And something will come up, and there'll be like a month gap but he'll call ... and he's really good with Keon, but, you know, sometimes when stuff happens, he has to, like, I don't know.... People go through their little things, and I understand that, but at the same time, I get a little bit frustrated cause he's the dad. I would rather Damian [the father] be, you know, in a more structured, not bouncing around.

Darlene implied although while her ex-partner's support financially benefitted her and her sons, she would actually lose a sense of autonomy through receiving it.

Interviewer: Is it too much trouble to take, you know, his help?

Darlene: Yes! Yes, it is. That's the thing: I don't want, tomorrow, for him to be saying "because of me, you know, you have this. Because of me, you're surviving. Because of me." You know what I mean?

Lone mothers' stories of waiting on fathers and of wondering whether their support of their children would materialize can be understood as stories of statelessness. The same can be said for stories of feeling anxious about future support. Kyla spoke further about how when she exits the rehousing program, she would be uncertain if she would be able to access what she needs for herself and her children.

> Kyla: I'm about to die as far as my resources are concerned. I'm seriously seeing the light … take what you can cause after that you're done, you know.
>
> Interviewer: Okay, that's a scary thought. Yeah.
>
> Kyla: I know! Because I have relied on them not just since my kids were born but since literally before they were even thought of. I had just turned sixteen. But I've been working with them [the organization that runs the rehousing program] for almost ten years now, not a consistent basis. But they have always been that place I know I could go to. So it was kind of like that home I had. And now it's going to be gone.

Sen maintains that while deprivations may create social exclusion, social exclusion may exacerbate them (5). Mothers' stories of feeling stigmatized or embarrassed were suggestive of the subjective impact of mothers' jeopardies through their relational deprivation. Margaret recalled how it felt to access supports that were readily available:

> I tried the food bank once. That felt like there's, I don't know. I was just carrying this stigma on my face that day I suppose, you know. But I had a bad experience in there too, like I was choosing from a spot I thought that I was told was okay to choose from so I did. I put it in my buggy and the lady says "well, you can't touch that stuff" and took it out. And I'm like "you know what? Fuck you, excuse me." But I don't even want to be here in the first place. So I was already embarrassed being there. But, you know, like I wanted to get stuff for the kids, right.

Georgia spoke about how she was aware of supports in her community, specifically subsidized childcare, but she was embarrassed to access it. The following quote illustrates how difficult it was for her to visit the local day care centre and apply for subsidized spaces for her children:

> You know, I've always, up until now I was like so embarrassed. Like going there and asking them for subsidy and stuff, like. So every time I make a point to go there, 'oh there's no people in there. I don't want to. But this time I really did. I really want to do something and I figure if they get in, okay. So if I get embarrassed for the first day that I register ... but like there's probably twenty other kids that are in the same boat, you know they're on the subsidy you know.

The perception of stigma associated with lone mothering in low income actually exacerbated relational deprivation for some mothers. Thus, social support networks have the potential to create social inclusion. Yet as mothers' experiences reveal that the quality of the support in the network are more indicative of their actual impact rather than their size.

Contradictions and Conclusions

In this chapter, we drew upon qualitative interviews with mothers to reveal that their social exclusion can be created by their experiences of multiple jeopardies and liminality. We then considered whether social support networks could mitigate social exclusion. Herein, we find contradictions.

Indeed, we can tentatively conclude that, on balance, mothers who create extensive networks of social support are perhaps less socially excluded than other mothers. Yet when we consider how multiple jeopardies and liminality infuse an understanding of mothers' social exclusion, this seems an inadequate and simplistic conclusion. Mothers' liminality can intersect with their gender, class, race, citizenship, and eligibility status to inhibit their social inclusion, as in the case of liminality circumscribed by policy (i.e., Jayla). Other mothers had extensive sources of support, as in Kyla and Darlene, which would suggest their greater likelihood of feeling a sense of social inclusion. Yet even for these mothers, social exclusion was possible in the future, via liminal existence (Kyla) or inhibitions of autonomy (Darlene). Indeed, the outcome of supportive relations is rather more complex when we consider the liminal existence created by some of them.

There is congruence, then, between theorizing lone mothers as socially excluded and the stories of their lives. There is, additionally, much to gain from emphasizing structural inequalities and the workings of multiple jeopardies in mothers' lives and their liminal states and spaces into a theory of social exclusion. From this perspective, we see that lone mothers' burden to create and manage social support networks—and therefore inclusion—is deeply problematic. For example, state agencies increasingly expect poor, racialized women to engage in "volunteerism" in lieu of paid employment—often to maintain their eligibility for income assistance—to demonstrate their civil virtue (Hyatt 205-07). As well, social support networks do not erase the structural injustices of racism, sexism, and the stigmatization of poverty.

There is a compelling need to understand mothering as a collective, social project—one that entails multiple supports and one that profoundly shapes healthy communities for everyone. Broad reaching structural changes to policies, labour markets, and cultural attitudes need to occur to embrace the collectivity of this mothering project. Only then will mothers experience adequate instrumental and expressive supports that can inhibit the experience of multiple jeopardies and liminality and actually facilitate their social inclusion.

Endnotes

1. The interviews with lone mothers we feature in this paper materialized from a larger project that explored how families create social support networks, including formal and informal sources and instrumental and expressive types of support in order to manage low income. Within this larger project, ecomaps were drawn for each participant to visually depict the types and sources of support and relations they relied upon.

2. The qualitative software NVivo 8 was used to analyze mothers' transcripts. Transcripts were coded by first assigning codes to capture key words, ideas, or experiences. We then categorized the codes thematically, with these words, ideas, or experiences organized by a central topic. Some examples of the central topics or themes from which we select interview quotes in this paper include

quality of support, conditional or unconditional support, money and finances, and future challenges.

3. The Canadian income survey defines families as economic families—those groups of persons who share a dwelling and are related to each other through marriage, common law, blood, or adoption.

4. Ontario Works is a means-tested financial and employment assistance program for individuals in need. The Canada Child Benefit is a non-taxable direct transfer of funds for low-income and modest-income parents with children under eighteen years old.

5. The respondents' names were changed for this research.

6. Two of the mothers interviewed defined as lesbian. All other mothers partnered with men who fathered their children and with whom they had a relationship, albeit sometimes a very brief one.

7. Ecomaps are visual diagrams of mothers' informal and formal supports. They note the direction of supports (one way or reciprocal) and their relative strength.

Works Cited

Caragata, Lea. "Lone Mothers: Policy Responses to Build Social Inclusion." *Public Policy for Women: The State, Income Security, and Labour Market Issues*, edited by Marjorie Griffin Cohen and Jane Pulkingham, University of Toronto Press, 2009, pp, 162-83.

Carrier, Tracy, and Jennifer Mitchell. "Immigrants on Social Assistance in Canada: Who Are They and Why Are They There?" *Welfare Reform in Canada: Provincial Social Assistance in Comparative Perspective*, edited by Daniel Béland and Pierre-Marc Daigneault, Oxford University Press, 2015, pp. 305-22.

Fingerman, Karen L., et al. "'I'll Give You the World': Socioeconomic Differences in Parental Support of Adult Children. *Journal of Marriage and Family*, vol. 77, no. 4, 2015, pp. 844-65.

Galabuzi, Grace-Edward. *Canada's Economic Apartheid: The Social Exclusion Racialized Groups in the New Century*. Canadian Scholars' Press, 2006.

Gazso, Amber, et al. "Networks of Social Support to Manage Poverty: More Changeable than Durable." *Journal of Poverty*, vol. 20, no. 4, 2016, pp. 441-63.

Gazso, Amber, and Ingrid Waldron. "Fleshing Out the Racial Undertones of Poverty for Canadian Women and their Families: Re-envisioning a Critical Integrative Approach." *Atlantis: A Women's Studies Journal*, vol. 34, no. 1, 2009, pp. 132-41.

Gazso, Amber, and Susan McDaniel. "Families by Choice and the Management of Low Income through Social Supports." *Journal of Family Issues*, vol. 36, no. 3, 2015, pp. 371-95.

Gerber, Linda. M. "Education, Employment, and Income Polarization among Indigenous Men and Women in Canada." *Canadian Ethnic Studies/Etudes Ethniques Au Canada*, vol. 46, no. 1, 2014, pp. 121-44.

Hopper, Kim. *Reckoning with Homelessness*. Cornell University Press, 2003.

Hyatt, Susan Brin. "From Citizen to Volunteer: Neoliberal Governance and the Erasure of Poverty." *The New Poverty Studies: The Ethnography of Power, Politics, and Impoverished People in the United States*, edited by Judith Goode and Jeff Maskovsky. New York University Press, 2001, pp. 201-235.

Leginski, Walter. "Historical and Contextual Influences on the US Response to Homelessness." *Toward Understanding Homelessness: The 2007 National Symposium on Homeless Research*. Office of Policy Development and Research, 2007, pp. 1.1-1.36.

National Council of Welfare. "Poverty Profile Special Edition: A Snapshot on Racialized Poverty in Canada." *National Council of Welfare Reports*. National Council of Welfare. 2013, www.canada.ca/content/dam/esdc-edsc/migration/documents/eng/communities/reports/poverty_profile/snapshot.pdf. Accessed 15 May 2019.

Pearce, Diana. "The Feminization of Poverty: Women, Work, and Welfare." *Urban and Social Change Review*, vol. 11, 1978, pp. 28-36.

Rosenfield, Sarah. "Triple Jeopardy? Mental Health at the Intersection of Gender, Race, and Class." *Social Science & Medicine*, vol. 74, no. 11, 2012, pp. 1791-1801.

Sen, Amartya. "Social Exclusion: Concept, Application, and Scrutiny." *Asian Development Bank*, Social Development Papers No. 1. 2000, www.adb.org/sites/default/files/publication/29778/social-exclusion.pdf. Accessed 15 May 2019.

Statistics Canada. "National Household Survey, Statistics Canada Catalogue No. 99-014_X2011048." *2011 National Household Survey: Data Tables. Statistics Canada*, 2011, www12.statcan.gc.ca/nhs-enm/2011/dp-pd/. Accessed 15 May 2019.

Statistics Canada. "Canadian Income Survey 2013." *The Daily. Statistics Canada*, 2015, www150.statcan.gc.ca/n1/daily-quotidien/150708/dq150708b-eng.htm. Accessed 15 May 2019.

Swanson, Jean. *Poor-Basing: The Politics of Social Exclusion.* Between the Lines, 2001.

Turner, Victor. *The Ritual Process: Structure and Anti-structure.* Aldine Publishing Co., 1969.

Widom, Cathy Spatz, et al. "Do the Long-Term Consequences of Neglect Differ for Children of Different Races and Ethnic Backgrounds?" *Child Maltreatment,* vol. 18, no. 1, 2013, pp. 42-55.

Chapter 14

Assumed Assumptions

Rae Griffin-Carlson

Identifying as a queer mother as well as a partner and parent of
Anishinaabe people has given me a multitude of unique experiences
in social exclusion. With this insight, I will be sharing a short
creative piece narrating my internal and external observations.

Heteronormativity is at best an uneducated assumption and at worst
a situation I need to explain to my clever three-year-old when he is
asked about a father who doesn't exist. Stay-at-home parents combat
thoughtlessness airings of "what do you do all day" through superhuman feats of raising real-live people, whom we urge to think of
someone based on their heart and morals, rather than their salaries.
Protecting my family from those who quantify the measure of
Anishinaabe in my children based on skin colour should not be in my
job description.Yet these are some of the thoughts and experiences that
have become common place throughout my day, my community, and
my life. I hope to weave a quilt of images for readers to witness in what
ways I experience social exclusion as a mother.

I stretch
This most peaceful part of my day
Waking beside a child, my child, one of my children
Is it morning Mama he asks
Let's go check the blinds
We meander across the bed
Still warm from our nightly cuddles
And greet the sun with smiles
Do you think Maman and my sister are awake he asks
We listen quietly as to not disturb them should they still be sleeping
But we hear them
We pinball across the room, through the door and down the hallway
Into the master bedroom
The other half of our family lights up when we see them
Four warm, content bodies embrace
We laugh
We cuddle
We stretch

This is how our mornings begin
Perhaps similar to how mornings begin in other households
Some configuration of parent and child
Eager to start the day
It's also the part of the day where it's just us
The outside world is still outside
There are no questions
As our whole truth exists simply
The four of us are unquestionably a family
Why wouldn't we be?

We start the morning off reading a new book from the library
While the books we own have been meticulously screened
To include representation of all families, a variety of gender
representation, race, culture and religion
Books from the library
Chosen by little hands
Aren't always inclusive

And the questions begin

Some outwards, and answerable
Some inwards, and there they will remain
The questions that aren't asked are the most damaging
They fester
They create doubt
They manipulate how young minds grow

The four of us sit down for breakfast
My wife eating quickly as she needs to get going to work
The kids and I taking a bit more time
The littlest imitates her older brother as he sings Pow Wow music
We only have one destination today
Preschool for the oldest
While this preschool was chosen after serious consideration
He still arrives as the only same-sex parent household
The only cisgender boy (at this point) to wear dresses and tights
And on opposite days, hockey jerseys and shorts
We have to invest in defensive language for a three year old
In case his choices of clothing encourage others to question his identity
At his preschool we are lucky
They speak of parents, rather than mommies and daddies
At least they try to
They encourage all children to play with the dolls, cars, kitchen and
art centres
We are welcome to bring books that include examples of our family
As the fifty that are already there do not
We are encouraged to bring literature and share experiences about
our Anishinaabe culture
As we would be the only ones to do so
There is openness, and yet we are still outsiders
And this is a more inclusive school

The littlest and I leave to go to the park
A new park celebrating Canada's 150th birthday
Cheers to settlers
Cheers to the demise of Native peoples

Native Culture
Native Lands
Let's honour this history with a playground
Let the native children climb cartoon-esque totem poles
That should fill their cultural void
Let the white children climb there too
Move over little one, make some space
You'll always be making space

When the littlest and I go out
I don't hear people say
She looks so much like you
The way I do with my son
The opposite true for my wife and daughter
People need to categorize to make sense of others
Phrases of "real mother" replaces "birth mother"
Instead of simply mother
I am her mother as much as his
But head tilts from strangers trying to understand our story
Try to chip away at that truth
Why should strangers feel they deserve to know private details
About our family
Or make assumptions
As a minority
Assumptions aren't something we make of others

Picking the oldest back up from school
We drive home
He sees people walking and assumes their gender
School teaches more than ABCs and 123s
I have to unteach him
We don't assume someone's gender based on their appearance I say
He corrects himself and uses the pronoun they
He reminds me that he has chosen to be a boy
I remind him that he can always change his mind
I know this may seem tedious
Some think this continuous reminding isn't necessary
They don't know

They identify with the body they were born in
Their sexual orientation aligns with ninety percent of the population
They don't need reminding when their reminders are all around them
My children are inundated with heteronormative messaging
Television, radio, literature
Statistics say that my children will be heterosexuals themselves
Regardless, they will always be queer spawn
And thus, members of the LGBTTIQQ2SA community

I love my children
I love teaching them
But sometimes it hurts me how much they need to learn
Some of it from me
But more from the world around them
I can only prepare them for so much
So I grow the community around them as a safety net
We educate ourselves and our allies
And those outside our immediate circle
Why did it become my job to educate others on basic humanity
A friend once noted to me
That it was minorities who always seemed the most compassionate of
other minorities
We know what it feels like to be assumed upon
Overlooked
Judged
Hurt
Hated
And we don't want to be one of the haters

So what do we do
We are slowly working through every children's library book
available to us
And those that aren't available
Requests are put in for their purchase
The library can learn too
We attend cultural gatherings, both of our own and of others
We are always eager to learn more
Inclusion vs. Exclusion

We talk about skin colour
We talk about the role of people of authority, of power
And how sometimes these people need our help to remind them
what's appropriate
We talk about different family models, all equal in their importance
Supporting people's gender identity
No assumptions
We talk about standing up for our friends
And those who don't have anyone standing up for them
Our children are being raised by two strong women
Two mothers who have had to carve out what that means for our family
While it can be exhausting
I know that my children will be stronger for it themselves
They too will be exhausted in their role as educators
But they will be better for it
For they will know

Chapter 15

Woman from Thessaloníki / The Step of the Door

Donna J. Gelagotis Lee

Woman from Thessaloniki

Your prepubescent son
pulls like a kite
at the end of a string.
The Aegean wind
stings your mouth, the
Lésvian sun
at your brow.

Village women fling
glances like spit
into the dirt.
Village soil
boils in the blood.

The gnarled olive trees
have stories to tell.
Their arms
are far reaching.
Their fruit is
bitter.

Cicadas call
on moonlit evenings,
make you cry.
The sun has dried
the tears into paths.

And you are
father and mother
in a land
now foreign to you,
without kerchief or
husband tying you—
only the echoes
of your grandmothers'
mothers, their faces
like moons in the dark.

In the *platía,* a village man
drops in dips and circles as he twists
the white handkerchief
and wanders...

Outside a souvenir shop,
you finger doilies,
hand crocheted.
Do they remind you of
years you spent
threading someone else's
dreams?

Now you watch your son
run with the breeze,
unencumbered,
and wonder...

Description of "Woman from Thessaloníki"

In "Woman from Thessaloníki," a mother, divorced ("And you are / father and mother / in a land / now foreign to you, / without kerchief or / husband tying you"), experiences social exclusion on an island. For this woman traveling with her son, even the weather is harsh: the "wind / stings your mouth," the "sun / at your brow."

What do we learn of the woman from Thessaloníki? What ties her to the land but "the echoes" of her "grandmothers' / mothers"? The land is foreign to her. Cicadas make her cry. "The gnarled olive trees / have stories to tell." Are those the stories of history, culture? She fingers doilies, and the poem questions, "Do they remind you of / years you spent / threading someone else's / dreams?"

Her "prepubescent son / pulls like a kite / at the end of a string." He appears both to seek and to experience, "unencumbered," a sense of freedom. Does the woman's freedom from her husband seem to result in the same "unencumbered" freedom? What are the social interactions of this mother? Are the women's glances flung "like spit / into the dirt" because of social norms?

The poem ends with the woman's contemplation: "Now you watch your son / run with the breeze, / unencumbered, / and wonder..." What is the significance of this ending in relation to her own sense of freedom and the possibilities for her? Does it appear that she has, or will ever gain, the support of others?

The Step of the Door

Over the doorstep: feet, shoes, bodies
on the move—the run of children,
the slow step of grandparents,
deliberate parents, and teens in a hurry
toward hormonal balance. The doorstep
swept daily, clean,
presenting an arch, an altar
to the house. One step in, one out—
home, family life protected
as a sacred right.

The door held a curtain by day.
At night, a woman lifted the curtain
onto a nail, and closed the door
(the lock used only in tourist season,
the lock like a new invention). No
one was locked in or out—no
one was denied.

Women kept the food prepared,
the food of sustainment, of fulfillment.
On the step, you were lifted, the breeze
pulled in by the house, breathed
by the house, exhaled by the house.

Our lives formed
by the breath of the house,
and the sounds of the sea and the constant
current leading us out and back into
the house. The pivot point, the step

of the door that hung on many hinges—
the swinging door
before the swinging moon.
At dawn, the door opens.
Over the doorstep, the first steps
and the last.

Description of "The Step of the Door"

In "The Step of the Door," the mother's role as keeper of the home and home life can restrict her to that space, largely limiting her social interactions to those ("children, / ... grandparents, / deliberate parents, and teens in a hurry") who pass over the "doorstep" and into, or out of, the home. The step of the door separates, and joins, the inside from the outside. We do not learn of a woman's role, if any, outside the home. But within the home, it is important: "Our lives formed / by the breath of the house." As the poem places the woman within the house, the closest she is to the outside is at the "step // of the door": "At night, a woman lifted the curtain / onto a nail, and closed the door." The "step // of the door" is the "pivot point," the door "hung on many hinges." What do those hinges represent? The doorstep is "swept daily, clean, / presenting an arch, an altar / to the house." What, if anything, is sacrificed on this altar, and by whom?

Chapter 16

Teen Pregnancy, Motherhood, and Social Exclusion

Heather Jackson

I was a teen mother and have been a single mother since my daughter was a toddler. Now, I am a thirty-something-year-old mother of a teenager. It has been difficult, and we have had scary times of financial instability, food insecurity, mental health disasters, breakdowns, and general instability. Even through all of that, I know that I am living because I had my daughter when I did. Having her has made my life more positive, and I certainly gained a better understanding of my life and the struggles of the world.

With that, this chapter is about my experience as a teen mother and the social exclusion I have experienced. I will also explore the statistics and consequences of teen pregnancy and will argue that blame is often placed on the individual instead of the large society. However, I do not want this chapter to focus on the negative aspects and consequences of teen pregnancy and parenting. Being a teen parent was very hard and scary, but it was also something I am so glad to have happened to me. Overall, it has been a positive experience, and I cannot imagine my life any other way. To create inclusion for teen parents is to change the narrative of how we talk about teen parents and to provide support and empowerment. That is part of what I will do in this chapter, but inclusion also involves increased access to resources, particularly education.

Becoming pregnant in high school was a trying time. I was born and grew up in North Dakota, a conservative state. My mother and stepfather assumed I would wait until marriage to have sex. That was almost an unspoken rule. There was no comprehensive sex education at school, either. My parents certainly did not tell me anything about condoms, birth control, abortion, or consent. Of course, I, the introverted shy girl who went to punk shows, got pregnant. The girl who hardly dated and had barely just started making out with people got pregnant.

When I started having sex, I was secretly getting birth control and sex tips from friends and my younger sister. My younger sister went on birth control and told me she went to the family planning clinic up the hill from the high school. After I met my baby-daddy, we had sex pretty quickly. He was the first person I had sex with. After using condoms for a short time, I decided to go the family planning clinic for the pill. I took the pill every day after school; I never missed one. But I got pregnant! A month after having sex for the first time and shortly after starting the pill, I got pregnant.

While terrified and in denial, I finally decided to take the pregnancy test. Even though I knew the test would be positive. I took it anyway. And it was positive. I sat there, staring down at the stick, the positive sign, in the bathroom with my sister and her girlfriend at the time. To make the matter more confusing and scary, I was a teenager in high school. My boyfriend at the time, whom I got pregnant by, was also a teen in high school (in fact, a grade lower). We were no longer together when I found out I was pregnant. He had cheated on me and started selling and doing drugs (again) and was eventually dating someone else. However, I called him to tell him about the positive test; he told me he did not want to hear it. So I said fuck off and told him anyway. He said nothing and listened to me freak out, and then hung up the phone.

I hid my pregnancy from everyone. I held in my puke during gym, band, and art class only to run to the bathroom to throw up in the toilet, sometimes puking in the trash bins, as fellow students bustled to their next class. I missed gym class a few times, but I never had to make the class up like we usually had to. Perhaps my gym teacher knew about my pregnancy before me and felt bad.

I thought about and considered adoption and abortion. I did not know how and where to get an abortion or even how to find that information. I looked up adoption agencies and called them. One person at an agency told me to enroll in Medicaid, which I did. I didn't even know about Medicaid until that person told me. I even went to an adoption agency and browsed photos of couples wanting to adopt a child. I remember thinking how much better these parents would be. They were stable and had an education and resources (I assumed). I was the opposite. How could I provide a decent life for the growing fetus inside me? I had a difficult time deciding who would raise my child: strangers who were, maybe, better suited or me? I also had to decide whether it was going to be a closed or open adoption. These were overwhelming choices for me to make at that age. But I also feel these choices would be difficult for anyone at any age. I didn't even know where to look to consider abortion. (There is still only one abortion clinic in North Dakota.)

An important question remains: why did I feel like I was opposite of these parents in the adoption book? Children from all sorts of households can have positive and/or negative outcomes. The outcomes of children in teen and single parent homes are not always as positive as children in homes of coupled and married parents. However, I would that this is not a simple problem of the parent or the individual; it is a societal and structural issue. Furthermore, there are patriarchal assumptions of how families should be, and all of us have to figure out where we fit into that mould. Capitalism and the state can push us away from each other and from our supporting communities. We are shamed for not fitting into various expectations, and we are shamed when we seek the state's support (e.g., social services, welfare, and so on) because we need it to survive. Literally. When we go against all of these expectations, we feel lowly and ashamed. Since I did not fit into these expectations defined by so many institutions, society, and individuals around me, I felt inadequate and an unacceptable parent. That is why the married, more stable couples in the books at the adoption agency seemed better suited to parent my child than I did because that's how I should have been. I should have been married to a man, older, educated, and had a home. However in the end, I kept my baby.

When I gave birth, the hospital staff assumed I was not going to breastfeed and made a lot of judgments about my life. They assumed I was going to choose adoption or foster care. They were judgmental because my baby-daddy had just been arrested the weekend before. His arrest had been published in the paper. No one tried to provide encouragement or empathy. One nurse told me how hard it was to be a single, teen parent. She was a single, former teen mother. The chaplain came in and told me that my baby-daddy was being selfish. My midwife highly encouraged me to put my daughter into foster care for at least a month.

In the end, I left the hospital with a new baby. I moved out of my parents' house while I was pregnant and during senior year, so I had my own apartment. But I needed to figure stuff out, so I moved back in with my mother and stepfather temporarily. During that time, I was negotiating my relationship with my baby-daddy. I desperately wanted to be a family. It felt right; it felt like that's what I should do. He told me he was clean and sober and no longer dating his girlfriend. In fact, he moved out of her apartment and was living with his mother again. However, I was in denial, sad, and so desperate to have a family with him (because I wanted my daughter to have a dad) that I ignored my intuition about him and how I felt the relationship was going to be.

Because my baby-daddy was arrested the weekend before I gave birth for selling drugs, he had court dates to follow up on. He went to jail when my daughter was about four months old. He was sentenced to eighteen months, and all but six were suspended. My daughter and I visited him twice a week, as, luckily, he was in the county jail that was located in the town we lived in. I wrote him letters every day, sent him stamps and cash, and also wrote letters to his judge asking for his early release. He got out about six weeks early and had a difficult time finding work because he had a felony charge.

Our family unit survived until my daughter was four years old. The three of us moved to Minneapolis, and I went to a community college. Our relationship was rocky and unhealthy. He was emotionally manipulative and abusive. He had drug problems. I was passive, had very low self-esteem, and could not stand up for myself. We were two young parents, and it did not work. But being young parents was not the only why the relationship did not work. It did not work because I could not take how he was treating me anymore, and I realized that I did not want my daughter to be around that and think that was okay. I had to break this cycle of abuse, as my mother was in an abusive relationship with my father. Although leaving him was so hard, it was the best decision I made for my daughter and me. I was very calculated about it. He had moved out of the apartment to work on our relationship and have a break, but we were still together. My daughter went to visit my mother for a couple of weeks, so I broke up with him then. He took it hard and would not leave me alone, but I made it through. Somehow.

Almost a year later, I moved back to North Dakota and starting working towards my BA, MA, and MPH. I started counseling sessions, and over the years, it has included a lot of trauma work, group therapy, abstaining from alcohol, eating disorder treatment, assertiveness training, dialectical behavioral therapy, and feminist therapy. It's been a long road but well worth it. My daughter has also been in counselling off and on and has been hospitalized, but we are working through it. We are also very close, and we are stronger today because of being on our own.

My daughter is well into her teens now, and we live in another state that's far from where we think he lives. We have not seen her father since she was eight years old. She has not talked to him on the phone in probably five or six years. We do not even have a phone number for him. She found him on social media at one point and was able to tell him her feelings about him not being engaged with her. He did not hear her because he became very defensive, but at least she had the courage to say something to him, and in the end, it helped her. She did not expect him to change, but she had to tell him it for herself. I do not have a relationship of any kind with him because he is not healthy for me. I tried for a few years after we broke up, but in the end, it was far more negative than positive.

Statistics on Teen Pregnancy and Parenthood and Social Exclusion

Teenage pregnancy is defined as a teenage girl, usually between thirteen and nineteen, becoming pregnant (UNICEF). Teen pregnancy has many negative consequences. Some of these consequences are that teen mothers are less likely to obtain a high school diploma or GED by age thirty, and they can expect to earn approximately $3,500 less annually than others who wait to get pregnant; also, they are more likely to receive financial aid for longer durations, and their children appear to have lower cognitive attainment and behavior issues (Healthy People 2020). The cost of teen parenting on average, per year, is estimated at $9.1 billion in the United States (Hoffman), which includes the cost of birth, public assistance, medical care, and other related costs. The younger the teen mother is the more it costs.

These are serious issues. Yet prevention is placed on the individual, the teen mother, and the social issues surrounding her and her choices. The focus of social exclusion is focused on the pregnant or parenting teen. Social, education, and economic factors are rarely blamed. Furthermore, most research focuses on teen pregnancy and parenting as a problem because of the costs, not because of the social issues surrounding how difficult it is to parent as a teen (Bonell).

Social exclusion and disadvantages are both consequences and contributing factors of teen pregnancy (The Evidence for Policy and Practice Information and Co-ordinating Centre 3). This is important. Teenage parenthood is complicated, and there are various factors that go into a teen getting pregnant, continuing the pregnancy, and the resulting consequences. Teenagers are autonomous and sometimes choose to become pregnant; they do not always know about abortion access, and they may have learned nothing about contraception.

Will teen pregnancy ever go away? For as long as humans have kept records, some mothers have been teenage mothers (Seamark; CDC). Although social and culture norms have changed, it may not be realistic to focus strictly on the prevention of teen pregnancy (Ingelhart and Norris; Cialdini and Trost). This is why I advocate for the social inclusion of teenage mothers. Maris Vinonskis has pointed out that teen pregnancy has declined since 1950s: "The rate of teenage childbearing increased sharply after World War II and reached a peak of 97.3 births per 1000 women ages 15-19 in 1975. After 1957 the rate of teenage fertility declined to 53.7 births per 1000 women ages 15-19 in 1977" (208). And according to the CDC, "In 2014, a total of 249,078 babies were born to women aged 15-19 years, for a birth rate of 24.2 per 1,000 women in this age group. This is another historic low for U.S. teens and a drop of 9% from 2013. Birth rates fell 11% for women aged 15-17 years and 7% for women aged 18-19 years." The current interventions are not failing, yet teen pregnancy is still modelled as an epidemic (Hoffman). Prevention is obviously important (Coreil). And continuing to have access to birth control, abortion, and educational programs to prevent teen pregnancy is also important.

The Rhode Island Alliance is an organization aiming to prevent teen pregnancy, but it also works to empower teens that become pregnant or are already parents. The group points out how teen pregnancy is viewed as a moral failing:

Traditionally, unplanned teen pregnancy has been viewed as a moral failing and a drain on public systems of support. In the U.S., where sexually charged images sell everything from toothpaste to automobiles, it seems odd that we spend so little time discussing with youth the rights and responsibilities of sexual activity, then condemn them for receiving the consequences of our silence on the issue (7).

The organization brings up an excellent point. Even though capitalism uses sexuality to make a profit, when a teen is sexually active, as evidenced by her growing belly, she is condemned. The moral failing is not the pregnant teen. The moral failing is the social structures failing to provide adequate support for the teen mother and her child to create a better life.

This is the beginning of inclusion—changing the framework and narrative of teen pregnancy and parenting. Instead of seeing the issue of teen pregnancy and parenting as a moral failing of the individuals involved, we can, instead, focus on how society routinely fails pregnant and parenting teens. Society can strive for access to resources that can prevent the issues that Healthy People 2020 highlight in regard to teen pregnancy, such as access to education, childcare, housing, parenting courses and support, life skills and financial management courses, other economic resources. We also need to acknowledge how hard it is. Being a mother is hard, but when you are young and trying to go to school and navigating all the other things a teen does, it is even more difficult.

Towards Inclusion

To work towards inclusion, we need to change how we see and talk about teen pregnancy and parenting. It is not a moral failing of individuals. Teens are sexual and have sexualities and sexual needs and desires. Some will engage in sexual activities. Some will choose to use birth control, and some may not. Sometimes birth control fails. Sometimes teens get pregnant. Sometimes they choose abortion. Sometimes they have supportive families who will support them no matter what they choose and sometimes they don't. Sometimes they have access to childcare in their schools, but usually they don't.

We need to work towards changing and reframing the narrative of teen pregnancy and parenting. Part of this includes excepting teen's autonomy and choices and realizing that some teens choose to become pregnant and continue their pregnancies when they have an unplanned one. We need to trust teenagers.

For many teens, their pregnancy is seen as an opportunity and has made them feel stronger (Duncan). One study followed several teen mothers over eight years and found that motherhood made them more mature and provided a positive catalyst for change. Many of the mothers felt motherhood helped them get over their desolate past (SmithBattle). The mothers also felt mothering anchored them and helped them discover more about who they are. Another study researched women living in rural areas and found that motherhood increased their self-esteem, positively influenced their lives, and provided a sense of stability and security (Bell et al.).

Websites such as #NoTeenShame (www.noteenshame.com), MA Alliance on Teen Pregnancy (www.massteenpregnancy.org), The Push Back (thepushback.org), Teen Mom NYC (www.teenmomnyc.com), Strong Families (http://www.reproductivejusticeblog.org/), Not Another Teen Mommy (https://notanotherteenmommy.com/), and Girl-Mom (http://www.girlmom.com/) are positive and empowering online resources. Each website aims to change the way people see teen parents and teen parenting. Many of these websites are run by teen or former teen mothers and feature stories, resources, activism, and more.

These resources are what we need to change the framework of teen pregnancy and parenting. They change the focus and add teen mothers' stories to the conversation. Instead of focusing on the potential negative outcomes, which many public health campaigns do, we can talk about how positive teen parenting is for most mothers. These frameworks see teen pregnancy and parenting beyond the social consequences and costs. They look at teen pregnancy and parenting with more humanity and trust, and they value the opinions and autonomy of teens and their families.

Furthermore, including teenager mothers in a positive light in stories, research, and academia is so important towards inclusion. The MTV show, *Teen Mom*, paints teen mothers' stories as dramatic and negative. We need a different light to break social exclusion.

Summary

My personal narrative has been very important in how I see teen pregnancy and parenting. Having been there myself, I have witnessed and experienced the judgment and comments of others and the poverty and lack of support that is so prevalent when it comes to being a single, a teen mother. Since I have also read positive stories and know other teen and single parents, however, I know that teen mothers are amazing mothers and deserve support and praise. Changing the framework and including the positive stories of teen in academia and elsewhere is important and critical for social inclusion.

Works Cited

Bell, Jo, et al. Living on the Edge: Sexual Behaviour and Young Parenthood in Seaside and Rural Areas. Department of Health. 2004.

Bonell, Chris. "Why Is Teenage Pregnancy Conceptualized as a Social Problem? A Review of Quantitative Research from the USA and UK." *An International Journal for Research, Intervention, and Care*, vol. 6, no. 3 2004, 255-72.

Cialdini, Robert B., and Melanie Trost. "Social Influence: Social Norms, Conformity, and Compliance." *The Handbook of Social Psychology: 2-Volume Set*. Oxford University Press. 2010.

Duncan, Simon. "What's the Problem with Teenage Parents? And What's the Problem with Policy?" *Critical Social Policy*, vol. 27, 2007, pp. 307-34.

The Evidence for Policy and Practice Information and Co-ordinating Centre. "Young People, Pregnancy and Social Exclusion: A Systematic Synthesis of Research Evidence to Identify Effective, Appropriate and Promising Approaches for Prevention and Support." *EPPI*, 2006, eppi.ioe.ac.uk/cms/Portals/0/PDF%20reviews%20 and%20summaries/pregnancy_social_exclusion.pdf? ver=2006-04-24-140619-143. Accessed 21 May 2019.

Healthy People. 2020. "Teen Pregnancy Prevention Initiative," 2019, www.healthypeople.gov/2020/tools-resources/evidence-based-resource/teen-pregnancy-prevention-resource-center-evidence. Accessed 21 May 2019.

Hoffman Saul. *By the Numbers: The Public Costs of Teen Childbearing.* National Campaign to Prevent Teen Pregnancy. 2006.

The Rhode Island Alliance. *Changing the Lens: A Reframed Approach to Teen Pregnancy Prevention.* 2012, rialliance.org/. Accessed 21 May 2019.

Seamark, Clare. "Design or Accident? The Natural History of Teenage Pregnancy." *Journal of Royal Society of Medicine*, vol. 94, no. 6, 2001, pp. 282-85.

SmithBattle, Lee. "The Vulnerabilities of Teenage Mothering: Challenging Prevailing Assumptions." *Advanced Nursing Science*, vol. 23, no. 1, 2000, pp. 29-40.

UNICEF. "Factsheet Young People and Family Planning: Teenage Pregnancy." *UNICEF*, 2008, unicef.org. Accessed 21 May 2019.

Vinovskis, Maris A. "An 'epidemic' of Adolescent Pregnancy? Some Historical Considerations." *Journal of Family History*, vol. 6, 1981, pp. 205-30.

Notes on Contributors

María Piedad Quevedo Alvarado was born in Bogotá, Colombia. She is the mother of eight-year-old Violeta. Her PhD is in romance languages and literatures from Harvard University. Her fields of research include colonial Studies, lettered Culture, New Kingdom of Granada, contemporary African literature, critical theory, Golden Age literature, and motherhood and literature. She currently works as an assistant professor in the Literature Department at Javeriana University, Bogotá, Colombia.

Lucy Baldwin is a senior lecturer in criminology, who is currently undertaking her doctoral research titled *Mothers Confined: Exploring the Emotional Impact of Imprisonment on Mothers and Grandmothers.* She has twenty-five years of experience in criminal and social justice settings. She is an experienced social worker and probation officer, having worked in a range of secure and community settings. Lucy has authored an edited collection called *Mothering Justice: Working with Mothers in Criminal Justice Settings* (Waterside Press 2015) as well as several journal articles and comment pieces—all of which focus on the issues surrounding mothers and their experiences in and around the criminal justice system.

Christie Byvelds is a mother and registered social worker. She is a sessional instructor with the School of Social Work at Carleton University, and she practices both clinically and as a private research consultant.

Clarissa Carden is a PhD candidate in sociology at Griffith University in Queensland. Her research focuses on disciplinary policies and practices in Queensland schools, both historical and contemporary. She is the mother of a two-year-old child.

May Friedman blends social work, teaching, research, writing, and parenting. Her passions include social justice and reality TV. Recent publications include work on digital media, transnationalism, gender fluidity, and Here Comes Honey Boo Boo. A faculty member in the Ryerson University School of Social Work and Ryerson/York graduate program in Communication and Culture, May lives in downtown Toronto with her partner and four children

Kelly Fritsch is an assistant professor in the Department of Sociology and Anthropology at Carleton University in Ottawa, Canada. Her research broadly engages crip, queer, and feminist theory to explore the relations of disability, health, technology, risk, and accessibility. She is the co-editor of *Keywords for Radicals: The Contested Vocabulary of Late-Capitalist Struggle* (2016, AK Press) and was from 2015 to 2018 a Banting Postdoctoral Fellow at the Women & Gender Studies Institute, University of Toronto.

Amber Gazso (PhD, University of Alberta) is an associate professor of sociology at York University. Her main areas of research interest include citizenship family and gender relations, research methods, poverty, and the welfare state. Much of her research explores family members' relationships with social policies of the neoliberal welfare state and has been published in such journals as the *Canadian Journal of Sociology, Citizenship Studies, Journal of Family Relations, Journal of Family Issues,* and the *International Journal of Sociology and Social Policy.*

Rae Griffin-Carlson is a queer, stay-at-home mother of two toddlers. A high school teacher in what seems like a past life, she is setting her sights at pursing a graduate degree in a counseling-related field in the near future.

Kathryn Huie Harrison, PhD, is a Marion L. Brittain Postdoctoral Fellow at the Georgia Institute of Technology. Her research investigates Victorian treatment of the female body and the ramifications of Victorian ideology on the contemporary conceptions of women's bodies. Her current work focuses on the breast and miscarriage. She has a history of recurrent miscarriage.

Heather Jackson, a former teen mom, is now a thirty-something single mom of a teen. She is often mistaken as her daughter's friend or sister. She is a former site producer of girl-mom.com. Currently, she works as a birth doula and an early childhood counsellor in Rhode Island. She published a chapter in *The Bakken Goes Boom* regarding the change of maternal health related to the oil boom in North Dakota, where she grew up. In addition to this, she is also the co-editor of *Feminist Parenting* and is currently co-editing *Motherhood and Abortion* anthologies with Demeter Press. Her writing has also been published on thepushback. org, hipmama.com, girl-mom.com, and muthamagazine.com, as well as in books, and zines. She loves bike riding, going to the beach, playing guitar, drums, and ukulele, going to shows, making zines (etsy shop: ramonegirl), and writing.

Romee Lee, Ph.D. is a research fellow in the Institute for Educational Research at Yonsei University in Korea. She received her B.A. and M.A. degrees from Yonsei University and her PhD from the University of British Columbia. She has been engaging in various research projects, particularly on planning programs for various groups of immigrant adults in Canada and Korea.

Donna J. Gelagotis Lee's book, *On the Altar of Greece*, winner of the Gival Press Poetry Award, received a 2007 Eric Hoffer Book Award: Notable for Art Category and was nominated for a number of awards. Her poetry has appeared in literary and scholarly journals internationally, including *Atlantis: A Women's Studies Journal, Canadian Woman Studies/les cahiers de la femme, The Dalhousie Review, Descant, Feminist Studies,* and *Vallum: contemporary poetry.*

Krystal Kehoe MacLeod has a doctorate from the School of Public Policy and Administration at Carleton University. She teaches courses on health discourses, the health of populations, policy analysis, and research methods and evaluation. Krystal has worked as a policymaker with the Ontario Ministry of Health and Long-Term Care, the Cabinet Office in Ontario, and the Department of Health in New South Wales, Australia. She is an Ontario Women's Health Scholar Award winner with research funding from the Canadian Policy Research Network. Krystal's primary research interests include home and community care, integrated care, and the linkages between gender, aging, and public policy.

Karen March is an associate professor in the Institute of Women's and Gender Studies at Carleton University. She published *The Stranger Who Bore Me: Adoptee-Birth Mother Relations* and conducted a Canada-wide survey of community attitudes towards adoption with Dr. Charlene Miall, McMaster University. Currently, Karen studies how losing children to adoption affects birth mothers.

Duncan Murray is a senior lecturer at the University of South Australia in the school of sport and recreation.

Christina Quinlan is a lecturer in criminology and criminal justice at De Montfort University, Leicester. With a background in social research, she has worked as a social scientist in third level education and in the community and voluntary sector. Her areas of interest include gender, crime and punishment, media and communications, and social research methods.

Nancy Sinclair is a mother of four children, with the privilege of being at home fulltime concentrating on parenting the newest family member's first eighteen months. When working outside of the family, she is a clinical social worker at a Canadian military garrison where clients are active military members. She likes to look for opportunities to dabble in the academic world, although she finds it a challenge with other commitments and living in a fairly rural area.

Flavia Nasrin Testa is a self-taught working artist and has been touched by many issues personally as a woman and mother. Her life experience includes international mothering and birthing (three children born on different continents), living in an abusive marriage, which included religious as well as psychological abuse, coping with PTSD, and experiencing single parenting. Yet, today, she finds herself in a happier place with a complete life. Her life and art are her testaments to the motherhood struggle. She feels she cannot separate the two, as they are born from the same place. Her work has appeared at the Museum Of Motherhood in NYC, at the Seconds Story Women Centre in Lunenburg NS, and at various university exhibits in Canada and the United States. Various magazines—including *Guided, Polluto,* and *Understorey*—have also published her work.

Chloe Trayhum is a self-taught artist and a mother of two, living in Cambridgeshire, U.K. She works in watercolour, ink and acrylic, and draws her inspiration from the beauty of the female form, motherhood, and physical connection. She is an advocate for gentle parenting, natural term breastfeeding, positive birth, and body acceptance.

Emily van der Meulen is an associate professor in the Department of Criminology at Ryerson University. Her research interests include prison health and harm reduction, the criminalization of sexual labour, and gendered surveillance studies. Her most recent co-edited books include *Red Light Labour: Sex Work Regulation, Agency, and Resistance* (UBC Press, 2018) and *Making Surveillance States: Transnational Histories* (University of Toronto Press, 2019).

Ashley Ward is the Research Director of the Making the Shift Demonstration Project at the Canadian Observatory on Homelessness. Her research takes a community-based, interdisciplinary focus, and includes the prevention of homelessness for youth, interventions for youth experiencing homelessness, evidenced-based program development and evaluation, criminalization and development, health and community systems integration, and critical research ethics.

Jason Webb (MA, York University, PhD-ABD) is a PhD candidate in sociology at York University. His main areas of research interest include citizenship, critical policy studies, homelessness, social and economic inequality, feminist political economy, and urban sociology. For his dissertation, he interviewed homeless parents residing in the Greater Toronto Area shelter system to understand how they practice social reproduction. His theoretical framework examines how welfare state restructuring shapes poor households' means to social provisioning.

Karen Williams is a current PhD candidate at the University of Adelaide (gender and social analysis) and is in the final year of her doctorate.

Yidan Zhu, Ph.D., is a postdoctoral research fellow at the Faculty of Dentistry, University of British Columbia. She obtained her Ph.D. in the Adult Education and Community Development Program at Ontario Institute for Studies in Education (OISE), University of Toronto. She is interested in studying the discursive and material dimensions of immigrant mothers' everyday experience and adult education. Her doctoral study focuses on Chinese immigrant mothers' learning in Canadian immigration settlement organizations. Her current work focuses on migrant mothers' lifelong learning and health professionals' education.

Deepest appreciation to
Demeter's monthly Donors

DEMETER

Daughters
Linda Hunter
Muna Saleh
Summer Cunningham
Rebecca Bromwich
Tatjana Takseva
Kerri Kearney
Debbie Byrd
Laurie Kruk
Fionna Green
Tanya Cassidy
Vicki Noble
Bridget Boland

Sisters
Kirsten Goa
Amber Kinser
Nicole Willey
Regina Edwards